Alex Cadogan

Xmas 2000 from

Chris.

HIDDEN AGENDA

Martin Allen

HIDDEN AGENDA

*How the Duke of Windsor
Betrayed the Allies*

MACMILLAN

First published 2000 by Macmillan
an imprint of Macmillan Publishers Ltd
25 Eccleston Place, London SW1W 9NF
Basingstoke and Oxford
Associated companies throughout the world
www.macmillan.co.uk

ISBN 0 333 90181 9

1 3 5 7 9 8 6 4 2

A CIP catalogue record for this book is available from
the British Library.

Typeset by SetSystems Ltd, Saffron Walden, Essex
Printed and bound in Great Britain by
Mackays of Chatham plc, Chatham, Kent

For my late father,
who left me the pieces of a jigsaw puzzle,
and for whom I have finished the work
he began twenty years ago.

Contents

CONTENTS

MAP I

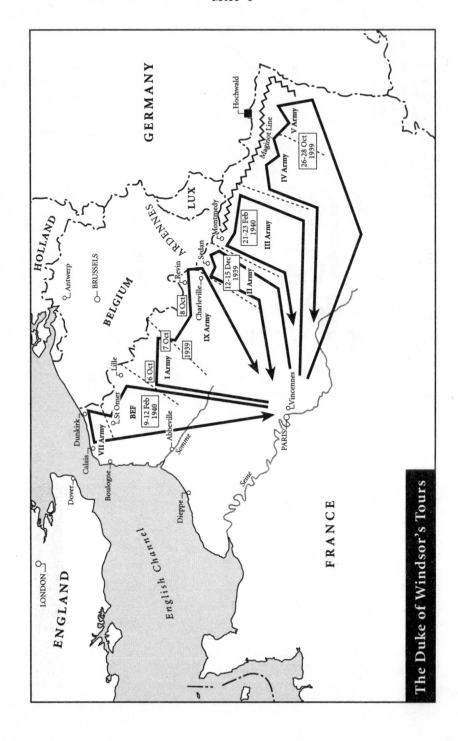

The Duke of Windsor's Tours

MAP II

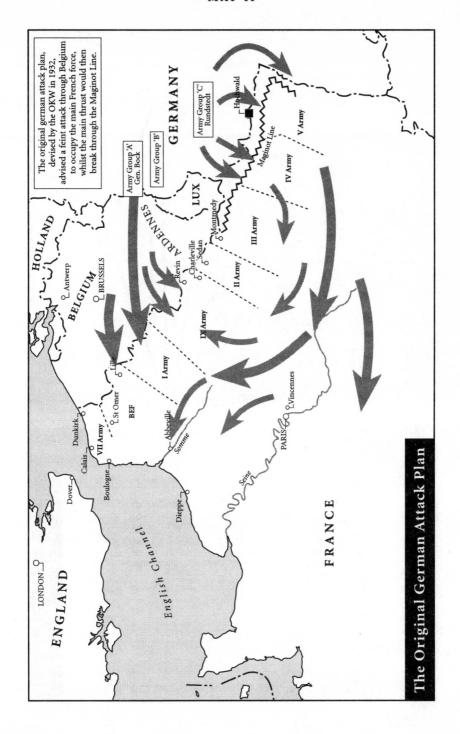

The original german attack plan, devised by the OKW in 1932, advised a feint attack through Belgium to occupy the main French force, whilst the main thrust would then break through the Maginot Line.

The Original German Attack Plan

MAP III

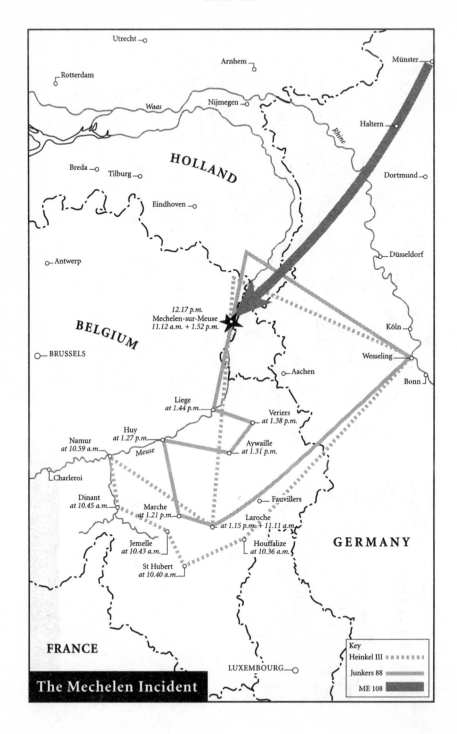

Utrecht

Arnhem

Münster

Rotterdam

Waas

Nijmegen

Haltern

HOLLAND

Rhine

Breda

Tilburg

Dortmund

Eindhoven

Düsseldorf

Antwerp

12.17 p.m.
Mechelen-sur-Meuse
11.12 a.m. + 1.52 p.m.

BELGIUM

Köln

BRUSSELS

Wesseling

Aachen

Bonn

Liege
at 1.44 p.m.

Veriers
at 1.38 p.m.

Huy
at 1.27 p.m.

Namur
at 10.59 a.m.

Meuse

Aywaille
at 1.31 p.m.

Charleroi

Dinant
at 10.45 a.m.

Marche
at 1.21 p.m.

Fauvillers

Laroche
at 1.15 p.m. + 11.11 a.m.

GERMANY

Jemelle
at 10.43 a.m.

Houffalize
at 10.36 a.m.

St Hubert
at 10.40 a.m.

FRANCE

Key

Heinkel III

LUXEMBOURG

Junkers 88

The Mechelen Incident

ME 108

MAP IV

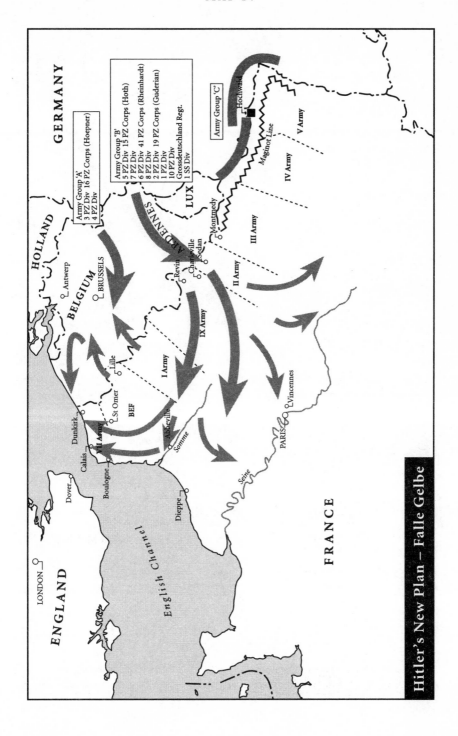

Hitler's New Plan – Falle Gelbe

Acknowledgements

I would like to take this opportunity to acknowledge and extend my thanks to all those people who have helped me with my research for this book. Some took the time and trouble to write to me, others granted an interview, and some assisted in translations, research, and providing information voluntarily that it did not occur to me to ask for. Without in any way depreciating the value of those persons assistance, I would like to pay a tribute to the following people in alphabetical order: Mrs N. Bleszynski, Mrs Wilmay le Bryce, Mr Stuart L. Butler, Major-General V. H. J. Carpenter (retd.), M. J. Caluwaerts, Mr J. Cronan, Mrs Jarmila Fialova, M. Frederic Grosjean, Joann H. Grube, Mr C. Heather, M. Daniel Farcis, Mr Michael Foot, Heer Van Gancuddam, Mrs Marta Kapalinova, Mrs Terri Land, Mr J. R. Lankford Jr., Dr Soos Laszlo, Brigadier Mike Lonsdale, Mrs Rebecca Lentz-Collier, Mrs Ewa Lipinska, Mrs Emma Lock, Heern Joost Klarenbeek, Dr Malcorps, Mde. Marie-Helene Marchand, Heern R. Martijn, Mr David Metcalfe, M. A. Muret, Mr A. Nikonov, Mr J. Novakova, Mr B. Ogibesov, Mr S. N. Robbins, Fred Romanski, M. C. Tricot, Drs Hans de Vreis, Lt Colonel A. Vyskrebentsev, Mr William J. Walsh, Mrs Linda Wheeler, and mgr Bronislawa Witkewska.

I am particularly indebted to the following institutions and government bodies for replying to my letters, or who otherwise gave me their time and assistance to aid my research to uncover the details that feature in this book: Archives Generales de Royaume, Bruxelles, Archivex ssro of Prague, the Archivio Storico Diplomatico, Rome, the Central Armed Forces Museum, Moscow, the Climatological Service, Bruxelles, Companies House, Cardiff, the Hoover Institution on War, Revolution and Peace, California, the Kent County Clerk's Office, Michigan, the Imperial War Museum, London, the Institut Pasteur, Paris, the Institut Royal Meteorologique de Belgique, the Magyar Orszagos Leveltar, Budapest, the Ministere de L'Interieur, Paris, the Ministerstvo Zahranicnich veci Ceske Republiky, Prague, the Nacelna Cyrekcja Archowow Panstwowych, Warsaw, the National Security Agency of the American Department of Defense, the National Archives, Washington DC, North Carolina Archives Service, the Polish Embassy, the Public Records Office, the Rijksinstitut voor Oorlogsdocumentatie, Amsterdam, the Templewood Papers and the Statni Oblastni Archiv V Praze, Prague.

I would also like to pay tribute to those friends, colleagues and translators who assisted in the logistics of writing this book: Mr D. R. Brown for providing me with information about aircraft of the Second World War, Mr F. P. Creagh for providing the security and chauffeur services necessary during the production of this book, Mr Pierre Vial and Mr Nick Burzynski for translations, and my agent, Mrs Sonia Land, who had the faith to stand by me during the writing of this book, and who gave her unwavering support through the many problems we encountered.

Lastly, I would like to express a very special tribute to Jean, without whose help in research, organizing ability, and talent on the telephone, this book definitely could not have been written.

Preface

IT IS IMPORTANT for me to state at the outset that *Hidden Agenda* is not the book I originally set out to write. Over three years ago I began researching material to write a book on a man named Charles Eugene Bedaux, and it was by this means that I eventually ended up with a book that heavily features the Duke of Windsor. It is almost impossible to conduct in-depth research into the Duke of Windsor's wartime career, for the vast majority of the more sensitive documents concerning him are officially listed as 'Lost', 'Withheld', or 'Not Available' until some distant date in the future. It was by researching Bedaux that I began to find information about the Duke of Windsor that had not previously been used, and I came in at a tangent to the story I have written. At the start of my quest I had no idea that I would travel many thousands of miles, conduct many months of research and interviews, and, finally, that my quest for evidence would incredibly take me back to my very starting point to search through my late father's papers. What I discovered amongst his records was a single sheet of paper, the contents of which made me gasp.

Back in the late 1970s and early 80s my father, Peter Allen, an author who specialized in military histories, wrote a book on the Duke of Windsor's exploits in Spain and Portugal in 1940.

During the writing of his book he researched and researched, dug out his old cronies from his time in Germany in the 1950s, utilized his contacts to gain access to men who'd been important within Hitler's dictatorship, and ever so slowly gathered the material for his book. Thus when his book, *The Crown and the Swastika*, came out in 1983 it was somewhat controversial, clarifying as it did the Duke's close association with the Nazis, and his contact with them in Lisbon in July of 1940.

In 1994, my father died after a sudden illness, and I packaged up his records, papers, and files into many, many boxes, placing them in the loft of my home where they remained, for I did not have the heart to get rid of them. In the autumn of 1996, I happened to be in the loft to look for a book, and found myself idly glancing through some of his paperwork when I came across something interesting. It was an intelligence report from 1917 on a Frenchman named Charles Bedaux, the man who had acted as the Duke of Windsor's host for his wedding to Wallis Simpson in 1937. This report stated that Bedaux had been suspected of spying for the Germans in the First World War. It was evident from the few sheets of paper in my hand that Bedaux was quite a character, and it occurred to me that it was surprising the Duke of Windsor had been permitted to marry Wallis Simpson in this man's home. Surely British Intelligence must have known about Bedaux's past?

I thought to myself that there had to be a story here.

Over the next two years I researched my book, visited archives across Europe, tracked Bedaux's life back and forth; from his Parisian birth registration in 1886, to his marriage papers in the United States in 1917, right through to the lab report on his urine sample taken at autopsy in 1944. From those few sheets of paper taken from my father's records grew a file well in excess of 2,800 documents, together with something else – the uneasy feeling that I had unwittingly uncovered a completely different story, that the papers I was gathering revealed a previously undisclosed secret about Bedaux's great friend, the Duke of Windsor. One of the major events in Bedaux and Windsor's association concerned a service that the wily Frenchman had undertaken for his friend, and the realization of what he had done on a specific date in 1939 ultimately sent me back to my father's papers to look for a letter.

Back in 1980, amongst his other contacts my father utilized his acquaintance with Albert Speer (Hitler's close friend, architect, and Reichsfuhrer, Minister of Armaments and War Production), one of the last of the high-ranking Nazis to visit Hitler at the Führer-bunker in the final days of the war. It was to Speer that my father had turned for information on his book about the Rhine Crossings of 1945, as well as other projects, and he felt that because Speer had been within Hitler's inner circle he might well have some information that could be of use. After writing to Speer in May 1980 requesting information on Hitler's relationship with the Duke of Windsor and Dr Robert Ley (a high-ranking Nazi), Speer replied in his usual friendly way saying:

> I am very pleased that your last book has been published and I wish you every success with it. Naturally, I would like to assist you with the research for your next book ... and would be very pleased to discuss your subject with you. The following dates would be most suitable for me: between 21–28 July, or as from August, either in Heidelberg or at my Allgau house, not far from Munich ...

My father travelled to Germany in July 1980, and during their meeting the two men not only discussed the Duke of Windsor, but also chatted about the economic policies of Nazi Germany, about the Reichsbank and the Office of the Four Year Plan. Towards the end of their talk, Speer leant over to a side table, pulled a single sheet of paper from beneath a newspaper, and handed it to my father.

'Here,' he told him, 'you can have that, but don't associate it with me.'

My father glanced at it, not fully understanding the letter for it was written in German, but he immediately recognized the recipient's name and noted it was signed with the initials EP. Puzzled, my father had pressed Speer to explain the letter, but he steadfastly remained silent. Since they had been talking about the Reichsbank prior to the letter's appearance, my father wondered if it was connected to that, and presumed that EP might be the initials of Erich Pohl, who had worked within the Finance Ministry. On his return my father had rather excitedly shown me his 'gift' from Albert Speer, and we sat down with pencil, paper, and a German–English dictionary to translate the letter. I must confess now, years later, looking at our scribbled notes, that our translation was not very accurate. However, our translation was good enough for us to roughly gather its contents, which was rather disappointing for the letter did not say anything very remarkable, in fact it seemed quite mundane, referring to a 'Mr B' and EP's holiday. The only importance seemed to be the letter's recipient. Unable to fathom Speer's reticence, or the letter, which we regarded only as an interesting curiosity, my father filed it away and eventually it was quite forgotten.

Then, on 4 August 1997, some seventeen years after Speer had given my father the EP letter, I received a photocopy of an intelligence report from 1939 that caused me to search through my father's records. At long last I knew who 'Mr B' was, and as a result now realized that EP was not someone's initials, but stood for *Edward. Prince.*

'Please, let the letter still be amongst these papers,' I thought, as I searched through the numerous boxes and files. Over an hour later, I sat perched on a box with the letter in my hand.

Knowing who 'Mr B' was, and by implication EP, I immediately got the letter properly translated, and discovered that the
letter said far more than my father and I had understood all
those years previously. Many more documents and letters had
been released in the intervening seventeen years and my understanding of the period, and consequently of those who took part,
had increased enormously.

At last the story was beginning to make sense.

There followed many more months of research as I was sent
off on another tack, contacting archives in Poland, Czechoslovakia, Russia, Bulgaria, Hungary, the United States, France,
Belgium, Holland, Italy, and Spain. I interviewed a Polish veteran
who lived near Land's End, wrote to Messerschmitt-Bolkow-
Blohm GmbH, manufacturers of the ME108 aircraft, took a
statement from an old farmer in eastern Belgium, contacted the
Institut Meteorologique de Belgique, faxed Companies House in
Cardiff, made use of the extensive FBI archives in Washington,
and requested information from a whole host of other obscure
holders of records and documents from the 1930s and 1940s.

Eventually, I had all the facts laid out before me in a pile of
documents four and half feet high, together with a bewildering
assortment of plans, maps and photographs – a vast jigsaw puzzle
that needed to be assembled. I had a story to tell breathtaking in
its audacity, yet it was not a book directly about the man I had
begun to research, he had merely proved to be the key to a
Pandora's box of perfidy, the ramifications of which are still
being felt today.

Martin A. Allen

HIDDEN AGENDA

Prologue

DURING THE FINAL days of the Second World War, Britain's King George VI entrusted a very secret and sensitive mission to a young MI5 officer, commanding him to travel into newly fallen Nazi Germany to protect the reputation of his elder brother, Edward, Duke of Windsor, and by implication that of the British royal family. It was to be only the start of an exercise begun in 1945 to keep secret the events surrounding Britain's former King, when he engaged in actions that could nearly have had the deadliest of consequences for his country. This extreme need for secrecy is continued even today with a fervour almost religious in its application, and any papers, notes, documents, or private letters from this period are still vetted and often removed, regardless of their location. It is the continuation of a panic and urgency started in Britain's darkest hour, and the first person charged with this protection of the royal image was MI5 officer Anthony Blunt. Ultimately Blunt was revealed as a traitor who had spied for Russia, and he in turn was protected by the royal family for over twenty years lest he reveal the details of the secret mission he had undertaken at the end of the Second World War.

In the spring of 1945 Anthony Blunt, having been provided with priority documentation and an army lorry, and accompanied by George VI's librarian, Owen Morshead, followed in the wake of General George S. Patton's Third Army as it rolled back the last remnants of Hitler's forces from the Taunus mountains. Blunt's objective was the mountain-top home of Prince Philipp of Hesse – Schloss Freidrichshof; his task the recovery of secret papers concerning the Duke of Windsor that Hesse had been charged to protect during the latter months of the war.[1] On arriving at Schloss Freidrichshof, Blunt and Morshead found the castle already occupied by American Third Army forces, Prince Philipp of Hesse was in custody for having been a high-ranking Nazi in Hitler's Reich, and the Hesse family had been evicted to a small house in the nearby village of Kronberg. Despite the set-back, Blunt presented his credentials to the American Commanding Officer in charge of the castle, and demanded access to the private papers that were rightfully, Blunt insisted, royal property. Evidently, the American senior officer was not over-awed by Blunt's papers, for he refused to recognize Blunt and Morshead's authority as representatives of King George VI, and they departed empty-handed, travelling back down the mountain to locate the remaining Hesse family in Kronberg.

Determined to complete their mission, Blunt and Morshead returned to Schloss Freidrichshof that night, having first been briefed on how to penetrate the castle by means of a back staircase. This time they would not approach the Americans, and they were armed with a letter from Prince Philipp's mother that instructed the remaining family retainers to assist the two Englishmen. Swiftly, the two Englishmen gained access to the castle's upper floors, located the papers they had been sent across war-devastated Europe to find, and surreptitiously succeeded in removing two crates of documents. With the crates safely secured in the back of their lorry, Blunt and Morshead then drove quickly through the night to reach the British zone before the American authorities discovered what had been done, and moved to repossess the papers that were vital to royal dignity and safety. A week later the documents were safely deposited in Windsor Castle, never to be seen again.[2]

Despite this concerted effort by the British establishment and royal family to maintain the secrecy about the Duke of Windsor's wartime activities, all Blunt's work would be jeopardized within a month by the Nazi's compulsion to hide their secret documents in the face of certain defeat. In the middle of May 1945, US General Courtney Hodge's First Army uncovered several huge caches of buried Nazi documents in Germany's Harz mountains amounting to four hundred and eighty-five dossiers of Germany's most secret papers, and sixty tons of bound material. Such was the quantity of documents that it took several days to dig all the papers up, and then many lorry journeys to transport it all to the huge gothic castle of Schloss Marburg, where a team of experts headed by Dr Perkins of the US State Department and Colonel Thomson of the British Foreign Office waited to examine them.

At the end of May, Karl Loesch, who had been assistant to Hitler's interpreter, Paul Schmidt, was captured on the road to Leipzig. Quickly it was discovered that the man was of some importance, and during his interogation by Colonel Thomson, Loesch tipped the British officer off that he had helped bury a vast microfilm archive deep in the Thuringia Forest. He had been making his way back home when he was captured. A few days later Loesch took Colonel Thomson deep into the Thuringia Forest, and in a secluded and thickly forested valley showed him the spot where he and Schmidt had buried the microfilm files of the Auswärtiges Amt (the German Foreign Ministry) in several metal suitcases. Amongst the substantive microfilm records recovered was a copy of State Secretary Ernst von Weizsacker's collection entitled 'German-British Relations', it included a volume on the Duke of Windsor, later to be called the 'Marburg File'.[3] After a cursory inspection of the 'Marburg File', its contents were immediately recognized as so dangerous and sensitive that

General Eisenhower quickly ordered the whole file be sealed. It was then removed from Schloss Marburg in complete secrecy before being taken directly to the security of his own SHAEF (Supreme Head Allied European Forces) Headquarters, where it was locked away in a safe.[4]

When exactly George VI learnt of the existence of the 'Marburg File' is not known, but on 25 October 1945, royal assistant Sir Alexander Cadogan noted in his diary 'the King fussed about the Duke of Windsor's file and the captured German documents'.[5] George VI was upset and very concerned that the highly organized mopping-up operation, set up to penetrate collapsing Nazi Germany and the Schloss Freidrichshof, might all have been for nothing. The closely guarded secret of Edward's actions, known by just a handful of people,[6] might now break with devastating repercussions, not merely for Edward, but more importantly the shock waves could rock war-weakened Britain to its very foundations. If the British people ever discovered what their former king had done, well, it seemed too horrible to contemplate. Faced with the appalling prospect that the royal secret might enter the public domain, Winston Churchill attempted to have all the captured German documents regarding the Duke of Windsor destroyed, including those that would later feature in the 'Documents on German Foreign Policy', Series D, Volumes IX and X.[7] It was only Churchill's defeat by Clement Attlee in the General Election of August 1945, that prevented his taking this extraordinary step, saving the less sensitive papers for posterity, and protecting the 'Marburg File' for just a little longer. Churchill's defeat by Attlee did not come in time, however, to countermand his orders to destroy Britain's code-breaking establishment – Ultra, at Bletchley Park – obliterating for ever all record of Britain's intercepted German messages, including many of the communications that must have featured within the 'Marburg File'.

In the latter half of 1945 the German files and microfilm record of the Duke of Windsor's wartime actions became split, with the original documents discovered in the Harz mountains ultimately ending up secreted deep within the Foreign Office in London, and the altogether more substantive and damaging microfilm discovered in the Thuringia Forest being deposited with the State Department in Washington DC. For the next eighteen months the German files on the Duke of Windsor were forgotten, whilst the Allied specialists examined the captured German Foreign Office and Chancellery records to evaluate the guilt of those Nazis implicated in the intent to wage war and cause genocide.

In early 1947 the 'Marburg File' at long last came under expert scrutiny, but almost immediately 'something so damaging was revealed that it required Anglo–American co-operation at the highest level' to prevent the file's contents from ever entering the public domain and becoming common knowledge.[8] Whilst in Moscow to attend a conference of Foreign Ministers, Foreign Secretary Ernest Bevan had an urgent and impromptu late-night meeting with his American opposite number, US Secretary of State General George Marshall. Immediately following their confidential discussion, and Bevan's revelation that it was vital any release of information from the 'Marburg File' must never be allowed to happen, General Marshall sent an urgent top-secret 'PERSONAL FOR YOUR EYES ONLY' telegram to Dean Acheson of the State Department in Washington, at midnight on 15 March 1947:

> Bevan informs me that Department or White House has on file a microfilm copy of a paper concerning the Duke of Windsor. Bevan says only other copy was destroyed by Foreign Office, and asks that we destroy ours to avoid possibility of a leak to great embarrassment of Windsor's brother. Please attend to this for me and reply for my eyes only.[9]

The result of Bevan and Marshall's intervention is that no record, file or microfilm copy of the 'Marburg File' now exists either in Britain's archives, America's National Archive, or amongst the Roosevelt, Truman or Marshall Papers. It was utterly destroyed, its contents for ever expunged from world history.

Despite this drastic act, royal paranoia and the search for damaging Windsor documents still continued. In August 1947 the rumour surfaced that the Duke of Windsor had communicated with Frederick William, Kaiser Wilhelm's son who had acted as a royal emissary for Adolf Hitler. Immediately, Blunt and Morshead were again despatched to the continent in search of embarrassing or damaging papers. This time their destination was Haus Doorn, the late Kaiser's residence in Holland, their mission: to obtain any remaining documents about the Duke of Windsor's wartime activities, and any and all copies of his letters to Frederick William.

About this time Anthony Blunt left MI5 to become Surveyor of the King's Pictures and Director of the Courtauld Institute of Art. He would retain this eminent position until his public exposure in 1979, revealed as a 'mole' who had supplied the KGB with information over a great number of years. Although his treachery was to be unearthed in 1963, he would be granted immunity from prosecution and allowed to retain his job within the royal household for a further sixteen years until his public downfall in 1979. In 1967 Peter Wright, an officer of MI5 and later author of *Spycatcher* fame, investigated Blunt with a wide remit to disclose all the man's perfidy. However, there was one subject he was not allowed to enquire about – the Palace emphatically insisted that any questioning of Blunt about his missions to Germany for George VI was out of bounds. Peter Wright was later to comment: 'In the hundreds of hours I spent with him I never did learn the secret of his mission at the end of the war,' adding, 'The palace is adept in the difficult art of burying scandals over several centuries, while MI5 have only been in business since 1909 . . .'[10]

Ever since the end of the Second World War, there has been considerable speculation about the Duke of Windsor's exact role during that conflict. After only eleven months of European war the Duke was dispatched to the 'safety' of a Caribbean appointment, far from the reach of Nazi plot and intrigue. That he did not want to go – he considered the appointment as Governor of the Bahamas as a banishment to an island quarantine – is without doubt. The Duchess of Windsor called the appointment 'The St Helena's of 1940', bringing to mind images of Napoleon Bonaparte exiled to an island existence with no chance of escape.

There have been claims that the Duke of Windsor was persecuted by the royal family and British government for putting his love-life before the needs of his country. It has also been alleged that the Duke was naïvely pro-fascist and recklessly indiscreet in his opinion about Britain's chances of surviving Hitler's onslaught. Worse epithets have been flung at him, and rumours have grown that during the first year of the war the pro-German Duke might actually have been a traitor,[11] that the Bahamas appointment was a ploy used by the British government to keep him far from Europe and away from Nazi compromise. However, the British government's dilemma with regard to the Duke of Windsor in 1940 is not that simple, and not merely about eleven troubled months of war. Often, when in need of an excuse to explain the Duke's behaviour at this time, it has been claimed that he was not a very clever man, prone to impromptu and petulant decision. This is not true. Edward, Duke of Windsor, was an intelligent man, who was bilingual in German and spoke French and Spanish with reasonable fluency, and, although no great mathematician, throughout his life kept a firm grasp on

7

his finances and business investments. It is probably not unfair to state that he was more intelligent than his younger brother, upon whom the mantle of king was thrust in 1936.

Moreover, it has been asserted that Edward was politically naïve, that he failed to grasp the complexities of politics. This is also not true. Edward, Duke of Windsor, had a firm understanding of modern politics (by 1930s standards anyway), and any claims that he was a political unsophisticate has less to do with post-war attitudes regarding what was politically acceptable, and infinitely more to do with the need to denigrate and write off his importance as a man who could have become a considerable, if not incredibly dangerous, political force in the late 1930s and early 1940s.

CHAPTER ONE

Born to be King

To understand the many complexities behind the Duke of Windsor's character, to comprehend how and why he became anathema to the British government and royal family, it is necessary to forget all the misconceptions and propaganda churned out about him over the years. The legend has been firmly established over the last sixty years that Edward VIII abdicated his throne and place in history for love, and that, as Edward the good, Edward, romantic of the twentieth century, he was to be for ever condemned by the royal family, slighted at every turn, never to be forgiven for abandoning his duty to be king. However, this is not the whole truth, for there is much more to Edward than has ever been revealed. To reveal that truth would severely damage royal dignity and cause outrage amongst the British people, possibly shattering the monarchy's untouchable image for ever.

It must be remembered that if Edward VIII had not abdicated in 1936, he would still have been Britain's Head of State well into the 1970s, and the likelihood is that world and British history post-1937 would have been very different had he remained on the throne. The reasons for this are many and complex, and despite the modern photographs and Edward's own aspirations of being a 'modern man', it is important to realize that he was

9

born a Victorian at the end of the nineteenth century. He experienced the end of the old world of empire and royal prerogative, and witnessed the emergence of the new, modern world of telephones, cinemas, liners, motor-cars, and aeroplanes. From birth it was imprinted upon his personality to expect deference and exclusivity. His own conviction was that he was one *born to be king*. It is for these reasons that the story of the real events of 1939–40 has to start at the very beginning, for Edward's actions were not impulsive or impromptu, but based on forty-six years of experience and a culmination of events.

Edward Albert Christian George Andrew Patrick David Saxe-Coburg-Gotha, known as David to family and friends, was born on the night of 23 June 1894 at White Lodge, Richmond Park, London. Born into the most powerful and extended royal family in Europe, Edward was destined from birth to become King of Great Britain and the Dominions, Emperor of India, and Head of State to the mighty British Empire. He was every bit Queen Victoria's great-grandson, and she looked upon him as her long-term progeny to reign her empire into the latter half of the twentieth century. Great-grandmother Victoria, who Edward called *Gangan*, had been a prolific supplier of royalty during her long reign, and nearly all the European monarchies were related. Of Edward's uncles, Tsar Nicholas II was also his godfather, and Kaiser Wilhelm II his summer holiday host at Bernsdorff Palace. Edward's world was one in which an extended family encompassed the world's empires and holidayed in one anothers' homes. National boundaries only applied to their respective territories and the subjects they ruled, the 'great-game' of power-broking they played between each other.

As a child Edward was described as 'shy and nervous …

modest, interested ... a little shy with his father'.[1] Edward's own opinion of his childhood was that, 'I had few friends, little freedom. There was no Huckleberry Finn around to make a Tom Sawyer out of a stuffy and too timid English prince. Growing up for me was a prolonged misery.'[2] It was a world belonging to a bygone age, and rapidly drawing to a close as the world entered the twentieth century. After the death of Queen Victoria and then his grandfather, Edward VII, Edward's own father became British Sovereign as King George V in 1910, and then, in 1911, Edward himself became Prince of Wales at the age of seventeen, complete with the income of £100,000 a year that came from the Duchy of Cornwall. He spent the last happy holidays of his youth in 1913 visiting Germany, staying with 'Uncle Willie', the Kaiser, and his queen; visits, it has been suggested, 'that inspired his lifelong admiration of all things German'.[3] Edward's mother, Queen Mary, was, after all, a German princess, Mary of Teck, and throughout his life Edward would feel a strong affinity to Germany.

When the Great War broke out in 1914, Edward was given a commission in the Grenadier Guards, and, although prohibited from front-line action, he spent most of the next four years in France. The war was a time of crisis for Edward as, from safe behind the Western Front, he watched both his British and German heritages determinedly try to obliterate one another. Life was not easy for his superior officers either. Edward was enjoying enormously the break from the rigours of princely etiquette and duty, and maintaining his safety could be an irritating distraction for those Commanding Officers responsible for the lives of many thousands. One General made responsible for him sourly commented that Edward was 'fearless, but a bloody nuisance!'.[4] Regardless of what Edward would do in later years, what he saw in the First World War made him determined that peace should prevail between Germany and Britain, and the results of his meddling in 1939 and 1940 would be all the more tragic for everyone concerned.

By 1917, the increasingly anti-German paranoia being expressed by the British populace caused George V to fear for the survival of his dynasty and have a momentary loss of nerve. In a public relations exercise aimed directly at national consumption, George V abandoned the family's Germanic surname of Saxe-Coburg-Gotha, and adopted instead the altogether more British cognomen of Windsor. Kaiser Wilhelm II immediately saw through the tactic when he heard what his cousin had done, and acidly commented that next time he went to the theatre he looked forward to seeing *The Merry Wives of Saxe-Coburg-Gotha*.

However, the Great War had more shocks in store for Europe's royalty than the mere changing of names, and this was Bolshevism – the very antitheses of Monarchy. Tsar Nicholas II and his family had been particularly close to the British royal family, and their murder at the hands of the new Russian political system was to trouble George V's thoughts until the end of his days. Edward was to record that:

> Just before the Bolsheviks seized the Tsar my father had personally planned to rescue him with a British cruiser, but in some way the plan was blocked ... Those politicians ... if it had been one of their kind, they would have acted fast enough. But just because the poor man was emperor ...[5]

George V passed his fear of Bolshevism and social revolution on to his son, Edward, catalyzing the prince's thoughts into an anti-Bolshevik sentiment that would last the rest of his life, and threw him towards the other end of the political spectrum, a force that would prove all the more dangerous in the late 1930s. The years following the Great War were not easy for the British royal family, and the tone for the future was set just a few months after the Armistice when a meeting of Trade Unionists at the Albert Hall made it known that their ultimate intent was to see the red flag of socialism flying over Buckingham Palace. Viscount Esher, who foresaw problems ahead as millions of men were demobbed and now expected the promise of a 'land fit for heroes', wrote to George V's Private Secretary, Lord Stamfordham, in November 1918: 'The Monarchy and its cost will have to be justified in the future in the eyes of a war-worn and hungry proletariat, endowed with a huge preponderance of voting-power.'[6]

As Britain struggled through the depression-hit twenties and the anger of the 1926 General Strike, the spectre of class unrest rose its head and it became more important than ever for royalty to be *seen* to be playing an important role. Edward and his younger brother Prince Albert, later to become George VI, played a vital part in this campaign of 'selling' the family image, taking the public's attention away from the concepts of social upheaval and the preoccupation with royal cost. It is a little acknowledged but important fact that in the early 1920s, whilst Edward was sent to travel the Empire, showing the flag and selling the family 'firm', promoting trade and taking the headlines as the bright new force that would one day be king, Prince Albert played an equally important role in industrial relations. Everyone remembers Edward's visits to the Welsh mines in the 1930s, his comment that something 'must be done', even his later tour of Nazi Germany ostensibly in the cause of social welfare and working conditions, but it was Albert *not* Edward who was the expert in this field. Whilst Edward travelled the world making his mark, it was the altogether quieter, frailer, and more steadfast Prince Albert who helped set up the Industrial Welfare Society, aimed at improving working conditions in industry. His elder brother on the other hand travelled the world visiting Britain's colonies, receiving the adulation and press coverage more akin to a modern-day pop singer or movie star, fêted wherever he went. It was a task he would continue throughout the 1920s, presenting the world with the public face that was Edward, Prince of Wales. However, there were other sides to Edward, the private life that took a back seat and was never seen by the British populace – his poor relationship with his father, his political views, his penchant for affairs with married women.

Edward's penchant for having short-lived relationships, usually with married women, was a constant thorn in the lives of the royal courtiers for he frequently dodged his 'princely' duties to accommodate it. There were longer-term relationships too: his affair with the married Freda Dudley Ward for example, or his long-term relationship with Lady Thelma Furness. But often the briefer encounters were never reported in the press and were covered up for him by loyal retainers. Alan Lascelles, Edward's private-secretary, was often infuriated by the Prince's behaviour, finding it unacceptable in the prudish society of the inter-war period. Eventually the two men had a serious falling out during Edward's 1928 tour of Kenya, when news was received that George V was seriously ill – perhaps fatally so. Edward obstinately refused to cut short his tour for an early return to Britain. Lascelles recorded the confrontation in a letter to his wife:

> Then for the first and only time in our association, I lost my temper with him, 'Sir,' I said, 'The King of England is dying, and if it means nothing to you it means a great deal to us.' He looked at me without a word, and spent the remainder of the evening in the successful seduction of a Mrs Barnes, wife of the local Commissioner.

On another occasion, Lascelles was to write: 'I can't help thinking that the best thing that could happen to him and the country, would be for him to break his neck!'7 Alan Lascelles had a long memory, and in later years he would crop up time and time again to expound his dislike of the prince, often giving valuable insights into Edward's character.

Then, in the late autumn of 1929, Wallis Simpson entered Edward's life and his world began to turn upside down.

Edward first met Wallis Simpson whilst attending a party at the home of Lady Thelma Furness. Both Wallis and her husband Ernest Simpson were friends of Thelma's, and they began meeting Edward regularly at the Furness home until Edward and Wallis were coming into contact with each other on an almost weekly basis. This evolved into Edward dropping in for tea with Wallis at her Bryanston Court home, and then the friendship expanded to Wallis and Ernest being invited for weekends back at Edward's country retreat and home – Fort Belvedere. It was a slow passion that flourished between them, not an instantaneous affair, and whether Wallis set her sights on the prince from the start is not clear. What is known, however, is that after becoming well acquainted, Wallis began to insinuate herself increasingly into Edward's company until a deep relationship developed between the two – and Edward fell head over heels in love with her. Indeed, Kenneth de Courcy, a close friend of Edward's, was later to say: 'I have never known anyone so utterly possessed by another as he was by her. It was a form of Possession!'8 Yet, despite Edward's belief that his new romance was a well-kept secret from his father, George V knew full well of the relationship that was blossoming between the two, and the fact that she was an American divorcee of dubious background was causing shock waves to ripple through the Royal Court.

However, at the same time that Edward was falling for Wallis Simpson, another influence entered his life, an infatuation that was also to cause shock waves in the Royal Court, anxiety to George V, panic in Whitehall and Downing Street, and consternation in the diplomatic corp. It became a closely guarded secret within the higher echelons of British power that Edward, Prince of Wales and Britain's future king, had an all-consuming enthusiasm for the new political ideology and force in Europe – Fascism.

Ever since the murder of Tsar Nicholas and his family, Edward, in common with most other royalty, had an overriding fear of Bolshevism and a horror of unpleasant influences coming from the East – the unshatterable belief that Soviet Russia would attempt the ideological conquest of Europe. Bolshevism would be the pox that would infect the common man of Britain, bringing down its ordered social structure, and sweeping Edward's dynasty away. However, instead of reinforcing Edward's belief in the virtues of democracy, the need to present a united front and support a democratic system that required strengthening to fight off the threat, Edward flew to the other end of the political spectrum and saw fascism as the way forward. His support quickly developed far beyond just an inclination to look favourably upon the progress being made in Mussolini's Italy, to outright adoration of Hitler and the Nazis in Germany. He looked at Hitler's programmes to tackle mass-unemployment, the economic miracle that had turned Germany's economy around after the Nazis came to power, and greatly admired them. He even went so far as to publicly state that Britain should extend the hand of friendship to Hitler's new regime. A furious George V accused his son of unconstitutional behaviour by intervening in the foreign affairs of another state and making pro-German statements. Regrettably Edward took no notice of his father whatsoever, for he was by nature fascist, and gave further indications of where his sympathies lay by demeaningly referring to Britain and France as 'slip-shod democracies'.[9]

Whilst attending a party with Wallis in July of 1933, Edward found himself in conversation with Sir Bruce Lockhart discussing the most extraordinary political event of the year – the rise to power of Adolf Hitler and the Nazi Party in Germany. Lockhart later recorded that, 'The Prince of Wales was quite pro-Hitler and said it was no business of ours to interfere in Germany's internal affairs either re Jews or re anything else, and added that dictators are very popular these days and that we might want one in England before now.'[10]

Just four months later, on Armistice Day 1933, Edward had a long discussion with Count Mensdorff, the former Austrian Ambassador, and surprised the diplomat with his candour on where he thought Europe's future lay:

> It is remarkable how he [Edward] expressed his sympathies for the Nazis of Germany, [saying] 'Of course it is the only thing to do, we will have to come to it, as we are in great danger from the Communists here, too . . . I hope and believe we shall never fight a war again, but if so we must be on the winning side, and that will be the German, not the French . . .' It is interesting and significant that he shows so much sympathy for Germany and the Nazis.[11]

Two months before George V died, the old King confided to Lady Gordon-Lennox, 'I pray to God that my eldest son will never marry and have children, and that nothing will come between Bertie [George VI] and Lilibet [Elizabeth II] and the throne.' George V's health was beginning to fail seriously now, and very shortly before the end of his life, he predicted to Prime Minister Baldwin, 'After I am dead, the boy will ruin himself within twelve months . . .' King George V died in January of 1936, little realizing that both his prayer to God and prediction of the future would come to pass. Although Edward's star had now reached its zenith with his accession as King Edward VIII, it quickly began to fall as it became apparent to those in authority that his wayward ways, his insistence on meddling in politics, his dictatorial leanings and outright fascism, indicated he would become a political and constitutional problem of the first magnitude.

At the same time as Edward fell in love with Wallis Simpson and began to demonstrate an interest in fascism, some other characters now enter this tale. Their activities would set in motion a chain of events that would ultimately coincide with Edward's in 1939 and 1940.

In 1931 Baron William de Ropp, a Baltic Latvian who had served with the British Royal Flying Corp in the First World War, chased up an old acquaintance and fellow Flying Corp pilot, F.W. Winterbotham. By the early 1930s, Squadron Leader Freddy Winterbotham had become Head of the Air Intelligence Section of the British Secret Intelligence Service (SIS). Baron Bill de Ropp, who had spent several years living in Berlin, now contacted his old friend and told him that he had become a reliable conduit into the new force in Germany – the Nazi Party. After listening to de Ropp's information about the aims and methods of the Nazi movement, Winterbotham realized his old friend's access to the Nazi hierarchy was an intelligence opportunity he could not miss, and that it would be a good idea to learn all he could about this dynamic new force sweeping Germany.

As a result of this initiative Winterbotham, using de Ropp's assistance, invited Hitler's close confidant and editor of the Nazi newspaper *Volkischer Beobachter*, Alfred Rosenberg, to London for a whirlwind tour in the autumn of 1931. It is hard to judge who was profiting from whom, for Winterbotham and de Ropp proceeded to introduce Rosenberg to as many prominent British establishment figures as they could find, ostensibly promoting Anglo–German friendship. Rosenberg's visit to Britain in 1931 has always been shrouded in mystery, for it is not exactly clear what purpose it served, except that the snippets of information available show he was being introduced to useful future contacts. Rosenberg had meetings with Lord Hailsham, the British Secretary of State for War, and Lord Lloyd, whose Nazi sympathies would be discovered on the recovery of the Nazi archives from the Harz mountains in 1945, but undoubtedly the high point of his tour was his meeting with Montague Norman, Governor of the Bank of England. Montague Norman made substantial loans to Hitler's regime in the early 1930s and is now known to have done 'all he could to assist Hitlerism to gain and maintain political power, operating on the financial plane from Threadneedle Street'.[12] Norman, who liked to travel the world wearing an opera cape and using the alias of Professor Skinner, was an ardent supporter of Hitler, and later went on to play an important role in Czechoslovakia's downfall. In March 1939, the Directors of the Czech National Bank hid their country's gold reserve from the invading Nazis by transferring it to the Bank of England. After a request via the Nazi-linked Bank of International Settlement, Montague Norman promptly transferred a substantial sum back through the BIS in Basle, and the gold swiftly 'flowed into Berlin for use in buying essential strategic materials towards a future war.'[13]

After Hitler and the Nazis took power in 1933, Rosenberg returned to Britain for a second visit, only this time he made a beeline for the palatial Ascot home of Sir Henry Deterding (which, by a curious coincidence, was only a mere three miles from Fort Belvedere). It was reported in the press that:

> In light of the present European situation, this purely private talk between Hitler's Foreign Adviser (Rosenberg) and the dominant figure in European oil politics is of profound interest. It supports suggestions current in well-informed political circles that the big oil interests had been closely in touch with the Nazi Party in Germany.[14]

It was also claimed that Rosenberg had previously met Deterding during his Winterbotham sponsored visit of 1931. If Deterding and Rosenberg had met in 1931, then Winterbotham and de Ropp must have known. This is significant because Deterding was one of the wealthiest men in the world, and it can hardly be a coincidence that after Rosenberg's visit in the early 1930s, Deterding loaned Hitler almost £55,000,000.[15] Winterbotham was to spend a great deal of time in Germany in the 1930s, frequently meeting both Hitler and Hess, and was later to write:

> The Nazis, who were themselves daily gaining experience in the battle for men's minds, saw at much closer quarters than ourselves the tyranny of Communism ... in those early days the Nazis felt they had saved their country from Communism. Some of them even felt that we should help in this anti-Russian drive...[16]

In 1934, Winterbotham met Hitler in person, and during a frank discussion on foreign policy was told by the German Führer that, 'there should be only three major powers in the world, the British Empire, the Americas and the German Empire of the future,' which, he explained, 'would include the rest of Europe and the lands to the east. England, with one or two exceptions, would continue her role in Africa and India, while Germany would take Russia and together we could decide the policy for China and the Far East.' Hitler then declared, 'All we ask is that Britain should be content to look after her empire and not to interfere with Germany's plans of expansion.'[17]

However, unbeknownst to Winterbotham, this was also pretty close to what Hitler was whispering to Edward as well...

After being introduced into British society circles by Winterbotham in 1931, predominantly to those who had right-wing leanings, Rosenberg went on his merry way independently, expertly indulging in political intrigue and secret diplomacy on a highly organized scale. Having been introduced to many useful contacts, he spent considerable time and effort over the next few years cultivating a high-level network of people favourable to the Nazi cause. By January 1935, his activity began to pay dividends, for he received a strictly confidential report from de Ropp (who later turned out to be a double agent) advising him that he had succeeded in establishing a 'direct pipeline to Buckingham Palace'.

Late in the evening of 23 January 1935, de Ropp paid a clandestine visit to one of the royal residences specifically to meet Prince George, the Duke of Kent. According to Ladislas Farrago, a high official of the Spanish Foreign Ministry, de Ropp claimed that not only did the Duke of Kent definitely know he was a German agent and a conduit into the Nazi hierarchy, but that the initiative for the meeting had come from the Duke. George had pumped him for information, and de Ropp had been sure that the questions were being asked on the behalf of another. 'De Ropp recorded that the Duke declared Britain was reconciled to Hitler's determination to rearm Germany,' and 'was deeply interested, too, to know what made Hitler tick, and Hess, Göring, and Goebbels as well'.[18]

In the years ahead Prince George, Duke of Kent, would often act as an emissary for his elder brother – Edward.

Hitler, meanwhile, was never a man content to have only one string to his bow, and a completely independent line of communication was also developed to Edward. When Edward was thirteen he had his first meeting with his German cousin Karl Eduard, Duke of Saxe-Coburg-Gotha, and the two youths had become firm friends. Whilst Edward's life had gone on to include service in the Grenadier Guards during the First World War, and post-war travels around the world to promote trade and integrity within the Empire, Coburg had mirrored his cousin's career with service as an officer in the Prussian army, but had followed it through the 1920s and 30s with support for the Nazi Party. Coburg had fully embraced Adolf Hitler's doctrines, becoming a devoted follower of his Fuhrer and a senior officer in the Schutzstaffel, the infamous SS. Nevertheless, he was close to his British relatives, and whenever he was in London he stayed with his sister, Princess Alice, in her apartment at Kensington Palace. He would later be suspected of participating in the precision bombing-raid upon Buckingham Palace on 13 September 1940.

When the news broke on 20 January 1936 that King George V had died, Coburg immediately travelled out of London to Fort Belvedere to call on his cousin, the new King Edward VIII, who had just returned home having attended his father's death at Sandringham a few hours before. Coburg was the first political influence on the scene, immediately taking Edward aside to offer his condolences and engaging his cousin in a private conversation 'with pipe at fireside'. Coburg later reported to his Fuhrer that he had then 'accompanied him [Edward] on his journey to Bucking-ham Palace'. In fact, Coburg was Edward's sole companion on that journey to London, and the two men were virtually insepar-able for the next few days, often engaging in private lengthy discussions about the future direction that Edward wished his reign as king would take. Coburg's confidential reports to Hitler on these conversations show that as head of state of Great Britain and the British Empire, Edward was now in a position to realize his ambition of bringing Britain and Germany closer together. When Edward was asked by Coburg whether Baldwin would approve of these closer ties and would sanction Edward's meeting with Hitler, suggesting that perhaps Baldwin should take the lead, Edward had replied, 'Who is king here, Baldwin or I? I myself wish to talk to Hitler, and will do so here or in Germany.'[19]

Edward also made it very clear to Coburg that he had decided that his new role as king should not continue as the mainly symbolic position that the Monarchy had become, but that he intended the position should be one of real power, taking the authority of government and policy-making decisions back from Parliament and devolving them upon himself. Coburg assured Hitler that, 'King Edward is determined to concentrate the business of government on himself, although he admitted this was not too easy in England. The general political situation, though, especially the situation of England herself, will perhaps give him a chance. His sincere resolve to bring Germany and England together,' Coburg cautioned 'would be made more difficult if it were made public too early.' For this reason, he went on, 'I regard it as most important to respect the King's wish that the non-official policy of Germany towards Britain should be firmly concentrated in one hand and at the same time brought into relations of confidence with official policy.' Coburg concluded, 'The King asked me to visit him frequently in order that confidential matters might be more speedily clarified in this way, and to fly to London at any time he wishes.'[20]

Within two months of Edward's accession to the throne, Hitler would reap the benefits of his new-found ally by knowing that at long last the resolute defences of the West, the very foundations of the buttress that prevented German militarism and aggressive expansion, were being seriously undermined by a man whose pro-German inclinations would allow him to do exactly what he wanted. On the morning of 7 March 1936, Hitler took his first tentative steps towards war when he broke the Locarno Pact, ordering his troops to cross the Rhine bridges to re-militarize the Rhineland (the demilitarized zone controlled by France since 1920, and the West's guarantee that Germany would never again be able to invade Belgium and France). However, even as Hitler broke the treaties drawn up at the end of the First World War, he was still not too sure how secure Germany's position was, for he feared his actions might provoke France and Britain into a military counter-stroke, precipitating a war for which he was not yet ready.

In 1936, the might of Germany's war-machine was still very much a bluff, and Hitler knew all too clearly that Germany stood little chance of re-militarizing the Rhineland if France and Britain had a mind to stop him. As the troops of Germany's Reichwehr marched across the Rhine bridges at dawn on 7 March, Hitler nervously awaited the result of his actions aboard his special train as he travelled south to Munich. The atmosphere was tense, the Führer aloof and troubled until the train had stopped at a station and a message was handed aboard. Hitler read the message and sighed with relief, exclaiming, 'At last! The King of England will not intervene. He is keeping his promise. That means it can all go well.'[21] What Hitler had received was a ciphered telegram from his ambassador to London, Leopold von Hoesch. An extraordinary account of the events that day were recorded by Fritz Hesse, the German Press Attaché at the Embassy, who overheard the conversation between the British King and his ambassador. Edward had told von Hoesch, 'I sent for the Prime Minister [Baldwin], and gave him a piece of my mind. I told the old so-and-so that I would abdicate if he made war. There was a frightful scene, but you needn't worry, there won't be a war.'[22]

And a war there was not, for although French pride and political sense determined that Hitler should not get away with breaking the treaty that had kept Europe safe since 1919, they were reluctant to act without British support. On 11 March, Pierre Flandin, France's Foreign Minister, flew to London and begged the British government to back France in military action enforcing the Treaty of Locarno, but his pleas fell on deaf ears. 'The Germans, after all, are only going into their own back garden,' Lord Lothian declared. In the House of Commons, MPs listened to Anthony Eden who told them that the 'occupation of the Rhineland by the Reichwehr deals a heavy blow to the principle of the sanctity of treaties. Fortunately, we have no reason to suppose that Germany's present actions threaten hostilities.'[23] Hitler had won the first round, for he had known that France would be unlikely to take action without British support.

'The forty-eight hours after the march into the Rhineland, were the most nerve-racking of my life,' Hitler later confided to Schmidt, his interpreter. 'If the French had marched into the Rhineland, we would have had to withdraw with our tails between our legs, for the military resources at our disposal would have been wholly inadequate for even a moderate resistance.'[24] Had France ordered her vastly superior forces into the Rhineland and forcibly ejected the Reichwehr out of the Rhineland, the resultant fiasco would almost certainly have caused the downfall of the German dictator. 'That he survived at all has been attributed to his iron nerves, which alone saved the situation. But it is clear from the evidence that the arch schemer had laid his plans with Machiavellian precision, leaving very little to chance. He knew that Britain's reaction would be hamstrung by its pro-German king, who, if opposed, threatened to precipitate a constitutional crisis of the first order.'[25]

This was not the first occasion that Edward had interfered in a British foreign policy decision, directly challenging and opposing the course of action Stanley Baldwin and the British Government wished to pursue. Edward's defiance of his own government and determination to exert his own obdurate notions on how Europe should develop, made it clear to all that he intended to cast himself in the mould of his grandfather Edward VII, who on occasion had personally intervened between his cousins, the Kaiser and the Tsar. However, the world had moved on since the old-world diplomacy of the family grapevine, and it was now a much more dangerous place, especially since Edward VIII was not meddling in minor policy with his relatives, but openly siding

25

with Europe's aggressive dictators against his own government on matters of the utmost importance.

Edward's attitude to his government was succinctly put by Sir Henry 'Chips' Channon who commented at the time that Edward was: 'going the dictator way, and is pro-German. I shouldn't be surprised if he aimed at making himself a mild dictator, a difficult enough task for an English king.'[26] Just the previous autumn, in 1935, Edward had involved himself in the fate of Abyssinia, the vast and impoverished cotton-growing kingdom of Emperor Haile Selassie. His role in Abyssinia's downfall – invaded and brutally subjugated by Mussolini's forces in October 1935 – was not an honourable one, for, rather than defend an independent nation's right to self-determination, political ideology and fascist sympathy prompted his actions, and he threw the weight of his support behind the Italian dictator.

In the period between October 1935 and 20 January 1936, whilst he had still been Prince of Wales, Edward's influence had not been particularly great, except for his ability to meddle in Abyssinia's fate by meeting with an old acquaintance, the right-wing French politician Pierre Laval who sympathized with Mussolini's aims. Edward entered into discussions with Italian diplomats, and used his position and influence to oppose Anthony Eden's support of the League of Nations, who wished to press for sanctions. In December 1935, Edward flew to Paris for a private meeting with Pierre Laval, who together with the like-minded British Foreign Secretary, Sir Samuel Hoare, had devised the grandly named Hoare–Laval Pact – a plan whereby Mussolini would be allowed to keep his conquests in Africa. When Sam Hoare took his plan before the House of Commons, Edward took the highly unusual step of demonstrating his support for Hoare by attending the discussion and sitting in the Distinguished Strangers' Gallery. In a minority of one, Edward applauded Hoare repeatedly to show his approval of the plan, in stark contrast to the boos and cat-calls Hoare received from his fellow Members of Parliament. The Pact, by which Mussolini would relinquish a large, useless, tract of Italian Somaliland in exchange for a vast slice of Abyssinia's richest and most fertile cotton-growing region, was seen for what it was. Not only was the Bill thrown out by the honourable members, but so was Sir Samuel Hoare who was shuffled off to the Admiralty.

However, in his new role as head of state, King Edward VIII wielded a vastly greater authority than he had mere weeks before. He now met openly with Dino Grandi, Mussolini's ambassador to London, telling him that he wanted the Italian government to know he was on their side, and he regarded the British government's attempt to stop Mussolini by supporting the League of Nation's sanctions policy as 'grotesque and criminal'. He concluded his conversation with Grandi by commenting that, 'The League of Nations must ... be considered dead.'[27]

It became uncomfortably evident to Britain's senior politicians that Edward's increasingly pro-fascist and dictatorial leanings demonstrated that he intended to take the lead on policy, and they could now clearly see the situation developing before them where Edward would impose his will when opposed, threatening constitutional crisis whenever he could not have his own way. Edward's expressed intentions to cousin Coburg within the first hours of his reign, the principals of the *Führerprinz*, began to look like becoming a reality. Anthony Eden is said to have remarked that if Edward insisted on intervening in foreign affairs, there were ways and means of making him abdicate.[28] Although Edward had technically become British Head of State as King Edward VIII on his father's death in January 1936, his position was not completely secure for he would not fully become king until his Coronation on the 12 May 1937. It must have been blatantly obvious to everyone concerned, particularly Stanley Baldwin, that once Edward was officially crowned at

Westminster Abbey his position would become unassailable. It was impossible to gauge what would happen if it proved necessary to topple Edward once his position had become fully legitimized. Certainly it would have caused a dangerously unstable political environment, perhaps even precipitating a tumble into civil war, for who could tell that such a thing could not happen in Britain in the volatile Europe of the 1930s? Spain's monarch Alfonso XIII had been deposed, and civil war was raging in Spain; Britain had its own budding Franco in the form of Sir Oswald Mosley, and his support for Edward was well known. If anything was going to be done about Edward, it had to be done quickly and soon.

About this time, a three-sided correspondence began between Geoffrey Dawson, the editor of *The Times*, Canon Don of Westminster, who was understood to speak for the Archbishop of Canterbury, and a very senior official within Buckingham Palace (believed to have either been Alexander Hardinge or Alan Lascelles). After preliminary correspondence the three men agreed that as king, Edward was not much good, and as time went on things could only get worse. Something must be done. This resulted in Canon Don and the Buckingham Palace official asking Dawson to sound out the Dominions for their opinion on the prospect of Mrs Wallis Simpson becoming queen. They didn't want this 'opinion-poll' channelled through the Dominions Office for obvious reasons, and Dawson agreed to use his confidential acquaintances in Canada, New Zealand, and Australia, to sound out which way public opinion was running. The results of Dawson's enquiries began to return, and they were all of one accord – under no circumstance would the old Dominions accept Mrs Wallis Simpson as their future queen. It became clear to the three men that Wallis Simpson could become the excuse and means to remove Edward VIII from his throne.[29]

Shortly after this episode, a highly confidential and secret meeting took place between several government ministers, church leaders and senior civil-service mandarins at a secluded country house in Hampshire. They all met under the guise of a private shooting weekend, but what they really did was discuss their monarch and how he could best be manoeuvred off the throne. It was no secret to these men that as Edward's ever closer links to the Nazis developed, combined with his sense of security in his new position, he was becoming more blatant about his Nazi leanings, and increasingly inclined to assert his political will. This situation was additionally complicated by Edward's apparent inability, or unwillingness, to keep sensitive information and confidential briefings to himself, and it was known for certain that on several occasions when Edward had received a confidential briefing about a Cabinet meeting, diplomats in the German Embassy had known what had been discussed within hours. Additionally, his lax treatment of State papers sent to him for examination or signature had resulted in the ludicrous situation of the Foreign Office withholding sensitive information and diplomatic boxes from its own head of state. The participants at the shooting weekend were briefed that Wallis Simpson could become the tool to unseat their monarch.[30]

Although the accepted tale where Mrs Wallis Simpson is concerned has always been that as an American divorcee she would have been unacceptable as spouse to the British King, and by implication as queen, there have always been rumours that she had other less palatable qualities that made her unsuitable to the British establishment – the raison d'être for her exclusion. The first was that unsuitable as she was, Wallis had a hidden agenda behind her actions, that she was closely associated with prominent Nazis, particularly Joachim von Ribbentrop, whom she was known to be on very friendly terms with, and this made her a security risk. As a result, Britain's Intelligence Services ploughed considerable resources into watching Wallis, observing her comings and goings, whom she met with and so forth. As Frances Donaldson was to write in *Edward VIII*:

> One of the strangest aspects of Edward's reign is that he spent much of it under the surveillance of security officers. Mrs Wallis Simpson was the primary source of these attentions, but, they were so often together, it was impossible to take this kind of interest in one of them without extending it to the other.[31]

Wallis undoubtedly did know Ribbentrop, who by late 1936 had become the German Ambassador to Britain, and it is widely accepted that he went to considerable lengths to establish a cordial association with her. That she attended receptions at the German Embassy is also known, but her invitations could well have been the type of typically shrewd diplomatic move entered into by any embassy eager to curry favour with Edward. 'If one discounts the social backbiting, then it seems more likely to have been a useful ruse by the security services acting for the government to keep an eye on Edward, whose meetings with the Germans cannot have been ignored.'[32] Edward, with his connections through Coburg and de Ropp, certainly had much better lines of communication to Hitler and the Nazis than Wallis Simpson, and he is therefore most unlikely to have put Wallis at risk of compromise or worse by using her as a courier.

The second rumour about Wallis concerns the so called 'China Dossier', a file that contained all sorts of juicy and unsavoury facts about Mrs Simpson that made her unsuitable to be queen. This dossier had been compiled as the result of an investigation into Wallis, authorized by Baldwin shortly before the death of George V. It had started off as a search of American records in an effort to prove that Wallis had been born out of wedlock and had not been baptized, but had quickly gone on to allege that whilst living in China in the 1920s she'd indulged in 'perverse practices' in Chinese whorehouses, and that she'd been involved in drug dealing and gambling.[33] This document pandered to the establishment's paranoia that American divorcee Wallis Simpson was a mischievous, sinister figure, who had forced herself upon the royal family, and whose presence could only cause scandal. This document now came into its own for, as problematic as Edward was, support for unseating him could not be guaranteed and there were many for whom monarchy still meant unswerving loyalty, come what may. Any important person disssenting from the cause, any whose conscience made them feel ill at ease at toppling their monarch, was shown the dossier and told of its implications. It did much to bring dissenters into line.[34]

In August of 1936, whilst the various plots and intrigues against Edward were being initiated by private meeting, post, and shooting weekend, Edward, oblivious to the forces ranging up against him, decided to take Wallis on a Mediterranean cruise. He chartered a large yacht, the *Nahlin*, and cruised the length of the Mediterranean, taking in Yugoslavia, the Adriatic, Greece, the Aegean and Turkey. With him travelled his principal guest, Wallis Simpson, her close friends Herman and Katherine Rogers, and a smaller retinue of people who stayed a few days before departing; an ever changing range of conversation supplied by John Aird, Lady Diana and Duff Cooper (the British Minister for War), Mr and Mrs Humphrey Butler, and Edward's aides, Alan Lascelles and Godfrey Thomas. Whilst the world's newspaper readers gorged themselves on photographs of the British King stripped to his shorts splashing about in a row-boat, pictures of the romantic Wallis and Edward strolling hand in hand, and read the intense speculation about what might happen next, Britons were still blissfully unaware of their king's romance, for unofficial censorship in Britain still indulged Edward's sensibilities.

The cruise was an ill-considered move by Edward, indeed the

Foreign Office advised against it. There were certain practical and political reasons why the British government did not want their Head of State to go swanning off across the Mediterranean in the summer of 1936; the Spanish Civil War was raging at full force, and the Balkans – always a volatile region – were particularly dangerous. Only weeks before General Metaxas had seized power in Greece, and another European state had taken a leap into the world of dictatorship. Yet again Edward VIII, monarch of all he surveyed, deigned not to listen, for he had places to go, people to see, and politics to meddle in. Malcolm Muggeridge would later refer to the *Nahlin* as 'the good ship *Swastika*'.

After Edward's Mediterranean cruise was over, he returned to Britain by train, travelling through Bulgaria, Yugoslavia and Vienna on to Zurich, where a plane of the King's Flight awaited him. Several days after his return he paid a brief visit to London to see Queen Mary, and announced to his mother that he intended to take a two-week holiday at Balmoral in September. The old Queen's pleasure at what she took for a return to duty turned sour however, when instead of the usual band of dignitaries, Edward invited Wallis Simpson and her friends, the Rogers. Edward's brothers and their families, who traditionally holidayed in the area, were given extreme offence when on being invited to Balmoral they found their hostess to be Mrs Wallis Simpson, American divorcee. It was at this point that Edward began to alienate his subjects as well, showing scant regard for their sensibilities and feelings. Months before, Edward had been asked to open a new infirmary at a hospital in Aberdeen, but had refused on the grounds that he was still in mourning for his late father, George V. The Scottish populace were now scandalized and outraged when they discovered that, on the due day, Edward had avoided the duty to meet a train at Ballater Station with the sole purpose of escorting Mrs Wallis Simpson to Balmoral. 'Chips' Channon, an astute discerner of the situation later wrote that if:

The Mediterranean cruise was a press disaster, then the visit to
Balmoral was a calamity, after the King chucked opening the
Aberdeen Infirmary, and then openly appeared at Ballater
Station on the same day to welcome Wallis to the Highlands.
Aberdeen will never forgive him.[35]

The lid could not be kept on the press pressure-cooker for
much longer, for although the world's newspaper readers had
been agog for months – with speculation rife as to whether
Edward would marry Mrs Simpson – all but a very few well-
connected Briton's, those in the know or whose lifestyles permitted foreign travel, had ever heard of Mrs Wallis Simpson. This
was due to Edward's use of his old-boy network to keep the lid
on the story and keep his private life out of the public domain of
the newspapers.

In October, Stanley Baldwin returned from his own holiday
to find a vast assortment of letters of protestation from British
residents abroad denouncing their king's romance, proclaiming
that loyalty to the Empire would be stretched too far if Edward
inflicted 'that woman' on his subjects. To add extra seasoning to
the unwholesome brew Mrs Simpson was by then petitioning for
a divorce from her husband, citing adultery on Mr Simpson's
part. Edward's cause was not made any easier when it was
discovered that Wallis had sent personal congratulations at the
beginning of the month to Sir Oswald Mosley and his new wife
Diana, on the occasion of their marriage in the Berlin home
of Dr Goebbels, complete with Adolf Hitler in attendance as a
guest.

Stanley Baldwin was a shrewd politician, although many
would have preferred the epithet 'crafty'. He was a solid, rather
old-fashioned, kindly man who had the reputation for laziness,
but this was a deliberate almost rural manner that avoided
precipitate action. His inclination was to let things run their

natural course before stepping in to reap the rewards.[36] The time had come for a confrontation with Edward, and thus when he went to see his king, Baldwin already knew the time was fast approaching when Edward would precipitate some action from which the government would reap the rewards.

During the meeting Baldwin told Edward that press coverage already spreading through the Americas, Commonwealth, and Europe, would soon reach British shores. The story could not be kept secret for much longer. Baldwin further advised him that Mrs Simpson would not be acceptable as queen, implying that if Edward insisted on his determination to marry her, he and his government would be forced to resign. Edward's response was to declare that he intended to marry Wallis Simpson, and that if it was not acceptable he would abdicate. He was later quoted as telling friends he'd had Baldwin over a barrel, saying, 'No wedding, no Coronation.' Little did Edward realize it, but he was manoeuvring himself into a position from which he'd have no choice but to go anyway. Edward's attempted negotiation proceeded through the remainder of October and all of November, with Edward endeavouring to find a solution – a compromise that would enable him to make Wallis acceptable to the Government – but unaware that *whatever* he suggested Baldwin would not agree.

In early November, Edward suggested that if he married Wallis using his title as Duke of Lancaster she could become his wife, but not technically queen – the suggestion was not accepted.

Towards the end of November Edward sent a friend, Esmond Harmsworth, to visit Baldwin to suggest a morganatic marriage. This legal loophole was a ploy by which a man of high rank might marry a woman of inferior status, but she would not acquire the man's rank and neither she nor any future children would be entitled to inherit his title or possessions. Reporting back to Edward after his interview with the Prime Minister,

Harmsworth revealed that Baldwin had seemed 'surprised, interested and non-committal'. A few days later Edward sent for Baldwin and asked him for his reaction to the morganatic marriage suggestion. Baldwin would not commit himself officially, but if Edward wanted 'a horseback opinion', he thought it unlikely Parliament would pass the necessary legislation. He then went on to point out to his king that before the proposal could be submitted to Parliament, it would first have to be considered by both the British and Dominion Cabinets. Placing the ball firmly in the King's court, Baldwin pointedly asked Edward if he wished him to submit the proposal to the Cabinets. Edward replied that he did. Edward had unwittingly handed Baldwin the chance to give the screw an extra turn, for the marriage would now have to be put before the Dominions, and the possible result of that had already been gauged several months before by Dawson of *The Times* – the suggestion of a morganatic marriage was refused.

December came, and with it ever increasing press speculation and public anxiety, for the story had by now broken in the British press as well. Edward's position was fast becoming most uncomfortable and Wallis, in a welter of photographers flash-bulbs and smothered by reporters, left for France on the night of 3 December with the intention of travelling onto the French Riviera home of Herman and Katherine Rogers. Edward's cause was hardly being helped by Sir Oswald Mosley's calls for a referendum, complete with a public announcement that he and his Blackshirts were entirely on Edward's side.

Edward had one last card up his sleeve, still believing that Might was Right, he went to Downing Street and announced to Baldwin that he intended to put his position to the people of Britain. He would make a radio broadcast, and appeal to their loyalty as his subjects over their elected government. The spectre of civil war peeked over the horizon, and Baldwin undoubtedly blanched. What Edward was suggesting was tantamount to 'A King's Party';[37] if Baldwin acceded to his wish, and allowed Edward to ask for the people's support over that of the government, the country might divide, splitting down the middle to pit Parliament against King, just as it had during the reign of Charles I. Baldwin braced himself and proclaimed that such 'an appeal to the people over the head of the government would be unconstitutional.'[38]

'You want me to go, don't you?' Edward had demanded angrily.

'What I want, sir,' Baldwin had replied calmly, 'is what you told me you wanted: to go with dignity, not dividing the country ... To broadcast would be to go over the heads of your ministers . . .'[39]

On 10 December 1936, Edward lunched with Winston Churchill. Throughout the autumn's discussions – the wrangling over marriage or abdication – Churchill had stood resolutely behind his king; it was to be a stance he was to pay for with continued banishment to the political wilderness for the next two and a half years, until Europe tumbled into war in 1939. By 1940 though, Churchill would eventually learn what Edward was really capable of in support of his absolute belief in his right to rule, and in the late summer of 1940 he would confide to Baldwin that he had been wrong in his support of Edward during the abdication crisis, stating it would have led to an 'eventuality too horrible to contemplate.'[40] This change in attitude, from unquestioning loyalty to the admission that his judgement in this instance was not all it should have been, was rare indeed in Churchill. However, he expanded this change of heart in later years by admitting his mistake to Lord Beaverbrook, another loyal Edward supporter. Beaverbrook later recorded a conversation he had with Churchill when the two of them had agreed that, since they always differed about everything, one of them must always have been right. 'Except once,' Beaverbrook had said, mentioning the abdication.

'Perhaps we were both wrong that time,' Churchill replied.[41]

Later that night Edward made his abdication speech from Windsor Castle and Britons listened to their radios as Sir John Reith announced, 'This is Windsor Castle. His Royal Highness, Prince Edward,' followed by a strangely wavering voice with an Americanized-cockney accent that proclaimed:

'At long last I am able to say a few words of my own.

'I have never wanted to withhold anything, but until now it has not been constitutionally possible for me to speak...' He went on to declare his loyalty to his brother, now King George VI, how he would not stay without Wallis, and how he had 'found it impossible ... to discharge my duties as king as I would wish to do ...'

Over sixty years later it is still possible to listen to Edward's abdication speech, hear the wavering voice, take note of the purposeful inflection Edward gave to the statement 'as I would wish to do,' hinting that he had not been permitted to rule Britain in the way in which he had intended, yet clearly not declaring his colours by stating outright that he had wished to devolve increased power upon himself at the expense of Parliament.

In central London five hundred of Oswald Mosley's Blackshirts gathered before Buckingham Palace, giving the fascist salute and chanting: 'We want Edward!' and 'One, two, three four five, we want Baldwin, dead or alive!' Other Blackshirts picketed the House of Commons waving placards that demanded, 'Sack Baldwin. Stand by the King!' The following morning fascists gathered for a mass rally at Stepney, and before an audience of three thousand, Sir Oswald Mosley demanded that the abdication should be put before the people. Windows were smashed, fascist and socialist fought openly in the streets. Britain seemed to momentarily teeter on the verge of an abyss.

At Herman and Katherine Rogers' French Riviera home, Villa Lou Viei, Wallis listened to Edward's abdication speech in the company of her friends. Wallis always claimed to have been quietly reserved and grief-stricken as she listened to Edward's abdication speech, but there are other versions of what happened that night. A maid who was present insists that a grim-faced Wallis muttered, 'The fool, the stupid fool.'[42] Katherine Rogers later claimed that after Edward's broadcast was over, Wallis flew into a tantrum, screaming with rage and smashing things.[43]

Late on that dark winter's night of 10 December 1936, Edward, now Duke of Windsor, was taken by car to Portsmouth where HMS *Fury* awaited to carry him across the Channel. After a mere 325 days as king he was being cast out – departing into exile with only the vaguest idea where he was going, for few plans had been made. He had wanted to go to France to be near Wallis, but his lawyers insisted that in the interests of her divorce he must keep a national border between them until her divorce became absolute. On entering France in the early hours of 11 December, he boarded the Orient Express and made his way to Austria where he stayed at Baron Rothschild's impressive mountain home – Schloss Enzesfeld. He would stay here for nearly three months, leaving in March 1937 to move to a smaller, more private establishment near Ischl.

On the morning following Edward's abdication, MP Harold Nicolson had a chance meeting with Alan Lascelles, and was taken aback by the man's anger and vitriolic tirade against his former employer. At long last, after years of serving Edward, Lascelles finally vented his spleen and said what he truly thought of the man who had been king for less than a year. Alan Lascelles observed angrily:

He was without a soul, and this has made him a trifle mad. He will probably be quite happy in Austria. He will get a small *Schloss*; play golf in the park; go to nightclubs in Vienna ... There is no need to be sorry for him. He will be quite happy wearing his silly little Tyrolese costumes. He never cared for England or the English. That was all eyewash. He rather hated this country.[44]

After spending a quiet Christmas with only a few aides and friends for company, January 1937 came and Edward discovered that his old friend, Major 'Fruity' Metcalfe was skiing across the border at Kitzbühel.

Major Edward Dudley Metcalfe, known as 'Fruity' to his intimates, had been one of Edward's few real friends since the early 1920s, when they had met in India. The dashing young cavalry officer had gone on to manage the Prince's stables, shared his company to hunt and play polo, and acted as friend-come-escort during Edward's excursions to London's night-clubs. Major 'Fruity' Metcalfe was also Sir Oswald Mosley's brother-in-law and a member of the January Club, a right-wing association affiliated to Mosley's Blackshirts, although there is nothing to suggest that he was actually of strong right-wing leanings, or ever involved in any of Edward's political machinations. This raises the interesting question whether 'Fruity', connected to Mosley through marriage, was actually engaged in intelligence work and keeping an eye on the right-wing in Britain. This would certainly explain the very strange coincidence that when Edward left for exile 'Fruity' should just happen to be skiing a few miles away, and would certainly explain much of what would happen to 'Fruity' later. There had been a brief lapse in their friendship over the past year of Edward's kingship during 1936, for having been a close friend for many years, 'Fruity' not unreasonably had expected to be offered a job in the new King's household.

However, Edward was ever expedient when it came to his friends, picking them up or dropping them as whim or usefulness suited him. There had been no job.

After receiving a lonely plea from Edward, however, the ever loyal and genuine friend 'Fruity' dropped everything and hurried to cheer up his ex-monarch. During the following months of Austrian exile, Edward was comforted by the companionship of his old friend 'Fruity' who would also become Edward's best man at his wedding. 'Fruity' was also destined to become Edward's on-off-on aide until June 1940, when Edward suddenly abandoned him in a Paris imminently to be occupied by the Germans, leaving him alone, without funds, transport, or any form of official assistance to aid his escape back to Britain – but that was three years away, and 'Fruity' Metcalfe was still a friend who would not openly judge him.

On 'Fruity's arrival, their friendship immediately took off again with great enthusiasm; 'Fruity' writing to his wife that Edward was in great form and a joy to be with. There were other disquieting features about the *new* Edward however, ones 'Fruity' was not quite sure about for he wrote, 'He has become very foreign – talks German all the time.'[45]

Edward threw himself enthusiastically into physical recreation, skiing all day, talking late into the night; but he was only killing time, ticking off each day until he could be with Wallis, remarking every night, 'One more day nearly over.'

'It's very pathetic,' Metcalfe commented.[46]

On 4 February 1937, Edward was visited by Franz von Papen, the dapper former German Vice-Chancellor whose slippery intrigues had backfired and helped Hitler into power in 1933. Von Papen had been sent to Austria in late 1934 to smooth over the mess left by the Nazi murder of Austrian Chancellor Dollfuss, and he was now busily undermining Austrian independence for the coming *Anschluss*, barely a year away. Edward and von Papen took themselves off into the seclusion of the library and had a long and very private chat.

Edward still did not clearly understand the implications of his abdication, and was telephoning King George VI virtually every night, offering his younger brother unwanted advice, guidance and policy 'suggestions', and generally treating him as a mere caretaker king, covering for his temporary absence. Often, Edward belligerently gave advice that 'ran counter to the advice that the King was getting from his responsible ministers in the government.'[47] The security services correctly suspected that the Germans were listening in on every call,[48] and Edward's complete obliviousness to the need for guarding what he said was still causing security leaks. His interference was upsetting George VI, disconcerting the young King and undermining his confidence as he valiantly tried to overcome his acute shyness and nervous stammer. Kingship was a responsibility George VI was ill prepared for physically or mentally; he had not been trained in the art of 'ruling', and as Duke of York had fully expected to live a quiet private life as a country landowner, managing estate matters, attending the occasional royal function. He had never dreamt that he would one day have the mantle of king thrust upon him, and it had come as an unpleasant shock.

In mid February Walter Monckton arrived at Schloss Enzesfeld, charged with the delicate task of informing Edward that the daily telephone calls to the new King had to stop. He sweetened the bitter pill of rejection by telling him that he had also brought news of the financial settlement that would enable him to survive comfortably as the Duke of Windsor. The calls stopped.

*

On 1 March, Wallis Simpson, who was still staying with Herman and Katherine Rogers on the French Riviera, wrote to a Mrs Fern Bedaux who lived near Tours:

> It is frightfully difficult for me to convey one tenth of what I feel about you and Mr Bedaux's kindness and generosity to the Duke of Windsor and myself. When we meet perhaps I can make you realize a little of it. I am so looking forward to our arrival at Candé on the ninth and I hope you will not have a shock at the size of the caravan.[49]

American multi-millionaire Charles Eugene Bedaux had philanthropically offered the use of his multi-turreted Renaissance castle, Chateâu de Candé, to Wallis as a retreat at the time of the abdication, and one of her first letters to Edward on 12 December referred to it directly. Correspondence between Wallis and Edward had resulted in their decision to take up the offer of the French chateau and use it as their place to wed.

George VI had been consulted. He'd approved the location, and all looked rosy.

Journalist Janet Flanner once asked Charles Bedaux about his friendship with the Windsors, and he'd replied in what she called 'his occasionally troubled English' saying, 'I never met them until I got to Candé as to her; as to him, until he arrived at Candé.'[50]

However, Mr Bedaux was not quite as innocent as he seemed, for, far from being a kindly, philanthropic gentleman who only wanted to see true love prosper in the gentile surroundings of his beautiful French home, Charles Eugene Bedaux had a past and pedigree that would have made George VI's hair stand on end, had he but been told the truth.

CHAPTER TWO

The Efficiency Engineer

WHEN CHARLES BEDAUX offered his chateau to Wallis Simpson in December 1936, it was no mere charitable gesture by an American abroad trying to help a fellow expatriate, and his agenda was not at all innocent. Had Downing Street and those Palace officials advising George VI known or guessed the truth about Mr Bedaux, and had they been given some intimation that a dangerous situation was developing around their vanquished former king, a panic should have flashed through Britain's corridors of power sending her intelligence defences swinging into action. However, nothing happened; no warning about Mr Bedaux's unsuitability surfaced, no hint that his very presence in Edward's company was a danger of the first magnitude. Yet Britain's Intelligence Services, whose responsibility it was, should and *must* have known about Mr Bedaux for he had been an undesirable element for a very long time. To appreciate the danger Bedaux posed it is necessary to know about his past, to understand *why* he would ultimately assist Edward beyond the bounds of perfidy, for he was an ambitious individual with a magnetic personality and not without a personal charm – a carefully managed public persona that was as different from reality as it is possible to imagine.

Charles Eugene Bedaux cut a flamboyant figure in 1930s

European society. A well-built man with Brilliantined dark hair swept back from a high brow and prominent ears, he habitually wore double-breasted jackets of the best cut, trousers with knife-sharp creases, and two-tone brogues known as co-respondents, nicknamed 'divorcees' for their ability, it was said, to carry the wearer in and out of a lady's bedroom without a sound. He was one of those men who had the ability to charm his way in or out of any situation, and his personality positively fizzed with the energy of a fanatic. His reputation as the kindly American philanthropist who just happened along was very carefully stage-managed indeed.

Bedaux was to play a key role in Edward's future, yet very little of real substance is publicly known about him, except for the benevolent and goodly image that was presented at the time. This was so firmly fixed in the popular imagination that it has lasted largely intact ever since.

To smash this false frontage one has to step back to a time when Charles Bedaux first came to the attention of the intelligence services in the United States.

On the morning of 5 December 1917, in a Washington swiftly chilling in the first weeks of winter, Colonel R.H. Van Deman (Chief of the Military Intelligence Section of the War Department) based at 1435-K Street, received a report from William S. Fitch, a field operative of the Intelligence Section of Camp Custer, Michigan. This report concerned a mysterious Frenchman who had recently moved to nearby Grand Rapids, and who was engaged in activities that could only be construed as spying. This was a particularly sensitive region to American security at the time as it was the heart of their industrial centre, between the manufacturing cities of Detroit and Chicago, and near the military establishments at Muskegon and Ludington, where a plant had just been established to build war planes. It was the start of an interest in Mr Bedaux that would, over the next twenty-six years, cross national boundaries, span continents, result in an FBI investigation conducted personally by J. Edgar Hoover, involve US Secretaries of State, and eventually reach the White House – yet today Mr Bedaux remains a virtual unknown.

What Van Deman read in William Fitch's report caused him great concern, and he immediately began marking sections with a red pencil. The report was supplemented by a letter from Fitch's superior officer, Major Gillespie, who wrote:

> Suspect claims to be of French descent and to have served in the French Foreign Legion as an enlisted man. Came to Grand Rapids, Mich. from France some time between Jan. 1915–17. Arrived without funds. Speaks English, French, and German. Is an efficiency expert. Always makes blue-prints of factories where he is employed which he reduces to postcard size. Has in his possession maps of Muskegon Harbor and Continental Motor Co. of Muskegon, Michigan. His associates at private dinners are all persons under suspicion by the government.[1]

Eighty years after Fitch's report was first written, it is now possible to reveal more about this man's background than American Intelligence could unearth at the time, setting Bedaux into context among the extraordinary events that were to develop around him at the start of the Second World War.

Charles Eugene Bedaux was born in Paris on Sunday, 10 October 1886, at 13 Avenue de Grenelle, within sight of where Gustave Eiffel would begin construction of his tower the next year. Bedaux's birth was duly registered the following day by his parents, Charles and Marie, in the presence of family friends Henri Gascougnoble and Auguste Hauvert.[2] Within a few short years this young thriving family, headed by father Charles Emile Bedaux, a mathematician and French Railway

Executive, had expanded until Charles Jr had three siblings – two brothers, Daniel and Gaston, and a sister, Marcelle. The young Charles Bedaux went through normal schooling and finished his education at the Say College, graduating in 1903 as a civil engineer.

On 4 February 1906, at the age of nineteen, Bedaux departed from Cherbourg aboard the *SS Staatinday*, bound for the United States of America and his first adventure, arriving in New York on 14 February. From here he travelled by train to Arkansas and Georgia,[3] where he became employed as a mining engineer. During his interrogation in 1943, Bedaux revealed that in 1907:

> I applied for my first [naturalization] papers in St Louis, Missouri, and I voted for President Taft in November 1908 without committing an illegal act. The law in Missouri permitting men having taken out their first papers to vote on the Presidential Election, and for that reason I voted for President Taft.[4]

It was during his time in St Louis that the first great change occurred in Bedaux's life when he met and married his first wife, Blanche Allen of Little Rock, Arkansas. Despite her Anglo-Saxon surname, American investigators suspected Blanche's parents were German. To explain this discrepancy in her surname, it is important to understand that it was a common practise during the great emigrations to the United States at the turn of the century for people with uncommon surnames often to have simplified names given to them by immigration officials overwhelmed by thousands of people a day. Thus, someone entering New York's Ellis Island as an Adlon, Aller, or Alois might well have become an Allen.

In June of 1909, Blanche gave birth to a son who they named

Charles Emile II in honour of Bedaux's father, and in December 1911 the whole family travelled back to France, ostensibly to visit Bedaux's relatives. However, they remained in Europe for six months, and when Bedaux returned to America in May of 1912, a fortnight after the *Titanic* sank, it was a quite different sort of person who returned. Evidently, during Bedaux's six-month stay in Europe something occured that changed the course of the rest of his life.

Up until now Bedaux's life had been quite unremarkable, however, it was now to undergo a sea change and his personality would radically alter, turning him into the ruthless efficiency expert and intelligence gatherer that he would remain until the end of his days. In fact, the differences between the man that departed American shores in 1911 and the man who returned in 1912 were so great that many in the FBI, particularly J. Edgar Hoover, didn't believe it was the same man. However, as easy as it would be to accept this as the cause for what was to follow, it was not the case. The Bedaux that departed for Europe with a new wife and young child was the same Bedaux that returned – except it was Bedaux's very personality that had radically changed. Perhaps his new life in America had not been all he had hoped for, or maybe the pressures of supporting a young family drove him into acts he would not normally have considered. The truth about what occurred in Bedaux's time in Europe will probably never be known, but it is possible to speculate on the various catalysts that may have turned him into an agent of Imperial Germany. To start with there is evidently a German connection through Blanche, and so it is possible that they visited her relatives in Germany as well as Bedaux's during that six months. It does not therefore take a genius to realize that if one of Blanche's relatives was connected to the German intelligence services in some way, they would have looked at Bedaux and realized he made the ideal agent – stable, established, and with the perfect opportunities for entering and examining America's most sensitive of industries. The other possibility is that it may have been an out-of-the-blue recruitment; such methods are not unknown even today, and Bedaux certainly was always a man with a keen eye for the main chance, particularly if good financial remuneration were on offer – which intelligence reports of 1917 made clear had been part of the inducements.

After a brief return to the United States in 1912, Bedaux was back in Europe by 1913, a resident in Alsace (always a source of Franco-German dispute) with a second home in Brussels, working as 'a German spy . . . doing efficiency work in Belgian factories for the German government'.[5] It was a remarkable jump in fortune for a man who only eighteen months before had been a humble civil engineer in the American mid-west. However, during Bedaux's first intelligence-gathering venture not everything ran smoothly. In early 1914 the Belgian authorities became aware of Bedaux's activities and *asked* him none too politely to leave their country forthwith, whereupon he removed himself back to Paris, staying in France for the rest of 1914, and was present in France at the outbreak of the First World War.

In January of 1915, Bedaux reappeared in the United States and moved into a set of rented rooms at 306 Eureka Drive, Grand Rapids, Michigan. Once established in this minor North American city on the shores of Lake Michigan, a mere 100 miles from Chicago and the centre of American industry of the time, he opened an office at 1112 GR Savings Bank Building, Grand Rapids, bought a motor-car, took out advertising, and announced himself open for business as an efficiency engineer.

Perhaps the only hint at the direction Bedaux's new career took comes from an American intelligence officer who surreptitiously managed to 'pump' Blanche (whom he also suspected of being a spy), during a train journey from Chicago to Richmond in the summer of 1916:

She was young and pretty, very clever, and spoke French, Spanish and German. She had a little boy with her about six years old. She told me her husband was a mechanical and electrical engineer whose business took him all over the world; that they had both just returned from Spain and France and that he was now getting ready to go to Japan and that she perhaps would go with him ... She told me her husband's office was at Grand Rapids, Michigan, in the Perkins Building; that her parents were German; that they lived in St Louis; that she spent most of her time with them while her husband was travelling.[6]

A later intelligence report made the agent's suspicions about Mrs Bedaux abundantly clear:

Bedaux's wife went to Japan last fall, taking with her, her young son and a young woman companion. Preparations for this trip were hastily made, and when statements were made that it was risky to cross the ocean at that time, Bedaux said a woman was not so liable to be suspected as a man.[7]

The implications were obvious; Bedaux was suspected of using his wife and young son as couriers. That it was financially rewarding there can be little doubt, for by 1916 Bedaux was earning in excess of $10,000 a year – a phenomenal sum of money at the time – and prone to much suspicion by those watching him, vastly exceeding as it did the earnings possible through his burgeoning efficiency business in the United States.[8] This money undoubtedly subsidized Bedaux's early business career, and gave him the financial backing and security to help him become the success he was in later years.

The core of Bedaux's efficiency business was very simple in fact; a factory owner would hire Bedaux to examine his production line, study the routine of his workers, and Bedaux would then set new work rates for the staff according to a 'formula' he'd invented – the grandly named *Bedaux System*. Those exceeding the new work quotas received a minimal bonus, whilst those who failed were penalized or fired; production was increased at less cost, and the factory bosses were delighted. It was not a very exhilarating enterprise, but it did have the distinct advantage of being a remarkably good cover for a man engaged in espionage, for by the very nature of Bedaux's business, any manufacturer wishing him to increase productivity and profits had to make Bedaux privy to the whole production technique.

Before long Colonel Van Deman was being informed that the expatriate French population of Grand Rapids shunned Mr Bedaux, convinced that he was a German spy.

The investigation into Bedaux established that his rooms on Eureka Drive were rented to him by a Mrs Lucie Margantin, whose husband had died a few months before. Being of French origin Mrs Margantin had advertised for a French lodger, and Mr Bedaux had duly appeared telling her he was a Frenchman who'd been in the French Foreign Legion. He'd described his past vaguely by telling her that he had fought in the French trenches during the latter half of 1914, before being injured and invalided out of the war, after which he had decided to emigrate to America. His wife was travelling, he confided, visiting her parents in St Louis.

It was not long, however, before Bedaux began to be suspected of being more than just a simple immigrant French ex-soldier. Firstly, Mrs Margantin maintained that Bedaux had swindled her out of a camera with a Bausch & Lamb Zeiss Tessars 8½ inch lens, a piece of equipment that was so specialized that the Signal Service of the US Army had actually been advertising for one in the press. This he used to photograph 'blue-prints of factories where he is employed which he reduced to postcard size',[9] before sending copies of them to his wife who was travelling extensively all over the United States, Panama, and making repeated trips to Japan. Bedaux was seen taking detailed photographs of factories, production techniques, munitions plants, docks, airfields, and Muskegon Naval Harbor, as well as having in 'his possession maps of Muskegon Harbor and Continental Motor Co. [who produced armoured cars] of Muskegon, Michigan.'[10]

Next, American Military Intelligence discovered that Bedaux's closest associates, a German music teacher named Carl Andersch and a Mrs W. Rowe, were also suspected of espionage and had been under constant surveillance long before Bedaux had ever arrived in Grand Rapids – the implication being that Bedaux had gone to Grand Rapids pre-informed of an espionage cell that he should contact. One of Van Deman's agents, operative E. Berkley-Jones, was referred to a chiropodist named Mr Labouslier who informed him that Bedaux occasionally gave lectures in the Grand Rapids Public Library. Labouslier had attended one of these lectures, but it had been so rabidly pro-German that he and his wife, as well as half the audience, had walked out. At Bedaux's last lecture his remarks had been so outrageous that the audience had shouted him down, calling him a German spy to his face; Bedaux had made no retort, merely picking up his hat and coat before walking out. On another occasion, Bedaux had shocked the assembled guests at a private dinner party by raising his glass and giving the toast, 'Prosit to the Kaiser!'[11]

Van Deman decided to check into Bedaux's past and he wrote to General Vignal, the Military Attaché at the French Embassy in Washington. Van Deman described Bedaux in detail to Vignal, telling him that Bedaux had a limp and claimed to have been invalided out of the war having been injured in the trenches, and all he had in his possession was a French uniform but no discharge papers. Two months later a reply came back from the French Embassy informing Van Deman that records on Bedaux had been found; he had enlisted into the Second Foreign Regiment on 22 August 1914, going straight to a military basic-training camp for instruction. In November 1914, Bedaux had gone on to receive Infantry training and had been promoted to Corporal. However, he had been placed on compulsory retirement from the army lists on 26 December 1914 with bacillary haemoptysis. Bedaux had been in uniform for four months, but had only ever been in basic training. He had never been in action.[12]

Puzzled, and more convinced than ever that Bedaux was a German agent, Van Deman wrote to Bruce Bielaski, the Chief of the Department of Justice's Bureau of Investigation. He enumerated his suspicions to Bielaski that Bedaux was a spy, and asked if he had come to anyone else's attention. Bielaski replied that his files contained no more information on Bedaux than Military Intelligence had already gathered, but asked if Van Deman would like the Department of Justice to start an investigation.

In January of 1917 Bedaux's first wife, Blanche, divorced him and a month later he married the new person in his life, society girl Fern Lombard of Kalamazoo, Grand Rapids. She would remain at his side through to the end twenty-six years later. That Bedaux knew Fern before Blanche divorced him there can be little doubt, for the intelligence operatives watching him could not fail to notice that Bedaux was a 'popular figure with the ladies', and they somewhat tongue in cheek recorded that, 'his escapades are not unknown to the public' and he married 'Miss Lombard of this city, evidently having violated the interlocutory decree'.[13]

Even Bedaux's wedding to Fern on 17 February 1917 had an extrovert image, for it was reported in the *Grand Rapids Herald* under the headlines: 'Punctures Tire – Lo! Society Girl is Wed'.

After beginning, 'A quiet country road! A glowing sunset! A punctured tire! A good Samaritan who happened along!' the newspaper report went on to tell the tale that Bedaux and Fern had been speeding along in their motor car en route from Kalamazoo to Grand Rapids when a puncture halted them. Whilst Bedaux had been struggling to change the tyre a vehicle pulled alongside.

'May I assist you?' enquired a passing motorist.

'If you are a minister you may,' replied Mr Bedaux, who happened to have a marriage licence tucked away in his pocket.

'I am!' said the Samaritan to the great surprise of the couple. Occupants of the clergyman's car acted as witnesses and the ceremony was performed at the roadside with a peach orchard as a background.'[14]

Despite the romanticism of the whole incident, Bedaux's wedding may not have been so completely innocent as it at first appears, for closer investigation of Charles and Fern's Marriage Certificate, held on record at the Kent County clerk's office,[15] reveals some rather intriguing facts. Of the three people involved in that unexpected roadside wedding, witnesses Mr William Geldersma and Mr Geoffrey F. Mueller, and Clergyman Frank A. Hess, both Mueller and Hess were ex-German nationals and known associates of Carl Andersch, and Geldersma was a lodger in the home of Mrs W. Rowe. The presence of these three men at Bedaux's roadside wedding could not possibly have been a coincidence, and so therefore the whole scene must have been a set-up, perhaps simply for the albeit innocent reason that James Lombard, Fern's father, disliked Bedaux. However, the incident is important for it demonstrates that when in need of accomplices for even the most innocent of tasks, Bedaux naturally turned to friends and associates who were exclusively those under suspicion of espionage.

Almost the last of Van Deman's file entries states that Bedaux had of late taken up 'going hunting very often in the vicinity of Ludington, Michigan, and appears to be watching an aeroplane plant'. He had also recently taken on an assistant – 'an ex-German national from Chicago.'[16]

Shortly after recording these last events during 1918, Colonel Van Deman died after succumbing to the Spanish influenza pandemic that was sweeping the earth, becoming one of the twenty-two million victims of the disease. The First World War ended a few weeks later and in the euphoria of an Allied victory, Van Deman's case against Bedaux was forgotten and his files abandoned to the Army Records Department. Bedaux took an extended break and vanished.

Interestingly, during the 1943 investigation of Bedaux, a statement was given to the FBI by one Fritz Wurmann, a German diplomat captured in North Africa. He reported that in a personal conversation he had with Bedaux in 1941, Bedaux claimed to him to have been a long-serving agent of the German Abwehr (Germany's Intelligence organ that had existed long before the Nazis came to power), and that he was personally acquainted with Admiral Canaris (Head of the Abwehr).[17] If Bedaux had served as a German agent in the First World War he would have been under the command of Colonel Nicolai, Head of the Kaiser's Intelligence. Unfortunately, efforts to pursue this line of enquiry failed because Colonel Nicolai's records were destroyed in the Potsdam firestorm of 1945,[18] and so we only have the evidence of the reports compiled on him by Colonel Van Deman, supported of course by Bedaux's own word for his activities.

We do however, have other tantalizing glimpses into Bedaux's inner personality that fit in with his activities in the First World War. FBI records on Bedaux reveal that in 1941, during the German invasion of Greece, Bedaux was a key-mover in the betrayal of two Greek Generals to the Germans, and in 1942 Bedaux even suggested to the German government that he would be prepared to organize an uprising in Persia to cripple Britain's main source of oil at Abadan. He suggested that, at a given time, he would organize two thousand natives to pour sand into all the machinery in the area, thereby destroying the equipment necessary to drill, pump, refine, and transport oil. The Germans, who were keen on the plan, eventually concluded that Bedaux's set-up lacked the security to ensure the plan's success and abandoned the idea, but not before listening to his terms for supplying this tactical coup – German citizenship, the rank of General, and the equivalent of one million dollars divided into various currencies.[19]

After a decent lapse of time, Bedaux resurfaced in 1920s America with a string of successful companies that promoted his 'efficiency system' philosophy. On his arm he had his refined socialite wife, Fern, and in his hands a range of active efficiency offices spread across boom-town America. He became an adviser to Henry Ford, speeding up the vehicle production line systems and greatly increased Ford's profits, he then swiftly went on to apply his efficiency expertise to General Motors, Du Pont, ITT, Standard Oil, the Texas Corporation, Sterling Products, and a whole host of smaller companies spread across the United States. His business was a roaring success due in no small part to his astute production of booklets which he circulated to prospective clients enumerating his philosophy on workers and production. His methods and views did nothing to enamour him to the Unions, but made him the darling of the 'company boss', be he manager or director. Bedaux opened lavish new offices on the fifty-third floor of New York's Chrysler Building, and made a particular point of entertaining his best clients such as Henry Ford, Walter Teagle (Head of Standard Oil), and members of the Du Pont family to lunch in the Chrysler Building's top floor restaurant, The Cloud Room. Within a few short years, he and Fern moved into a magnificent apartment, 12-C, 1120 Fifth Avenue, New York. In later years he would rent this out to his private-secretary, Mrs Isabella Waite, who became a close confidante and important within his organization, whilst he moved into an apartment in the New York Ritz, which Fern equipped with their own furniture.

It was at this time Bedaux made a friend that would ultimately prove useful in his contact with Wallis Simpson and the Duke of Windsor in 1936. Bedaux, by now a wealthy man due to his business success, engaged in an activity that was popular in the inter-war period – that of expeditions. He decided to drive across Canada, North British Columbia and into the Yukon. One of the main members of his small expedition was a recently made acquaintance from Washington, a banker by the name of James Rogers, the son of Colonel Rogers who was the next-door neighbour of Franklin Delano Roosevelt, but more importantly, James Rogers would turn out to be the brother of Wallis Simpson's long-time friend Herman Rogers, with whom Wallis Simpson lived at Villa Lou Viei, the Rogers' home on the Riviera, during the abdication crisis. It is entirely possible that suddenly aware of this useful route to the Duke of Windsor, Bedaux himself suggested contacting Wallis, for, as we shall see, at the time he offered Château de Candé, Bedaux was in the closest possible proximity to the highest Nazi of them all.

Suddenly, and out of the blue, in late 1926 Bedaux moved back to Europe, rarely setting foot in the United States again unless he was required to do so for business reasons, even though his American companies continued to tick over quite happily, generating vast revenue. The explanation for this sudden move was actually remarkably simple. Although Bedaux was an efficiency and mass-production genius backed by a successful business empire, throughout his magnificent career he hardly ever paid a cent in US taxes; quite simply he was the ultimate free-marketeer and he positively begrudged surrendering a single dollar or cent of his hard-earned cash. He would spend the rest of his life in a battle of wills between himself and auditors, outwitting the world's tax men at every turn.

Once back in Europe, Bedaux started a new range of companies in Italy, Holland, France, Sweden, Britain, and Germany, all promoting his 'speed-up system' and imaginatively called: Italian Bedaux, Internationale Bedaux Mij. of Holland, Bedaux Cie of Paris, Bedaux Company of Sweden, Bedaulim Limited of London which was to become British Bedaux Limited . . . and Deutsche Bedaux-Gesellschaft. He consolidated these with a string of branch offices in Belgium, Czechoslovakia, Poland, Hungary, Greece, Turkey, even attempting to open an outlet in newly communist Russia, although he was quite literally booted out of the People's Paradise for promoting a management and work ethic that was completely at odds with the communist way of thinking. The majority of these companies were formed in the late 1920s, and were intended to herald Bedaux's presence onto the European stage as the world master of business efficiency – the expert in modern mass-production.

Bedaux augmented his launch onto the European social scene by buying a string of homes ranging from a hunting lodge in Scotland, a villa in Spain, even a castle in Hungary, but without a doubt his pride and joy was the imposing Château de Candé near Tours in France. He bought Candé from the Drake de Castillo family in 1927 for the princely sum of 1.6 million francs,[20] and immediately set about renovating the stately pile, spending another six million francs putting in over half a mile of plumbing, adding bathrooms, garage blocks, a swimming pool, tennis courts, and even his own private golf course.

By the mid 1930s Bedaux's European efficiency businesses were a great success and he had made his mark on Europe as the 'Speed-up King'. In Britain alone, British Bedaux Limited's profits for 1935 were £50,024,[21] and he had other enterprises that were just as successful, if not more so, in all the other major European countries. He travelled continually, always on the move, always one step ahead of the tax man. One week he would be in London, the next Brussels, a flying visit to Paris before a weekend at Candé, and then he was on the move again, to Amsterdam to consult Mrs ter Hart – his personal appointee to head Bedaux Internationale Mij, not to be confused with Internationale Bedaux Mij – for the two were very different companies.

Bedaux Internationale Mij was Bedaux's main holding company for his European enterprises – and his clearing bank. All the profits from his various companies were channelled into this company headed by the ubiquitous Mrs ter Hart, and she used every means possible to hide the money. Mrs ter Hart, formerly Miss Lubowski of Polish origin, had once been Bedaux's private secretary, but he had soon recognized not only her multi-linguistic genius, but also her talent for financial finagling. A Dutch Department of Justice report of the time describes how Mrs ter Hart, married to a painter and decorator to gain Dutch nationality, was able to hide vast financial sums of money by continually moving them between countries. She opened companies in Africa to hide share allotments and capital, signed Bedaux's and other directors' names to documents and boardroom minutes when they were not even in the same country, found ways of paying Bedaux's personal living expenses out of company sums, and was generally able to give any European tax collector apoplexy by the mere mention of her name.[22]

However, despite his business acumen and success, his methods of tax avoidance, there was still the other side of Charles Bedaux – like a shadow that for ever kept pace with him.

In the immediate years following the First World War there is no evidence to suggest that Bedaux maintained his career of espionage agent. He had no need of it, for despite the previous marriage tie to Germany, and the undoubtedly large financial remuneration he received for assisting the Kaiser's interest during the First World War, he was now successful enough for the money to be of little consequence. What returned Bedaux to his former career of spy, agent, and political manipulator, was something far greater than financial reward. He became enamoured of a new political ideology and force on the European stage, and his own prospects for power that could hatch from it – Nazism.

In the latter 1920s one of Bedaux's new enterprises opened for business in Germany. He had looked at the economic disaster and social disintegration that was devouring Germany, and decided she was ripe for the 'Bedaux efficiency system'. His production and efficiency system would sweep the German industrial landscape clean, he would be the saviour, and Germany would be leaner, stronger, and healthier for it. After some consideration, and probably a lot of research or forethought, for Bedaux rarely made a mistake, he created a German Bedaux company – Deutsche Bedaux-Gesellschaft – with a swanky new building as its headquarters in Hanover.

To start with all went well, and two major German industrial concerns, Continental Gummi and Guttepercha AG, were converted to the Bedaux system. However, the German economy at that time was notoriously unstable, the political battle-lines were drawing up and the communist and left-wing unions were particularly strong. They would have nothing to do with a system in which their members were watched, timed, filmed, and the information put through a complex Bedaux calculation, that always resulted in their members having to work dramatically faster, for longer hours, but for less money.

In the United States when there had been dissension amongst the workforce the factory owners had merely fired and re-hired, or contracted in thug 'security-men' who used intimidation and threats, bludgeoning a striking workforce into submission with clubs. America in the 1920s was, after all, the world of the bootlegger, crime gang, and Al Capone, and the conglomerate bosses were not beyond using a few 'hood' tactics of their own. Europe, particularly Germany, however, was an entirely different proposition, and Bedaux's Deutsche Bedaux-Gesellschaft was soon in serious difficulties.

If the unions got word that Bedaux's company had been contracted in to examine or reorganize production, everyone downed tools and walked out. German workers were already having to quite literally cart their wages home in wheel-barrows anyway, so bad was the inflation. Any wage reduction due to Bedaux's system would have meant starvation for them and their families. Thus they had nothing to loose. Bedaux badly miscalculated, for he had failed to discern that in a successful economy like America, his system could be made to work because the wages were considerably higher, and the population could be easily intimidated by the factory bosses with their draconian measures for anyone who fell out of step. A good example of this was the riot that ensued outside the Ford Detroit plant at this time in which several demonstrators were killed. When one German company in Dortmund tried these strong-arm tactics to disperse a several hundred strong picket, the hired heavies were set upon by the local communists and given a good hiding. The workers stayed out on strike and Bedaux's company was dismissed forthwith.

At this point in time a new element and ideology entered Bedaux's life, probably for the first time. Bedaux was still a consultant to the Ford organization and a personal friend of Henry Ford himself, so the connection probably came via this route. During the 1920s, Henry Ford, the puritanical, simple living, abstemious, multi-millionaire, was also the same fanatically anti-Semitic Henry Ford who contributed financially to support the new rising political force in Germany – the Nazi Party. In a 1919 edition of the *New York World*, Ford was quoted as saying, 'International financiers are behind all war. They are what is called the international Jew: German-Jews, French-Jews, English-Jews, American-Jews ... the Jew is the threat.' It could have been a speech written for Adolf Hitler at his most vitriolic. At Adolf Hitler's 1924 trial for the failed Beer-Hall Putsch, it was testified that Henry Ford was one of his major backers. In 1927 Henry Ford wrote an appalling anti-Jewish book called *The International Jew*, which Hitler admired so much that at the Brown House in Munich he had copies stacked on tables outside for anyone who wanted a copy, and inside, in pride of place on his office wall, Adolf Hitler hung a large photographic portrait of Henry Ford.[23]

Bedaux's introduction to Nazism was not by this means alone, for by the very nature of his business he became closely involved with Germany's biggest and most successful companies from Krupps and Mercedes, to Opel and IG Farben – all companies that would become the Nazi Party's financial backers, and the heads of these companies, leading Nazi Party supporters. Through Bedaux's association with these financial giants he came into contact with Dr Hjalmar Schacht, Head of the German Reichsbank and Hitler's future Minister of Finance. Schacht was the financial wizard who turned Hitler's new Reich into an economic powerhouse of the mid 1930s, doing more than any one man in Nazi Germany to provide the financial muscle that paid for Hitler's re-armament programme. Indeed, he was hailed by the Nazi hierarchy and the German General Saff as the man who had done more than any other to make Germany's re-armament programme possible. In 1945, Schacht would sit in the Nuremberg dock alongside Dr Robert Ley, Head of the German

Labour Front, and in the company of Göring, Hess, Speer, Ribbentrop, Keitel, Streicher, Frank, Funk and Seyss-Inquart; but that was all still a decade and a world war away.

In the 1943 FBI investigation into Bedaux, the US Judge Advocate in Algiers tracked down one of Bedaux's former directors, Dr Robert McChesney who was then residing in Khartoum, and asked him: 'How did Bedaux come into contact with the Nazi Party?' McChesney was also asked if it was for financial remuneration or out of sympathy with Nazi ideology. His answer was recorded and sent to Special Agent J.E. Thornton in Washington who passed it on to J. Edgar Hoover:

Bedaux's [first] Company started in Germany . . . and was a complete failure. It was a perfectly genuine engineering venture and its failure was not a matter of it being a difficult struggle resulting in the decision to abandon; it was a complete rout; both labour and employers refused to have it. This was unusual. After the suppression of the Trade Unions [by the Nazis], however, Bedaux painstakingly built up another approach. The details of the preparatory work are not known, but by 1935–36, Bedaux was on very intimate terms with Dr Schacht and Dr Ley. The upshot of the manoeuvres was that the three agreed to a large-scale application of the Bedaux system to German industry. The set-up was that Dr Schacht would *impose* Bedaux on a selected group of industrialists, and Ley undertook that labor in the plants concerned would not be allowed to voice any dissent.

It is unlikely that Germany paid him anything at all in exportable marks. In fact, Bedaux related to me one isolated incident which showed how tight was the control, and even how Dr Schacht himself was not adverse to getting a few hundred pounds outside of Germany. Dr Schacht's mistress was an extremely clever sculptress and Bedaux intimated that he wished to buy a statuette by her as a wedding present for the Windsors. Dr Schacht asked that payment should be made in francs; Bedaux went further than this and held an exhibition in Paris and his own purchase (costing £500) was only one of several made by his friends.[24]

Thus, during the pre-Nazi era of the Weimar Republic, Bedaux had found it impossible to make his mark in Germany, but once the Nazis came to power he knew he was onto a winner, for he had spent considerable time and effort during the early 1930s cultivating Nazi contacts, men he knew would one day run the country. He had examined the literature, read the books, and listened carefully to the conversations that did the rounds in Nazi circles before they came to power, and, by the time Hitler became Chancellor in 1933, Bedaux was a devoted Nazi follower. During the early years of the new Reich, Bedaux's talents as the 'Speed-up King', with his time-and-motion-study of working practices, became invaluable to the Nazi hierarchy and his system, advocated by Schacht and Ley, was applied to the German munitions and military production industries. He took on yet another apartment, Room 106 at the Hotel Adlon, Berlin, so often was he in that city, and he was appointed as Head of I.G.'s (of IG Farben fame, and later the industrial giant that manufactured Zyclon B, the gas used to poison the Jews) commercial operations by Fritz Weidmann, Nazi diplomat and Hitler's personal adjutant.[25] Bedaux and his efficiency system became very important in the 1930s for he was a key component in Hitler's economic miracle, and a major influence and designer of Germany's re-armament programme. His was the mass-production expertise that assisted the German manufacturing capacity of munitions, military vehicles and aircraft, to increase by the magnitude. It was at this time that Bedaux also became closely associated with the Commissioner of the Four Year Plan, Hermann Göring, who at that time had been placed in charge of the ministry organ whose purpose was to reorganize German industry and gear up the system for rearmament production.

It is important to note that although Bedaux was a fanatical Nazi, he was not necessarily a fascist. The distinction between Fascism and Nazism was noted by J. Edgar Hoover in 1943, and the point was made that Bedaux believed in a new order – a Nazi Order – developed by Hitler in Germany, which at length he was convinced would be applied throughout Europe before spreading to the United States.[26] By the mid 1930s, Bedaux was known in European Society for being able to converse at great length on Nazi ideology, and he would hand out vast quantities of pro-Nazi literature to anyone he thought susceptible to indoctrination. His parties at the Château de Candé were noted in French society as hot-beds of Nazi intrigue and propaganda.[27]

It is all the more intriguing therefore, given the facts known about Bedaux and his parties at Candé, that Edward was permitted to associate with this advocate of a Nazified Europe, and that George VI was not forewarned of the unsuitability of Bedaux's offer.

However, Nazi intrigue was not confined to the Château de Candé alone. If it had been, it would have been far easier to contain. Early within Germany's new regime under Hitler, thoughts had spread not just from a new German order or even European order, but to a new world order – one that would last a thousand years. Organizations committed to this ideal began to spring up all over Europe and America, from the French Fascist movement of the Croix de Feu (a leading member of which was Armand Grégoire – a close friend of Charles Bedaux), the Dutch Nazi leader Anton Mussert (again personally known to Bedaux), through to Austria, Spain, Portugal, and surprisingly, the United States of America.

Directly after the Nazi's rise to power in 1933, the powerful Du Pont family in the United States began financing right-wing political groups, from the anti-black Liberty League to Clark's Crusaders. By 1934 their activity had expanded by an incredible rate, even to the extent of planning a coup d'état, and they invested $3 million into funding a private army with the aim of toppling Roosevelt to replace him with their own man. Fortunately, Roosevelt got wind of the conspiracy and it collapsed before it really had a chance of succeeding, but not before over a million men had joined the illicit organization, with a pledge of arms and munitions from Remington – a Du Pont subsidiary. The Special House Committee set up to investigate the plot took four years to reach its conclusions, but eventually admitted that 'certain persons made an attempt to establish a fascist organization in this country.' Although this plot failed, the right wing of America was not beaten yet, and the Nazi orientated American Liberty League, set up with funding of $500,000 a year, advocated anti-Jewish sentiment, pro-Hitler comment, and distributed fifty million Nazi pamphlets nationwide.[28]

In a second attempt to topple Roosevelt, the Du Ponts and the America Liberty League, together with the German-American 'Bund' (Brotherhood) and the American Nazi Party, tried backing Republican Alf Landon in the 1936 election. However, Roosevelt won a landslide victory, and to the fury of the Du Ponts and their supporters, announced it would be a key policy of his new administration to improve the working conditions for the common man – better pay for shorter hours. In outright defiance of this attainable policy, the Du Ponts, General Motors, and their other supporters in 'big' industry instigated an accelerated plan of 'speed-up production' organized by their friend, close associate and fellow thinker, Charles E. Bedaux,[29] through the use of American Bedaux Associates.

Back in France, Bedaux had been just as active in promoting Nazi aspirations of European domination, and through his association with Schacht he became closely involved in the economic penetration of French industry by Germany's bankers. Foremost amongst these was the powerful Cologne banker, Baron Kurt von Schroeder, whose Parisian representative, Worms Banque et Cie, was actively financing acts hostile to the Third Republic. It engaged in the transfer of French industry to German ownership, and supported the Cagoulard Plot headed by Lemargue-Dubreil, yet another long-time friend and associate of Bedaux. In 1940 virtually the entire board of the Worms Banque et Cie would become Ministers of the Vichy Government under Marshal Pétain.

In January 1937, the right-wing Cagoulard organization attempted a coup d'état aimed at the overthrow of the legitimate French Government. The Cagoulards were very well organized and superbly equipped, even down to shiny brass helmets being issued so they could recognize one another should street fighting ensue. They drew members from all walks of life, business, military, justice departments, even government officials, and counted Bedaux as a leading member. It was only the result of a tip-off just before they were ready to take action that forestalled the coup that was imminently about to take place. A thorough police investigation at the time came to nothing, for the trails led to such high officials that it was feared that any prosecutions could lead to civil war. Instead, the dossiers which listed top businessmen, generals, and marshals of the army, were classified and secreted in the Ministry of Justice. During the Second World War, Pétain's Vichy government went to great lengths to hide the incriminating evidence, and the documents might never have been found but for the wife of the concierge at the Bordeaux tribunal, who showed Free French officers where the files were hidden behind a false wall. But this was to be in the future, and in the intervening period many Cagoulard members would become part of the sophisticated organization that assisted Germany to run occupied France. Bedaux himself would become the Reich's Economic Adviser to the Occupied Territories, a position of enormous power in a land under the control of Hitler's armies.

This then was Charles Eugene Bedaux, the man who offered Wallis Simpson and Edward, Duke of Windsor, the use of his home in December of 1936; he was no mere philanthropist who had taken pity on the hapless Duke and decided to do a good turn for a fellow American, Wallis Simpson.

He was the covert former German agent of the First World War, the ruthless efficiency expert with the backing of an enormous business empire from America to Turkey, from Sweden to South Africa; he was the foreign specialist who had developed his friendship with Schacht, Ley and Göring to make Germany's rearmament programme a reality; he actively promoted Nazism on a continent-wide basis, and was thus fêted by the Nazis wherever he went. Bedaux was also personally acquainted with Adolf Hitler, Rudolf Hess, Joachim von Ribbentrop, Joseph Goebbels, and a whole host of lesser but important Nazi minions. However, there was yet one more fascinating fact about Mr Bedaux that should have set alarm bells ringing within Britain's Intelligence Services – in 1935 Bedaux was allowed to take on a villa at Berchtesgaden,[30] the Nazi holy of holies, within sight of Hitler's personal mountain retreat at Obersalzberg – the Berghof. A Berchtesgaden residence made a statement in Hitler's Nazi Germany, it was the equivalent of a Russian having a Dacha home near Stalin. It said: 'I am an important asset to the State and my services have been recognized.'

Bedaux was *important* in Nazi Germany.

That does not mean, however, that British Intelligence had never heard of him, for there was little of importance that escaped the eyes and ears of the intelligence services in the 1930s, particularly where their former king was concerned. It would therefore be intriguing to know why they kept this particular titbit of intelligence from Downing Street and George VI – i.e. where Bedaux was living when he made his offer of the Chateâu de Candé to Wallis and Edward.

In his 1943 interrogation Bedaux was asked, 'How did you come to meet [the Windsors] and why did they come to your house, for the purpose of getting married?'

To which Bedaux replied:

> Because they were friends of Herman Rogers, the brother of the young man we took [to the Yukon] in 1926 ... Mrs Simpson, when she left England, sought refuge in their home on the Riviera, and her life was considered endangered and the place too small, easy to expose. My wife and I were in Midway, South Carolina. I was there weekends working in Georgia during the week, and we cabled the Rogers offering our home as a protection for Mrs Simpson.[31]

However, like much of Mr Bedaux's interrogation and testimony recorded in over 218 pages, when asked a question to which he had an unpalatable or damning answer, what he told his interrogators was a lie. Firstly, the offer of Château de Candé was made by letter, not cable, and secondly, far from Bedaux being in South Carolina, he was not even in the United States.

Evidence gathered from Immigration, State Department records, and Bedaux's own passport (number 330783 issued on 17 July 1936), shows that whilst he travelled Europe extensively in 1936, during the period Bedaux claimed he was in the United States, he had actually been in Europe. However, he was not at Candé in France, nor his other home in Scotland, nor attending to the business of Bedaulim in London, nor his Hungarian, Borsodivanka Castle. Neither was Mr Bedaux incommunicado whilst travelling, for he was somewhere much more sensitive, and if he had revealed his location to his interrogators in 1943, he would have laid himself open to questions for which he could not, and dare not, supply the answers. At the time in question, Charles Eugene Bedaux was residing at his alpine home in Berchtesgaden. It was from this substantial house, within sight of Hitler's Berghof and surrounded by Nazi Germany's hierarchy, that Bedaux wrote to offer the use of the Château de Candé to Wallis Simpson. It was an offer meant to show the Duke that he had not been forgotten by his right-wing friends, that it did not matter to them that he was no longer king – for it might only be a temporary interlude.

The initial coming together of Charles Bedaux and the Duke of Windsor has never been satisfactorily explained, and it has often been claimed that there was absolutely no connection between the two men, and that neither party had ever met or had any associated links with the other. However, the links between Wallis, Edward and Bedaux were more than tenuous and the threads were many. Firstly, Wallis Simpson's lawyer, Armand Grégoire (described in a French security report as one of the most dangerous Nazi spies) was a personal friend of Bedaux's. Grégoire was also lawyer to Joachim von Ribbentrop, Rudolf Hess, and Hermann Göring, all men who were also acquainted with Bedaux. Bedaux stayed regularly at Ribbentrop's Berlin home[32] and Ribbentrop also knew Wallis, as well as having an interest in Edward. Edward was closely acquainted with Pierre Laval, and Bedaux and Laval had known each other very well since their early teens.[33] It is a strange recurring pattern within this tale that virtually everyone involved knew everyone else; the threads are multiple, criss-crossing like a spider's web, and just as intricate to unravel.

A most spooky and telling comment on the whole episode comes from a deposition that Mr and Mrs Herman Rogers made to J. Edgar Hoover, which he passed on to Major-General

George V. Strong, Chief of Staff, G2 (intelligence) of the War Department:

> Mr and Mrs Herman Rogers have been interviewed and stated that Bedaux ... offered his castle for the wedding of the Duke and Duchess of Windsor since he believed their chateau would not be large enough for the event. In March 1937, the Rogerses stated they sent a cable to Bedaux asking if his offer was still open. Bedaux had a villa at that time in Berchtesgaden where he had spent two summers and they described Bedaux as a great admirer of Hitler and stated he was anxious to see England and the United States go Fascist. In Bedaux' opinion, the Duke of Windsor would be a good man to head a Fascist Government in England, whilst he himself would head a regime of this type in the United States.[34]

CHAPTER THREE

Marriage and Exile

DESPITE CHARLES BEDAUX'S chequered career, his undoubted eminent connections into a regime that was the very antitheses of all things British and democratic, King George VI was ultimately responsible for the choice of Château de Candé for Edward and Wallis Simpson to wed in. The alternate suggestion for the marriage ceremony had been La Croë, a rented villa on the French Riviera, but George VI considered this location unsuitable because of the region's reputation as a playground for the rich. It was to be a devastating mistake, for Edward was now propelled headlong into the Nazi fold, into the company of those very agitators and manipulators working towards a new world order. Thus George VI, uninformed by Britain's intelligence services of Bedaux's dubious past and current political inclinations, approved the use of Candé for Edward and Wallis Simpson to marry at, permitting Bedaux to establish himself in Edward's company, and Edward to firmly insinuate himself into the shady world of right-wing politics.

In the 1930s, many of the men running Britain's intelligence services saw Bolshevik Russia not Germany as the threat, and members of the intelligence community communicated in an unofficial and open fashion with the various branches of the Nazi political machine. These same men, virtually all from the upper-

71

classes and fearing socialist ideals, were convinced of the necessity to maintain a strong Germany as a bastion against Communist incursion into Europe. They feared with good cause that Russia's long-term aim was to topple their ordered, class-orientated society, and saw Hitler's regime as the best defence against this. However, it must be remembered that although these men were possibly right-wing inclined, they were not Nazis themselves, but saw Hitler as the lesser of two evils. They believed that Communist Russia and Nazi Germany would eventually slug it out on the plains of Eastern Europe, destroying each other in the process, and leaving the true victors as democratic western Europe – safe in its social order, undamaged by war, and secure for the future. Thus, when the offer of Candé came from Bedaux, they may well have known who and what Bedaux was, realized the intent to usher the willing Edward into the Nazi fold, but were not inclined to suddenly pull up the political draw-bridges and cause the Nazis offence.

Quite simply they completely under estimated the situation, thought Edward a spent force, and declined to warn George VI of Bedaux's unsuitability.

The use of Candé approved, Wallis Simpson, together with Herman and Katherine Rogers, arrived at Château de Candé during a dismally wet evening in March 1937; Wallis was greeted at the door and welcomed by Fern Bedaux and the uniformed Candé staff. Although Charles Bedaux was not present, being in Amsterdam to consult with Mrs ter Hart, his wife made a great effort to make Wallis feel at home, and gave her a personal tour of Candé.

Edward at this time still languished in Austria, not daring to cross the border into the same country as Wallis for fear of damaging or delaying the divorce petition. However, they spoke on the phone that evening, and he was reassured about Candé's suitability by Wallis's praise of Mrs Bedaux and her French home. Edward was not having a happy time of his exile from Britain nor indeed his enforced separation from Wallis, and by this time was writing furiously to his beloved: 'God's curses be on the heads of those English bitches who dare insult you!' He had recently moved to a smaller hotel called the Appesbach Haus, at Ischl, hoping to find more privacy, but had become increasingly plagued by raging toothache; so much so, that he ordered his private dentist Dr Sumner Moore, of Wimpole Street, London, to fly all the way out to Austria to take care of him.

Throughout the early spring an almost daily correspondence flowed between the pair expressing their wrath at their perceived ill-treatment; on 22 March, Edward wrote saying he would one day 'get back at all those swine [in Britain]' and make them realize how 'disgusting and unsportingly they have behaved.'[1] Throughout the remaining weeks of their enforced separation, the two continued to brood at numerous slights that had been heaped upon them; Edward at the loss of his throne, Wallis at the lack of any kind of recognition, and their letters began to take on an increasingly frantic tone. Referring to fantasies of a triumphal return to Britain, which he would change into a Republic with himself as President and Wallis as his First Lady, Edward wrote, 'WE [Wallis & Edward] will soon be back in glory sooner than WE think.'[2] On 14 April, Wallis wrote bitterly of George VI, 'Well, who cares, let him be pushed off his throne.'

By the latter half of April the agonizing limbo of Wallis' divorce began to draw to a close, allowing events to begin moving again. On 27 April her divorce was declared absolute, and on 3 May Edward's solicitor, George Allen, telephoned his client to pass on the good news. In a mood of unbridled joy Edward gathered up his bits and pieces, loaded his private compartment on the Orient Express with his seventeen suitcases, and in the company of Dudley Forwood (his new equerry), Thomas Carter (his private secretary) and his bodyguard in the form of Chief Inspector Storrier, headed for France, Candé, and Wallis.

The following morning the Orient Express was halted at Verneuil for Edward and his entourage to disembark, and he was met by an ecstatic Wallis.[3] A cortège of Candé vehicles supplied by Bedaux, including his own chauffeur-driven Rolls Royce, swept the pair back to the château, accompanied by a police car and motorcycle escort. Edward and Wallis were together at last.

Charles Bedaux had arrived at Candé about a week before, and his flamboyant charm immediately endeared him to the Duke. Edward found a kindred spirit in his new friend, and the two men settled into an easy friendship, playing golf on Candé's private course, entering into long discussions on politics and the way forward for Europe, and arguing the need for a strong Germany as a bastion against Communism.

After spending a week in the company of Edward, and engaging him in some deep and private discussions, Bedaux, accompanied by Fern, departed from Candé, and made a beeline straight to Germany. Whom he met and what he discussed at this time has never been discovered, and all Bedaux would disclose during his interrogation in 1943 was that he went to Hitler's Reich 'to arrange for a bronchial cure,'[4] which unbelievably took him a fortnight to arrange. There can be little doubt, however, that he met with Nazi officials at that time, either to report on his initial discussions with Edward, to receive instructions, and perhaps receive dispatches, for Bedaux never did anything on impulse. Perhaps the only clues that arise from the mire are some of the peripheral incidents that occured after Bedaux's return. During the latter half of May, Edward and Wallis selected Schloss Wasserleonburg, in Austria, as their honeymoon base, a gothic alpine castle owned by Count Paul

Munster, a dual British and German citizen, who together with 'Fruity' Metcalfe was a member of the January Club – the society allied to Oswald Mosley's British Union of Fascists who were at that time receiving substantial funding from the Nazi Party, channelled through Wallis Simpson's lawyer, Armand Grégoire.[5]

On the final evening before their wedding, the Duke received his latest and most stinging rebuke from Buckingham Palace to date. Walter Monckton – again destined to be the harbinger of bad news – brought a letter from George VI which coldly informed Edward that Wallis would not be allowed to use the title of 'Her Royal Highness'. As he read the letter, Monckton later said, 'He [Edward] was transfixed, as if pole-axed. Then an oath burst from him: "*Damn* them! Damn them *all*! I'll make them pay for this!"' After months of anxiety and anguish, Edward finally cracked and broke down in tears.

The Windsor's wedding day, Thursday, 3 June 1937, dawned bright and clear, but was an altogether much quieter affair than Edward had envisaged – far removed from the royal occasion he had planned – and not a single member of his family accepted his invitation to attend. This obvious and very public snub offended Edward greatly. Wallis was later to write '. . . the unspoken order had gone out, Buckingham Palace would ignore our wedding. There would be no reconciliation, no gesture of recognition.'[6] Ostracized by his family, Edward found that most of his friends stayed away too, in deference to royal pleasure. There had even been major problems in locating a clergyman who was prepared to perform the ceremony for them, for the Church of England refused to countenance a divorcee's marriage. In the end a Reverend Jardine offered to marry the couple, although he was later to fall foul of the Church authorities for performing the ceremony. As a consequence, the number of wedding guests attending the ceremony was pitifully small, even by modern standards, and Edward and Wallis had to content themselves with a ceremony in Candé's dining room attended only by sixteen close friends.

And so the wedding took place, Wallis garbed in pale blue, Edward in formal dress, and after the civil ceremony necessary under French law, followed by the religious ceremony, it was all over by 3.30 p.m. 'Fruity' Metcalfe's wife, Lady Alexandra, later wrote:

> We shook hands with them in the salon. I realized I should have kissed her but I just couldn't ... If she occasionally showed a glimmer of softness, took his arm, looked at him as though she loved him, one would warm towards her, but her attitude is so correct. The effect is of a woman unmoved by the infatuation of a younger man. Let's hope she gets up in private with him otherwise it must be grim.[7]

Although Charles Bedaux, together with Fern, was a major guest at the event, he kept a very low profile. Fern appears in several of the wedding pictures, but Charles Bedaux made a point of always being on the wrong side of the camera, for he was not entirely sure of his security in this environment yet, and, should anything have gone amiss, nothing aids like a little anonymity. However, he did content himself with giving the Duke and Duchess a rather special wedding present – a sculpture entitled 'Love' by German sculptress Anny Hoefken-Hempel, Dr Schacht's mistress – the piece of art he had paid £500 for in British currency as requested by Schacht. Amongst the other gifts the Windsors received that day was a small inscribed gold box – a wedding present from Adolf Hitler.

The Windsor's honeymoon started with a regal procession aboard the Orient Express that took them, 226 pieces of luggage, 7 servants and 2 dogs, across France to Italy and Venice. The American press in particular drew attention to the thoughtlessness of such decadence in a world that was still struggling out of the depression, but they completely missed the point, for Wallis was not flaunting their vast accumulation of luggage through imprudence, she was making a statement as much to her new husband as to anyone else, meant to intimate to all: the loss of a throne doesn't mean the end of the cornucopia of luxuries, privileges and attention ... he's just a king without a throne. It was a resolve that was to harden within her, corrupting her values as time went on.

Edward and his new bride arrived the following day at St Lucia train station, Venice, to an adulatory welcome by a vast cheering Italian crowd that repeatedly gave the fascist salute to the famous couple. The fasces banners of Mussolini's Italy fluttered gaily in the bright afternoon sun, and Edward, no longer constrained by the British government or the Foreign Office, delighted the crowd by raising an outstretched arm, fingers straight, and returned the fascist salute of Italy's ruling order. He continued to salute the crowds frequently as the ducal entourage, protected by an escort of Italian police, swept through the crowded station, and out onto the Piazza where an assembly of gondolas waited. These had been ordered by Mussolini and were to take the royal party to the Lido, where arrangements had been made to receive them at the Hotel Excelsior.

The Windsor's only stayed in Venice for three and a half hours, before continuing the journey to their Austrian honeymoon retreat at Wasserleonburg. During their time in Venice, accompanied by the smiling crowds and a flotilla of brightly painted gondolas, they crammed in St Mark's Cathedral, the Doge's Palace, and St Mark's Square, before strolling to the Excelsior for afternoon tea. They then returned to the station where an official handed Wallis a bouquet of a hundred carnations sent by

Mussolini. They boarded the train, the whistles blew, and as the train began to move, a smiling Edward stood in the open window and gave the crowd a departing fascist salute. A rapturous cheer and a thousand outstretched saluting arms sent the Windsors gaily on their way.

They arrived at Villach, Austria, at 11.45 p.m. that night to an altogether different reception. The crowd that had gathered to welcome them had been turned away by the police before the train arrived, and they were met instead by only a few local dignitaries and six journalists. Edward, however, was in buoyant mood as he and Wallis climbed into a waiting Mercedes that took them up the steep dangerous road to Schloss Wasserleon-burg, their honeymoon base for the next three months – a fifteenth-century, forty-room, mock-gothic edifice set against a backdrop of mountain crags and perched on the edge of an escarpment that would offer the new couple all the privacy they desired.

Wallis immediately set about making the castle more homely. She removed the worst of Count Munster's hunting trophies, and reorganized the castle's heavy gothic furniture to her taste. Count Munster's home-on-loan was not entirely gothic though, for it did boast a heated swimming pool, tennis courts and an extensive stable. There were chamois and stag nearby for Edward to stalk, and a golf course for him to play on. They took frequent day trips in the car until they found somewhere for lunch, and gave the outward appearance of the happy couple. Asked by an American reporter if they had enjoyed Austria, Wallis later replied, 'We adored Austria! Oh, we were so very happy there! We could go about peacefully and not be bothered. Best of all was being together again.'[8]

The truth was somewhat different though. Miss Benton, a secretary borrowed temporarily from the British Embassy in Vienna, perceived that Edward was deeply lonely. He had 'a nagging home-sickness for England . . .' she later recounted, and 'a troubling inner conflict'. Wallis later admitted they spent much of their honeymoon 'endlessly rehashing' the events that had led to the abdication. Edward was at a loss to understand how he'd been so completely and totally wrong-footed, and it undoubtedly played on his mind. He had been outwitted by Baldwin, those around him had given him bad advice, and he had lost his throne. It must have been very humiliating.

On 20 June the Windsors drove to Vienna for a few days' stay at the Hotel Bristol, and attended a dinner party in their honour at the Brazilian Embassy given by the British wife of Sam Gracie, the Brazilian Ambassador. During dinner attended by a number of important dignitaries from the diplomatic circle in Vienna, including an attaché from the Italian Embassy, George Messersmith, the American Ambassador, listened carefully to everything Wallis said, and later reported to Washington that she was particularly bitter about the American press.

After dinner had finished and coffee was being served in the drawing room, Messersmith found himself been drawn to one side by Chancellor Schuschnigg's Private Secretary, who had just arrived and asked for a confidential word with him. The Austrian handed Messersmith a sealed letter from his Chancellor, which informed the American Ambassador that a few hours before there had been a train crash in the mountains. Police on the scene reported that it was a German train bound for Italy, and that 'a very large quantity' of naval shells had been found amongst the wreckage. Austria had thus found her neutrality impinged upon and it was a matter of the gravest concern to the United States, for the shells were undoubtedly bound for Mussolini's navy and intended for use in Italy's war against Abyssinia. It was top-secret information for it proved that Germany was aiding the Italian war machine, and thus breaking the sanctions imposed by the League of Nations.[9]

When Messersmith rejoined the other dinner guests, Edward asked him why Schuschnigg's secretary had taken him to one side. Was it a problem he should be aware of? he asked. Messersmith hesitated for a second before handing Edward the secret letter to read for himself. Soon afterward Messersmith was more than a little perturbed to see Edward deep in discussion with the Italian attaché, on the far side of the room.

The following morning the American Ambassador was handed an urgent dispatch by his military attaché that shook him to the core. It was a telegram that the American Intelligence Service had intercepted and decoded during the night from Prezziozi, the Italian Ambassador, to his Foreign Office back in Rome; in the telegram Prezziozi reported that the Duke of Windsor had approached one of their attachés at the Brazilian Embassy and informed him there had been a train crash in the Alps the previous evening. Prezziozi directly quoted the Duke of Windsor as telling the Italian attaché that: 'The cat is out of the bag so far as the naval shells are concerned.'[10] Edward had betrayed Chancellor Schuschnigg's confidence to Messersmith, and warned the Italians that the American government now knew that Germany was breaking the League of Nations Munitions Sanction Agreement imposed on Italy, and that Germany was supporting Italy with military supplies.

After spending much of July back in Austria, the Windsors returned to Venice on the 28th and attended a party on the terrace of the Grand Hotel, put on in their honour by the Woolworth heiress, Barbara Hutton and her husband, Count Haugwitz-Reventlow. Amongst the sixty guests attending the party were the Maharaja and Maharani of Jaipur, Wallis's old friends Kitty Bache and her husband Gilbert Miller, and Mussolini's daughter Edda with her husband, Count Galeazzo Ciano, the Italian Foreign Minister.

Documents on record at the National Archives in Washington

reveal that Wallis, whilst married to her first husband, naval officer Lieutenant Winfield Spencer, had been romantically involved with Count Ciano in Shanghai in 1927 and so the two were already well acquainted, although Barbara Hutton's diary does not record their reaction to each other. It does however record that throughout the evening, the Duke and Duchess repeatedly emphasized the virtues of Fascism to the other guests, and that the Duke 'sees it as the great way forward'.[11]

Before departing Venice, the Windsors attended a performance of *Romeo and Juliet*, by the Monte Carlo Ballet at the Teatro la Fenice; where from the Royal Box, to the delight of the Venetians and the absolute horror and consternation of Whitehall and Downing Street, Edward stood in his box before the assembled theatre-goers seated below, and gave them the fascist salute before taking his seat.

Once back in Wasserleonburg, events started to take on a momentum of their own. Charles and Fern Bedaux visited the Duke and Duchess, and whilst Wallis showed Fern about the castle, Edward and Bedaux settled down to a leisurely discussion in the library. Whilst the Windsors had been on honeymoon, Bedaux had again been to Germany and engaged in a little behind-the-scenes organizing to aid the former British King. After a series of high-level meetings with the Reich's hierarchy a plan had been hatched. The Duke of Windsor would visit Nazi Germany ostensibly as the guest of the German Labour Front, headed by Dr Robert Ley. The resulting tour would have the two-fold effect of elevating the Duke of Windsor's standing on the international stage and restore him to the limelight, whilst at the same time it would be a propaganda coup for the Reich, enabling them to show the working masses of Britain and the world that their way was the best – the future, in fact. Bedaux also brought news that the ever penny-pinching Duke (he wasn't known as the 'millionaire miser' for nothing) would not have to spend a single pfennig on his trip. A substantial payment from the Hitler-controlled Reichsbank would cover all expenses. All Edward had to do was sit back and enjoy the ride back onto the world stage. It was perhaps understandably an all too tempting offer.

During their meeting, Edward and Bedaux plotted a similar visit to the United States, so that he could view working and housing conditions at the other end of the spectrum; from the ordered ways of Nazi Germany, to the free-for-all that was democratic, capitalist America. The very idea appealed to Edward, for he saw a role forming for himself as a champion of the working classes. Visiting the desperately poor, expressing a concern at their plight and saying a kindly word about their appalling working conditions, had been one of the ways he'd gained popularity and recognition in Britain when he'd been the Prince of Wales. The formula had worked once before and he evidently saw no reason why it should not work again. He ordered Bedaux to organize the tour. Bedaux then invited Edward and Wallis to end their honeymoon with a stay at his castle at Borsodivanka in Hungary. Edward agreed, and Bedaux went off happily to make the arrangements.

On Bedaux's arrival in Hungary, whilst Fern prepared Castle Borsodivanka for their important guests, hiring locals to clean it from top to bottom, engaging servants, ordering food and flowers – Bedaux began preparing the logistics of a grand tour by an ex-head of state.

On 19 August Howard Travers, the chargé d'affaires at the American Embassy in Budapest, was surprised to receive a visit from Charles Bedaux. What Bedaux told the American diplomat had him leaping for his cypher-pad the moment the Frenchman left. He sent off a frantic 'Strictly Confidential' message back to Washington, and very soon alarm bells began to ring in Whitehall as well, for Travers cabled Washington that he had that day received Mr Bedaux, who'd informed him he was acting on the

Duke of Windsor's behalf, and that, 'The Duke of Windsor is very much interested in the lot of the lower classes and desires to make a complete study of working conditions in various countries with a view to returning to England at a later date as a champion of the working classes.'[12]

It was a devastating statement for Bedaux to make, for it implied that if Edward could not have his throne then he intended to enter politics, and that would be a direct threat to the new King, George VI, who was still struggling to find his feet.

Back in London, upon seeing the memo concerning Edward's future career plans, Sir Alexander Hardinge immediately wrote to Sir Robert Vansittart, the Permanent Under Secretary of State at the Foreign Office, to say:

> His Royal Highness the Duke of Windsor and the Duchess should not be treated by His Majesty's representatives as having any official status in the countries which they visit ... His Majesty's representatives should not have any hand in arranging official interviews for them, or countenance their participation in any official ceremonies.[13]

It became imperative to Downing Street and Buckingham Palace that Edward's activities should not be aided or legitimized by the support of the British State or her diplomatic representatives abroad. Foreseeing trouble ahead, Vansittart wrote an urgent dispatch to the British Ambassador in Hungary, Sir Geoffrey Knox, clarifying the Foreign Office's position regarding the Windsors, hoping to defuse any potency Edward's foreign adventures might have back home. They were not to be accorded the status of visiting royalty on a state tour, but 'should be treated on the same lines as a member of the royal family on holiday'.[14]

However, Vansittart's problems were only just starting for he then received a cyphered message from Sir Robert Lindsay, the

British Ambassador to Washington, which clearly stated in black and white that Edward had contacted him personally to inform him of his forthcoming American tour, and that he (Edward) had great hopes for what he might accomplish through it. Lindsay ended his message by warning Vansittart that he thought Edward was about to attempt 'to stage a semi-fascist comeback in England by playing up to labour in America'.[15]

Whilst the Windsors were staying at Castle Borsodivanka from 6–16 September, Howard Travers received another visit from Bedaux. This time Bedaux informed him that the German government had placed eight motor cars and two aeroplanes at the Windsors' disposal, and that Adolf Hitler had personally issued an invitation to the couple for a twelve-day tour beginning on 11 October. He went on to explain that the Duke and Duchess would then embark for the United States aboard the SS *Bremen*, on 11 November.[16] Travers' communications back to the State Department in Washington began to take on a frantic quality.

After ending their honeymoon with a ten-day stay with Bedaux in Hungary, Edward and Wallis returned to Paris where they installed themselves in a suite of rooms at the sumptuous Hotel Meurice, and set about looking for a Parisian home. All seemed peaceful and quiet for the moment. But, events were now to take a bizarre turn.

Six months before, Errol Flynn, American actor and swash-buckling movie star, had sailed into Europe aboard the *Queen Mary*. On his person he carried a banker's draft for $1.5 million which had been raised by pro-Communist and Loyalist sympathizers in Hollywood to aid the legitimate Spanish government based in Valencia, against Franco's forces. However, the money never made it to the legitimate government, for Flynn arrived empty-handed. Rumour had it that the money had actually been given to the Falangists, the very people it was meant to be used against, for it is a little known fact that Errol Flynn was extremely pro-Fascist.[17] As a result of several damning intelligence reports compiled against him in the mid 1930s, Flynn had been followed to Europe by two FBI agents. They watched him travel frequently between France and Fascist Spain for several months before his activity seemed to suddenly cease and he settled peacefully into the Hôtel Plaza Athénée in Paris. There, Flynn's activities were also watched by two MI5 men, for British Intelligence mistakenly suspected he was a courier for money which was funding IRA operations. It was all rather convoluted and not a little boring for the watchers, for Flynn did nothing; he seemed to be waiting for something.

Then, on 26 September, Flynn suddenly began to move. He unexpectedly breezed through the hotel foyer, suitcase in hand, and leapt into a taxi. The following agents gave chase and were surprised when Flynn travelled to Gard du Nord and boarded an express bound for Berlin. Both British and American concern and stupefaction was to gradually rise though, for, on arriving in Berlin, Flynn was met at the train station by none other that Charles Bedaux, who immediately after the Windsors' departure from Hungary on the 16th, had journeyed straight back to Berlin. The agents watched as Bedaux and Flynn climbed into a taxi and went directly to the Kaiserhoff Hotel, where Flynn did nothing again, remaining in the hotel for two days. Before there was time for London or Washington to assess the implications of what was happening, on the 29th, Flynn, bag in hand, left the hotel accompanied by two well-dressed gentlemen, who also carried suitcases. The tension in the watching men must have risen to fever pitch when they observed that Flynn was in the company of none other than the Deputy Führer of the Third Reich, Rudolf

Hess, and Adolf Hitler's Private Secretary, Martin Bormann. All three men then went to Friedrichstrasse Station where they boarded a train for Paris.[18]

Once they got to Paris, they were pursued directly to the Hotel Meurice, where the two following MI5 agents were surprised to recognize two fellow MI5 men standing in the foyer. Before the men could exchange any information or guess at what was going to happen next, the explanation took place before their very eyes. To the utter disbelief of the assembled agents, an immaculately dressed man of slight stature, sauntered down the grand staircase, reached out to Rudolf Hess, and shook him firmly by the hand. He then shook hands with Martin Bormann, and Errol Flynn. All three men then accompanied the Duke of Windsor back up the stairs to his suite.[19]

This bizarre meeting resulted in a positive snow-storm of telexes, cyphered messages, and memos that flew throughout Whitehall like a blizzard. At long last everyone began to realize the very real danger of what was going on. No record of what was said at the meeting has seen the light of day, the only clue as to what was discussed is Hess' personal report to his Führer which said, 'The Duke is proud of his German blood . . . says he's more German than British . . . [and is] keenly interested in the development of the Reich . . . There is no need to lose a single German life in invading Britain. The Duke and his clever wife will deliver the goods.'[20]

Just a few days after this meeting, on 3 October, Edward's Private-Secretary, Mr T.H. Carter, issued a statement on the Windsors' behalf, saying that:

In accordance with the Duke of Windsor's message to the World Press last June that he would release any information of interest regarding his plans or movements, His Royal Highness makes it known that he and the Duchess of Windsor are

visiting Germany and the United States in the near future for
the purpose of studying housing and working conditions in
these two countries.[21]

After hurried discussions in Whitehall, Lord Beaverbrook,
appalled at the idea of Edward's dealing with the Nazis, which he
emphasized would only further their cause and hand them a
propaganda coup on a plate, flew to Paris to see the Duke. He
urged Edward to go only to the United States, but this the Duke
refused to consider. In an attempt to dissuade Edward, Beaverbrook offered to send his private plane back to Britain to bring
Churchill out, hoping the great man might have some influence
over the obstinate Duke. However, Edward responded that it
didn't matter who was brought out, for his mind was made up.
The British government no longer had Edward's ear, for it was
less than a year since these same men had placed him in a
position that resulted in his abdication, and he refused to listen
or trust their judgement again.

Consternation swept through the halls of Buckingham Palace
for there was now the very real fear by the new King and his
advisers that Edward's actions could well be intended to initiate
some kind of constitutional crisis, leading perhaps to a usurpation
of power.

Following Lord Beaverbrook's report back to Whitehall that
the Duke of Windsor could not be stopped, a meeting was held
at Balmoral between George VI and his advisers. Queen Elizabeth
also attended the meeting, as did Sir Alexander Hardinge, Sir
Alan Lascelles and Sir Robert Lindsay, the British Ambassador to
Washington. Of the meeting, Lindsay was later to write to his
wife that:

[The general opinion is that the Duke is] trying to stage a
comeback, and his friends and advisers are semi-Nazi . . . What

if he were to go to a Dominion? Or to cross over from the United States into Canada? There was a lot of talk about a scheme by which ... [an] emissary should speed over and persuade him to decline. This absolutely horrified me and it was, thank God, discarded because 'that woman' would never allow him to decline, and because there exists no emissary who would stand the smallest chance of influencing the Duke.[22]

The Duke of Windsor's tour of Germany has always been played down in Britain, the impression given that his visit had a purely industrial and social flavour, punctuated at the end by an ill-judged visit to Adolf Hitler. However, the purpose of the tour was not really for the Duke to look at factories and working conditions, and there was much more to his visit than was made public at the time or has been generally acknowledged since.

The Duke and Duchess of Windsor began their tour of Nazi Germany on 11 October 1937, arriving by train at Berlin's Friederichstrasse Station to a vast glittering array of Aryan prowess. Several hundred German citizens lined up giving the Nazi salute, and rhythmically chanted 'Heil, Windsor!', and 'Heil, Edward!'. It was a spectacle that until that time Germany had reserved for her leaders alone. Awaiting them for what was ostensibly a private, non political visit, was Joachim von Ribbentrop, Germany's Foreign Minister, Fritz Wiedemann, Hitler's Adjutant and a close confederate of Bedaux, Arthur Goerlitzer, the Deputy Political Leader of Berlin, Paul Schneer from the Office of the Four Year Plan, Walter Hewel, Hitler's liaison man to Ribbentrop, and last but not least, Dr Robert Ley, Leader of the German Labour Front, long-time friend of Charles Bedaux and business associate of Bedaux's Nazi approved efficiency/consultancy firm of Gesellschaft für Wirtschaftsberstung GmbH.

Tucked discreetly amongst these knights of the Third Reich, the vast multitude of uniformed officers from the various branches of the Nazi political machine, the SS and Gestapo guards in black uniforms, was Mr Harrison the third secretary from the British Embassy. Mr Harrison stood quietly to one side in a neat suit with his overcoat casually folded over his arm, intentionally oblivious to all the Nazi showmanship, saluting, and prancing going on about him. The British Foreign Office in an attempt to diffuse the situation had ordered Sir Neville Henderson, the British Ambassador, to take a short vacation, and no one higher than third secretary was allowed to attend or legitimize the Nazi pageant now taking place for Edward's benefit. Harrison handed Edward a letter from Sir George Ogilvie-Forbes, the chargé d'affaires, which informed the royal personage that Ambassador Sir Neville Henderson had gone on vacation, and that he had been ordered to take no official interest or part in the visit.

Whatever Edward thought of the British diplomatic response to his visit is not recorded for he and Wallis were immediately ushered through the station, past the chanting and saluting crowd, and out to a vast, glittering, open-top black Mercedes-Benz that whisked them away to the Kaiserhof Hotel, and a suite with a view of Hitler's Chancellery.

After a brief stop off at the Kaiserhof for lunch, and whilst Wallis settled into their suite, Dr Ley took Edward out of Berlin to view one of the Reich's latest showcase factories at Grunewald, designed from its inception to incorporate the Bedaux philosophy. Here Edward was shown a brand-new manufacturing complex that employed several thousand workers. He viewed the extensive gardens and lawns that surrounded the factory, the clean, safe, modern working conditions, the recreation facilities available to the workers, including two halls, a modern well-furnished restaurant, and even a full-size swimming pool with changing rooms. Edward chattered in German with his host, Dr Ley, and was greatly impressed; Ley introduced workers to the Duke, cajoling them to tell Edward how wonderful life was, and slapping them heartily on the back and laughing. Edward learned of high wages, good health care, good food, and the Nazi method of management. It was all quite dazzling.

A concert was put on for Edward in one of the halls, and attended by the factory workers, to listen to the tenor Eyvind Laholm give a rendition of the 'Grail Aria' from *Lohengrin*. The concert ended when the assembled two thousand men and women struck up the Nazi marching song, the 'Horst Wessel'. It is perhaps understandable that Edward left his first encounter with Nazi organization and manufacturing greatly impressed.

Dr Robert Ley, however, was less impressive. A crude man whom Edward observed was fond of 'off-colour jokes', he had risen from a background of street brawling and fist fighting with the Communists, but then so had most of the Nazi hierarchy. Ley should not be under estimated though, for although he had a slurring speech impediment that often gave the impression of intoxication, a battered countenance from too many fights, and a crassness that would in 1945 lead him to vaingloriously proclaim the Reich had developed the 'deathray', he was a persistent and clever man. He was the Gauleiter of Cologne, an intimate of Dr Hjalmar Schacht, and had concentrated all German fashion production into one giant enterprise run by his wife. As head of the German Labour Front, Dr Robert Ley was a very powerful man indeed in Hitler's Germany of the late 1930s. That night, the Windsors were guests of honour of Ley's at a party at his magnificent Grunewald villa. Attending the party was the full dazzling spectrum of the Reich's Nazi élite and hierarchy, including Mr and Mrs Rudolf Hess, Heinrich and Marga Himmler, Dr and Mrs Hjalmar Schacht, Arthur Goerlitzer, Mr and Mrs Joachim von Ribbentrop, Mr and Mrs Walter Hewel, and Dr Joseph Goebbels and his wife.

Wallis later described these icons of Nazism in the following terms. Of Rudolf Hess, she thought him 'charming of manner and good-looking', Heinrich Himmler, a 'bespectacled meekness' and the appearance of 'a clerk caught up in politics', and of Dr Goebbels, 'a wispy gnome with an enormous skull'.[23] It was a dramatic underestimation of the three men, and a total miscalculation of the situation.

On the following day Edward went again with Dr Ley, this time aboard a specially constructed observation bus that had an upper seating gallery, dining salon, toilet facilities, communications room, and a bar. It thundered down the autobahn towards Pomerania at eighty miles per hour, occasionally slowing so that the Duke might observe some item of interest Ley would point out. Once in Pomerania, the coach paused to take on the local governor, before continuing to the élite SS Deaths Head, or SS Totenkopf, Division headquarters and training camp at Crossensee. Here, the SS Regimental band struck up the British national anthem, whilst a highly efficient Guard of Honour presented arms and stood to attention. Edward gave the Nazi salute and inspected the troops, walking up and down the lines with SS Reichsführer Himmler in attendance.

This was no mere Wehrmacht unit, this was the crème de la crème of the SS; the men who provided Hitler's honour guard, sworn to him in life and death, with their skull and crossbones emblem signifying the world beyond the grave. These were the best-equipped and trained men of the SS who could be entrusted with the most dangerous and unsavoury tasks within the service of the Reich – from a fight-to-the-death to the herding of Europe's Jews into the gas chambers.

Edward was then given a tour of the entire establishment, from its towering entrance gate to the quaintly thatched barracks, and onto the classes where recruits underwent the complete, full political–ideological training course that went with membership of the SS; he was shown classes where the young men were taught about their Aryan backgrounds, the hocus-pocus archaeology and false history that was necessarily tainted to make the facts fit Nazi ideology. After his tour Edward watched the élite of the élite show off their stuff on the parade ground; the bands played and banners flew, and Edward watched in awe.

On 14 October, the Windsors visited Field Marshal Göring at his great mansion, Karinhall, about forty miles north of Berlin.

Prior to the royal arrival, Emmy Göring had said to her husband, 'I don't understand this woman not giving up her marriage in view of everything that was involved.' Hermann had replied that, 'The natural opposition between British and German policy ... could easily be set aside with such a man as the Duke.'[24] And he held great hopes for Edward's conciliatory influence between the two countries.

Göring was an immediate hit with the couple, awaiting them at the door of his baronial mansion at the end of a mile-long driveway, a great mountain of a man in his gleaming white uniform – the ever jovial, sparkle-eyed 'Fat Hermann', as he was popularly known. He immediately took them on a tour of his huge home, taking great pleasure in showing them his well-equipped gymnasium, romping playfully on some of the equipment to demonstrate, the massive dining room that could accommodate a hundred guests in comfort, and even his attic 'playroom' where he had a complicated train network laid out. Here, he demonstrated his latest 'toy' – a wire-controlled model plane that could drop wooden bombs.

In Göring's study, the Windsors were treated to a glimpse of the future, for on the wall behind Hermann's desk was a large marquetry map of Europe. Edward took in the fact that it showed, with the sole exception of Britain, the whole of Europe and much of Russia as already being in German possession – the Greater Reich – and remarked with a smile, 'Isn't that a little impertinent? A little premature?'

'It is fated,' Göring replied with a shrug. 'It must be.'[25]

The Windsors attended another rally at Düsseldorf on the 16th, this time under the guise of a folk and craft exhibition, funded by the Reich's Strength Through Joy organization. Flanked by an honour guard of black-clad SS men, Edward wandered through the exhibition pausing here and there to look at the exhibits, the demonstrations of artificial textile weaving, and calmly returning fascist salutes to those he passed.

In Whitehall, alarm at the Duke's behaviour resulted in a censorship order going out to doctor the newsreels. It was considered inappropriate, if not downright dangerous, for the British public to see their former king walking through lines of adulatory young people with an escort of SS men, his arm in an almost permanent salute.

By the time the Windsors' tour reached Leipzig, Edward was utterly dazzled and completely flattered by the fawning respect Hitler's Nazi Reich gave him. Britain's politicians had rejected him, Buckingham Palace had insulted his new bride, and it was only in Nazi Germany that he and the Duchess were treated with the respect they were due. It is only human nature to want to feel valued, and the Nazis went to extraordinary lengths to make him feel just that. On arriving at Leipzig train station, Edward and Wallis were greeted by a several thousand strong crowd and forty enormous swastika banners. Edward posed dramatically before the assembled masses, waited a few seconds for effect, then gave them the Nazi salute. There was a roar of adulation in return, and a vast forest of saluting arms again flattered Edward's sense of standing and dignity. He went on to attend a Labour Front meeting with Dr Ley, and delivered a speech to the audience saying:

I have travelled the world and my upbringing has made me familiar with the great achievements of mankind, but that which I have seen in Germany, I had hitherto believed to be

93

impossible. It cannot be grasped, and is a miracle; one can only begin to understand it when one realizes that behind it all is one man and one will.[26, 27]

At an urgent meeting called at Whitehall to discuss Edward's forthcoming trip to the United States, it was revealed that Bedaux had approached Prentis Gilbert, the chargé d'affaires at the US Embassy in Berlin, to discuss the Duke's future tour. Bedaux had pressed Gilbert to urge the American government to treat the Duchess as visiting royalty, and then went on to tell him that after visiting America, the Duke intended to visit Italy and Sweden. In Sweden, the Duke would meet and join forces with Axel Wenner-Gren who 'was interested in world peace through labour relations. Bedaux said it was intended that HRH should take up this line, and even went so far as to express the opinion that HRH might in due course be the "saviour" of the monarchy!'[28] This caused great consternation, for it was known that Axel Wenner-Gren, the multi-millionaire owner of Electrolux and inventor of the domestic refrigerator, was closely connected with Bedaux's Swedish efficiency company Aktiebelaget Nordisk Bedaux of Stockholm, and was another close confidant and friend of Hermann Göring. It was also known that Wenner-Gren had decidedly pro-Nazi leanings, and it was inconceivable to the men in Whitehall that anything he was involved in was not under the control of Berlin.

What alarmed the men in Whitehall was the distinct possibility that the Nazis were setting into motion an attempt to destabalize and topple foreign nations, using fascist agitation and labour relations as a conduit. When it came to conquest, or furthering their interests, the Nazis were specialists at using the whole spectrum of methods available to them; from social, political or racial interference, through to assassination and ultimately military intervention where appropriate. Over the following two years these very methods would be used to devastating effect on Austria, the Sudetanland, Czechoslovakia, and Poland.

It was decided that Edward's venture into social welfare and labour relations should be scuppered at all costs.

Oblivious to the turmoil and plotting going on back in London, the Windsors' tour entered its final phase with a visit to Hitler at Berchtesgaden on 22 October. When the Windsors and their SS escort men arrived at Hitler's home, he was ready at the door waiting to greet them, then led them into the entrance hall, and gave them a tour of his sprawling Alpine home, before ushering them into a vast semi-sunken reception room, dominated by an entire wall of glass that gave an uninterrupted view of the Alps beyond. The Duchess noticed with interest that all the furniture covers had been stitched with tiny swastikas and national socialist mottoes.

The bulk of what Hitler and the Duke of Windsor discussed is not known, for the German account of the conversation, captured with the German Foreign Policy Documents in 1945, has never been released, with the reason given being that: 'Key parts of what passed between the Führer and the Duke at Berchestgaden, has been held ... until a disclosure will no longer be wounding to British sensitivities.'[29] What is known is that the two men undoubtedly discussed the core of Edward's visit, his admiration for Nazism, the efficiency in the workplace and the modern housing conditions; his views on a nation that was rushing away from the depression that had crippled it less than a dozen years earlier, to become a modern, right-wing, progressive society. However, apart from the polite chit-chat of one visitor to another, other matters were certainly discussed for what is known is that Edward told Hitler, 'The German races are one. They should always be one. They are of Hun origin.'[30] In 1966 the Duke recounted that 'Hitler for his part talked a lot, but I realized that he was only showing the tip of the German iceberg ... he encouraged me to infer that Red Russia was the only enemy, and that it was in Britain's interest and in Europe's too, that Germany be encouraged to strike east and smash Communism for ever.'[31] Apart from these statements, very little of any substance is known, for the Duke was always unwilling to disclose the finer details of his confidential discussion with Hitler, and in the light of subsequent events and his actions perhaps it's understandable.

At the end of their meeting the Windsors took afternoon tea with Hitler before he escorted them back to their waiting car. One of the few reporters allowed into Berchtesgaden to witness the meeting recorded that, 'the Duchess was visibly impressed with the Führer's personality, and he apparently indicated that they had become fast friends by giving her an affectionate farewell. He took both their hands in his saying a long goodbye, after which he stiffened to a rigid Nazi salute that the Duke returned.'[32] As the Windsors' car carried them back down the mountain, Hitler who stood on the steps of his Alpine home watching them depart turned to Schmidt, his translator, and remarked, 'She would have made a good queen.' The Windsors were rushed back to the station, and boarded a special train that would take them back to Munich, where they were welcomed by the former Grand Duke of Mecklenburg. That night they had a last dinner party in Munich with Rudolf Hess and his wife.

The Windsors' tour of Germany was finally over, and the couple returned to Paris to recuperate in the Hotel Meurice.

However, a storm was now brewing against them, for in America, the *New York Times* ran an editorial saying:

The Duke's decision to see for himself the Third Reich's industries and social institutions and his gestures and remarks during the last two weeks have demonstrated adequately that the abdication did rob Germany of a firm friend, if not indeed a devoted admirer, on the British throne. There can be no doubt that his tour has strengthened the regime's hold on the working classes ... The Duke is reported to have become very critical of English politics as he sees them and is reported as declaring that the British ministers of today and their possible successors are no match for the German and Italian dictators.[33]

By the time Charles Bedaux, travelling on the liner SS *Europa*, arrived in New York a week later to organize Edward's American tour, he was met by a full-blown hurricane. In just a week the US press turned against him to an extraordinary level. Bedaux's efficiency methods were condemned, and any defence or protection 'big business' in America had once given him, was swiftly yanked away from beneath his feet. He suddenly found himself a lone voice struggling valiantly against a gale of vilification, whilst at the same time trying to organize a dignified tour for the Duke.

The American unions, who had long hated Bedaux and his labour system, needed no prompting and swiftly swung into action. The American Federation of Labor and the Congress of Industrial Organization issued statements criticizing his companies and their efficiency policies, condemning Bedaux personally as 'an exploiter of labor' and 'a schemer who promoted the Duke's tour only to further his own nefarious interests'. Bedaux, until recently honoured wherever he went as the 'Speed-up King,' now found his company's reputation dragged in the mud, and himself reviled as the inventor of the 'Bedaux work-like-hell system' that exploited workers in 'the most completely exhausting, inhuman efficiency system ever invented'. Further, the Union of New York Longshoremen announced they would picket the Duke of Windsor's ship and refuse to unload a single item of luggage.

In Baltimore, Wallis' hometown, the American Federation of

Labor launched a scathing attack on the Duchess herself, saying they had never noticed her take any interest in the working classes, and stingingly urged other unions to ignore 'slumming parties professing to study and help labor'.[34]

Back in Paris meanwhile, Edward and Wallis attended a series of farewell dinners intended to send them merrily on their way to America. They attended a reception given in their honour by William Bullit, the American Ambassador, in the company of Léon Blum, the French Premier. The next day they were given a farewell luncheon by Sir Eric Phipps, the British Ambassador to Paris.

On 8 November, Bedaux received a message from his Board of Directors, summoning him to a meeting at the offices of American Bedaux Associates, in the Chrysler Building. The value of his company's stock, particularly Industrial Bedaux Limited, had plummeted in the week of the scandal surrounding him. It was as if all a country's resources had piled against him, from the press, through to the unions, to the very government itself – which is, of course, exactly what had happened.

The following morning, in the mock gothic boardroom of American Bedaux Associates, Bedaux fought a desperate two-hour battle for his commercial and business life. He was literally roasted by the very men he'd appointed to the board, and in the rabid argument that ensued, members of the board began to resign, threatening to bring the whole edifice of American Bedaux Associates crashing down. Realizing what was happening James T. Ramond called the meeting to order and presented Bedaux with an ultimatum. He would immediately suspend share trading of all Bedaux's American companies on the stock exchange, unless Bedaux relinquished the presidency of his own American Bedaux Associates, and all his authority over his companies that went with it. He would in effect, become a silent shareholder. In the deathly silence that followed a devastated Bedaux eventually nodded his agreement.

Completely outfoxed, boxed in at every turn, and vilified from coast to coast by the American press, Bedaux knew he was beaten. In a state of shock, he staggered from the boardroom and into his own office, stunned and powerless. After twenty years of unrivalled business success, Bedaux had finally been beaten – not merely lost a fight to come back another day, but quite literally blown out of the water, destroyed. He would never forgive the Americans. Ever.

Later that evening, having temporarily gathered his wits about him, for he was now heading towards a nervous breakdown, he sent a cable to the Duke:

> Because of the mistaken attacks upon me here, I am convinced that your proposed tour will be difficult under my auspices. I respectfully implore you to relieve me completely of all duties in connection with it.

Edward was uncertain what to do next; his luggage was awaiting him on the Cherbourg quayside, the more radically inclined of his friends were still urging him to go, and yet here was a clear indication that all was not well. That, combined with what he'd read daily in the American newspapers had an unsettling effect on him. He telephoned Sir Robert Lindsay, the British Ambassador to Washington, to ask his advice.

Should he go? he asked, or would it be better to postpone his tour till a later date?

Lindsay had replied, 'If you do [postpone], you will not be able to do it ever.'

'Are you alarmed?' Edward had asked.

There was a long silence before Lindsay replied, 'Sir, I feel the tour will cast a certain discredit on the American view of the British monarchy.'

Edward could see which way the wind was blowing, and the following morning in a damage limitation exercise designed to stop the pox spreading from Bedaux to himself he washed his hands of the whole affair, disclaiming any political inclinations by issuing a statement which said, 'The Duke emphatically repeats that there is no shadow of justification for any suggestions that he is allied to an industrial system, or that he is for or against any particular political and racial doctrine.'[35]

In New York meanwhile, Bedaux had been forced to sign over the controlling interest in his companies, and surrender the company assets he had the use of, such as the magnificent apartment that overlooked Central Park. On the morning of 10 November, having spoken on the telephone to the Duke who asked him: 'not to speak under any circumstances to the press',[36] Bedaux slipped quietly out of the Plaza Hotel by a back service door, avoiding the multitude of reporters and photographers that awaited him at the front. He jumped on a train bound for Canada and under the alias of 'Mr Jones', fled to Montreal where he took passage back to France. It would be almost five years to the day before Bedaux would see the United States again, only then he would be in custody and charged by the United States Government with trading with the enemy, and suspected of treason.

The Bedaux who returned to Europe was a man utterly shattered by the disasters that had befallen him. After twenty years of unrivalled success, having made himself a valuable asset to the Nazi's re-armament and political machines, he had suddenly found himself out on a limb and vulnerable. That the American State as a whole could turn on him, was such an utter shock that he effectively had a mental breakdown. The official diagnosis of his condition as a 'mental and physical breakdown from persecution',[37] was probably an understatement, and he spent from December 1937 through to March 1938 dosed up with the new German anti-depressant Medinol,[38] as a patient in the exclusive Munich hospital, Reichenhall, that was reserved for Germany's hierarchy and their families – to which grouping Bedaux, of course, belonged. When he eventually left hospital he took an extended vacation to convalesce in Tormina, on Sicily's eastern coast during April and May of 1938. However, something had happened to Bedaux during those dark depressing days of his illness. He had become someone who talked of the United States with detestation, declaring it decadent and ripe for social revolution that would turn it into an ordered modernistic society under a right-wing regime. His humiliation at the hands of the US press, unions and government officials, had turned him into a man bent on seeing the whole American edifice collapse.[39]

Over the next eighteen months, Europe became an increasingly unstable and unsettling place as Hitler continued his policy of expansion and consolidation, and the tumble towards the Second World War began to pick up an ever more certain momentum.

In March of 1938, Hitler annexed Austria to 'protect' the 10 million ethnic Germans resident there, then it was Czechoslovakia's turn to be destroyed, resulting in Neville Chamberlain's journey to Munich to appease Hitler for the sake of European peace. The Czechs were not even invited to attend, and Chamberlain's proclamation of 'Peace in our time' would turn out to be nothing of the sort.

In November the Nazis inflicted the Kristallnacht on their country, giving full vent to their anti-Semitic feelings, smashing Jewish shops and synagogues, and taking 30,000 Jews off to concentration camps. Anyone who had hitherto professed themselves ignorant of Hitler's long-term intentions towards the Jews could no longer be in any doubt. In March of 1939, Franco's Fascist forces were victorious in the Spanish Civil War, and another European state slipped into right-wing dictatorship. Throughout the continent, Europeans began to realize another war was coming and the political battle lines began to be drawn up between those of right-wing inclination, who saw Hitler and his politics as Europe's saviour, those who would become the appeasers of war, who were prepared to sacrifice territory and national dignity for peace, and those who swore to fight fascism to the bitter end.

During the last years of the 1930s, the Duke of Windsor had a much better time in France than Bedaux did in Germany, and despite perhaps coming to terms with his exiled life in France, Wallis did much to try and restore his light as an unemployed head of state. In short order they moved from their hotel suite into a beautiful home on the Boulevard Suchet, overlooking the Bois de Boulogne, and Wallis stripped the antique boutiques of Paris clean in her search for valuable furniture and objets d'art. Nothing was too outlandish in her pursuit of luxury for herself and the Duke, even down to carpeting their bedroom with yards of purest ermine (which everyone except the Duke and Duchess were afraid to walk on). About them they equipped their servants in uniforms of scarlet and gold livery – a parody of those uniforms issued to the Buckingham Palace staff, headed by Mr Hale, Bedaux's Head Butler from Candé, who left his former employer to join the Windsor household. Edward hung his banners and Orders of the Garter in the Mansion House's entrance hall, and the ducal pair gave parties at which they attempted to effect a royal presence – a poor imitation of a gone-forever past. They swiftly became a common sight in Paris, in their respective identical Buick limousines; the Duchess driven by her own French chauffeur, the Duke with his sturdy Austrian.

However, not everything was unhampered pleasure in the life

of the Duke and Duchess of Windsor. The Duke continued to fret about his loss of power, and the Duchess her all too public snubbing by the British establishment, and the pair always seemed to attract the most unfortunate of events.

In the summer of 1939, probably instigated by the Windsors' Berchtesgaden visit and Hitler's actions of Czech conquest, the Duke of Windsor became involved in a most unpleasant and dangerous incident at the Eiffel Tower. On 23 June, the Windsors attended a party at the first-floor restaurant of the Eiffel Tower, put on to celebrate the Duke's forty-fifth birthday. Sitting outside on a bright sunny summer's day to take in the magnificent view whilst they dined, all was elegance, good humour, and excellent cuisine. Meanwhile, 186 feet directly above them on the Eiffel Tower's second floor, an activity of a very different kind was taking place. Suddenly a protracted scream and a wildly flailing figure plummeted earthward, passing within feet of where the Duke and Duchess of Windsor sat. The Duchess screamed in unison with the body flying past. Instantly the Duke and Duchess' security swung into action, and they were quickly ushered away from the scene.

It was swiftly established that the broken body that lay smashed below the Eiffel Tower belonged to Bedrich Benes, the Military Attaché to the legitimate Czechoslovakian Government in exile, and that he had fallen from an access walkway suspended immediately below the second-floor observation platform. It was noted with curiosity and alarm that access to this walkway was restricted, and that Benes had obviously positioned himself with deliberate intent above the restaurant where the Duke and Duchess of Windsor had sat. Rumours began to flow, and the suggestion that it was a suicide was discounted because those so inclined invariably went to the very top of the tower, and never went to the trouble of surreptitiously clambering around the access ways. It was suggested that Benes might have been engaged in an assassination attempt on the Duke for his support of the Nazis and his well-known views on Hitler's expansion eastward – indeed, he had even supported Hitler's policy towards the Sudetanland. Because of this suggestion, the question 'did he slip or was he pushed?' was seriously asked, but since no one had seen Benes depart from the second-floor access way it was impossible to establish. It is unlikely anyone will ever know the precise details of exactly what happened that day up the Eiffel Tower, and additional enquiries into the event for the writing of this book were complicated by the inordinate difficulties in gaining access to the reports from the time, as was the attempt to establish whether Benes had a gun or not. However, the suggestion of attempted assassination was seriously looked into at the time of the incident, and rather more extensive enquiries conducted than one would normally have expected for a suicide.

CHAPTER FOUR

War

At dawn on 1 September 1939, Hitler's armies rolled across the Polish frontier, and the Second World War began. However, it was typical of Adolf Hitler's mendacious nature that the Second World War should begin with a lie, a character trait in which he manipulated events by deviousness, deceit and deception. It would be a ploy he would use time and time again, particularly in regard to the events of 1940.

Throughout 1938 and 1939, Hitler's policy of Lebensraum – an expanded living space for the German people that was to act as the lynch-pin for the new 'Thousand Year Reich' – repeatedly pushed Europe to the brink of war. Hitler had discovered very quickly that by adopting an aggressive foreign policy, backed up by the threat of military force if his demands were not met, Europe's appeasers would use their influence to prevent war at all costs; even at the expense of another country's sovereignty. Thus, when Hitler decided that the time had come for Germany to be once again united with Danzig and East Prussia at the expense of Poland, a necessity if the Reich was to expand eastward into Russia, he made great efforts to hide his intentions of conquest behind the legal niceties of defending his own territory against the aggressive and dastardly Poles. He had been assured by many sources, particularly Ribbentrop, that when faced by the

105

prospect of war the appeasers of Britain and France, backed by those politicians and statesmen who looked favourably upon Nazi Germany, would carry the day and Poland could safely be added to the territory of the Greater Reich.

However, the German war-machine could not simply role across her eastern frontier into Poland and expect the appeasers and right-wing politicians to carry the day in their own countries, as had happened in the case of Czechoslovakia. So, in typically Nazi fashion, fact and truth was manipulated to present German action as a legitimate reaction to events beyond their control.

Early in August 1939 the Reich's arch manipulator Reinhard Heydrich, Head of the SD (Sicherheitsdienst – the SS Secret Service), was ordered to initiate the first phase of the planned attack that would present Germany's actions on the world stage as a defence against Polish aggression. On the eve of the assault against Poland, Heydrich's SD men would travel to the German-Polish frontier, put on Polish army uniforms, and engage in several simultaneous actions: attack the German village of Kreuzburg, loot the frontier post at Pischen, and simulate a violent combat near the frontier post of Hochlinden. The last and most provocative action to be taken bore Hitler's personal stamp of approval and he gave the action a code name that drew on his own particular brand of humour – 'Operation Himmler'. A few hours prior to Y-Day (the German High Command code word for the attack on Poland) men of the SD, disguised as Polish soldiers, would attack the German radio station at Gleiwitz and deliver a vitriolic anti-German speech over the air-waves – to be listened to by millions, and be the straw that broke the camel's back, forcing a reluctant Germany to retaliate against wanton Polish provocation.

Having planned these actions down to fine detail, the SD men were dispatched to the German–Polish frontier with orders to start the war against Poland with an 'attack' timed to begin on the evening of Friday 25 August 1939, for Hitler wanted his war to begin at 4.45 a.m. on the morning of Saturday, 26 August. The might of the German war machine, Wehrmacht and SS units, were already established at their jumping-off points in final preparation for their imminent departure, and would attack promptly at the given time. It was no coincidence that Ribbentrop had flown to Moscow a mere two days before, on Wednesday, 23 August, to sign the Russo-German Non-aggression Pact, which included a secret agreement under which a defeated Poland would be partitioned between Germany and Russia.

Yet despite this overwhelming evidence of Hitler's intent at Eastern conquest, he hesitated. Hitler always liked to have an edge, some piece of inside knowledge that would ultimately project his image as the great seer (just as he had with the re-militarization of the Rhineland, and just as he would with the attack in the West in May 1940). He was not confident that he had all eventualities covered, and his intuition was to prove correct. A mere fourteen hours before the planned attack, Hitler met with British Ambassador Sir Neville Henderson at 3 p.m. on the afternoon of Friday, 25 August. Already aware that Britain had declared her support for Poland, Hitler now learned from Henderson about the signing of the Anglo-Polish Treaty of Alliance. It was a bitter blow. For the first time Hitler now risked outright European conflict, and if Britain declared war for Poland, France would soon follow suit. It was the one thing Hitler feared above all others – a war on two fronts, folly for a country like Germany, which under identical circumstances had proved to be the Kaiser's undoing a mere twenty years before. Two hours later, at 5.30 p.m., Hitler summoned the French Ambassador, François Coulondre, to the Chancellery to impress upon him that he did not want war with France. At 11 p.m. that night Coulondre telephoned Bonnet at the Foreign Ministry in Paris to report that:

This afternoon I had an interview with Herr Hitler . . . 'In view of the gravity of the situation,' he told me, 'I wish to make a statement which I would like you to forward to M. Daladier. As I have already told him, I bear no enmity whatever towards France . . . I do not want war with your country; my one desire is to maintain good relations with it. I find indeed the idea that I might have to fight France on account of Poland a very painful one . . .'[1]

Hitler's anxiety mounted over the next few hours as he agonized over the thought that something might go wrong. He was painfully aware that despite the Russo-German Non-aggression Pact, Stalin had still not sent a military mission to Berlin, Japan had turned a deaf ear to his offers of a tripartite pact, and Britain and France had just formally guaranteed Poland's sovereignty. After an hour of solemn contemplation, Hitler's anxiety and doubts overwhelmed him and a mere ten hours before the launch of his offensive against Poland he summoned Generals Keitel and Brauchitsch to the Chancellery at 7.30 p.m.

'Have the orders for the attack countermanded,' he ordered them. 'I must have time to negotiate . . . I must see if I cannot avert British intervention.'[2]

In the flurry of frantic telephone and radio communications that flew through the ether between the Chancellery in Berlin, the German High Command, the General Headquarters at Zossen, and the frontier east of Breslau, the emphasis of Hitler's order was the same – 'Stop everything!'

Back in Berlin the men at the Chancellery waited anxiously, for numerous army units had already departed their jumping-off points (past the point of reliable communication), and at that very moment were preparing to cross the Polish border all along the frontier the following morning. As the clock ticked toward midnight, news began to filter back. The attack had been stopped. The vast juggernaut of the German army had juddered to a halt – just, but not without the many creaks and bangs inevitable in stopping a huge force moving to attack another nation. On the frontier, the SD men allocated agent-provocateur duties leapt back into their cars and returned to Berlin.

For the next several days, whilst 1.5 million German soldiers waited, and every European held their breath, Hitler continued to hesitate. He proposed to the British that an alliance should find a joint solution to the Polish problem, that the Danzig question be found in Germany's favour – Britain prevaricated and Hitler became impatient. It was a week of pendulum swings in which the prospect of war loomed threateningly one day, and receded the next. On Tuesday, 29 August, Hitler decided to cool the situation and placate the western leaders by offering to receive a Polish envoy to discuss the predicament, still hoping he might take back Danzig without force; holding his troops back for another day. On the same day as Hitler made his offer, the Polish government, disturbed at the thought of having her fate decided by the very same European leaders who had looked after Czecho-slovakia's interests, ordered a full mobilization.

'Hitler was wild with rage. Was he manoeuvring for a diplomatic advantage when agreeing to receive a Polish envoy the next day, Wednesday, 30 August, or was it duplicity to keep Great Britain out of the conflict? Only Hitler ever knew the exact truth.'[3]

By Thursday lunchtime, 31 August, Hitler was decided. He had played his diplomatic hand, ironed out his last remaining doubts, and his confidence in ultimate success had returned. At 12.40 p.m. Hitler summoned General Keitel to his office and handed him 'DIRECTIVE NO. 1 FOR THE CONDUCT OF THE WAR'. The invasion of Poland was to begin on Friday, 1 September at 4.45 a.m. the following morning.

That night of 31 August, a few hours prior to Y-Day, the German towns of Kreuzberg, Pischen, and Hochlinden were shot-up and vandalized by Hitler's SD men dressed as Polish soldiers. At Gleiwitz, the German radio station was attacked and taken over. The few night staff on duty were unceremoniously roughed up by the SD men who shouted pro-Polish slogans across the German airwaves. Alfred Naujocks, the SD commander, recalled that one of his men shouted the slogans 'Germany's leaders are hurrying Europe into war . . . Peaceful Poland is being constantly threatened and bullied by Hitler, who must be crushed at all costs . . . Danzig is Polish . . .' whilst he cheered and fired his gun into the air. With typical SS ghoulishness the reality of the attack was enhanced by the scattering of a few bodies dressed as Poles – convicts who had been suitably attired in Polish uniforms before being shot and dumped.[4]

The following morning, the Nazi newspaper and Party mouthpiece, *Volkischer Beobachter*, blared the headlines: 'Aggressors Attack Gleiwitz Radio'.

> A group of Polish soldiers seized the Gleiwitz Radio building last night a little before eight. Only a few of the staff were on duty at that hour. It is obvious that the Polish assailants knew the ground perfectly. They attacked the personnel and broke into the studio, knocking out those they encountered on the way . . .[5]

At dawn the conquest of Poland began. Operation Himmler had achieved its objective, and Hitler now had the alibi for the conquest he required. 'The Führer [is] calm and slept well,' recorded General Halder. 'Opposed to evacuation . . . proof that he hopes Great Britain and France will remain at peace.'[6]

At 10 a.m. Hitler went to the Reichstag to deliver one of his most important speeches to the assembled gathering of the Party faithful, declaring:

> While recently twenty-one border incidents have been recorded in a single night there were fourteen last night, *three of them very serious*, so I have decided to speak to the Poles in the language they have used to us for months ... Last night, for the first time, Poland has opened fire on our national territory, with *soldiers of her regular army*. Since 4.45 we have been answering their fire. As from now we answer bomb with bomb ... I shall conduct this struggle against whomsoever until the safety of the Reich and its rights are secure ...[7]

There followed a frantic forty-eight hours whilst Britain and France hesitated, made last-ditch appeals to Hitler to stop his armies and withdraw them to within his own borders. He was calling their bluff and they knew it. That Hitler did not want war with Britain and France in 1939 is without a doubt, his plan was for eastward expansion, and the last thing he wanted was a war on two fronts.

On 3 September 1939, contrary to Ribbentrop's assurances that British and French appeasers, and those who had pro-Nazi leanings, would carry the day, Hitler's plans for eastern expansion were thrown into complete disarray when Britain and France fulfilled their obligations to Poland and declared war on Germany.

The Duke and Duchess of Windsor were at La Croë, their gleaming white villa on the French Riviera, when they heard that Germany had invaded Poland. They had spent the last long hot days of summer at their villa away from friends who, seeing which way the political wind was blowing, had found more important things to do – like tidying their affairs and leaving Europe whilst it was still possible to do so. On 3 September, after listening to the lunchtime news on the radio that told them Polish resistance to the German war machine was collapsing, Edward spent a frustrating hour battling with French telephonists as he tried to get through to London and find out what was happening. 'Fruity' Metcalfe, who had recently rejoined the Windsors' retinue, recalled that after Edward had been defeated by the overwhelmed cross-channel phone lines, as hundreds of expatriate British also tried to telephone home, he had given up in exasperation, saying: 'There's nothing we can do from here right now . . . I'm sure I shall hear from my brother the moment any decision is taken.'[8]

Wallis suggested they retire to the swimming pool for the afternoon, but no sooner had they left the house than a servant called the Duke back, informing him that Sir Ronald Campbell, the British Ambassador to Paris, was on the phone. Telling the others to continue, Edward returned to take the call. Wallis later recalled that when Edward returned, he said in a quiet voice, 'Great Britain has just declared war on Germany, and I'm afraid in the end this may open the way for world communism.'[9] And with that, he dived into the pool to join them.

That night, when the phone system was under less strain and reception was clearer, Edward sat in the library and eventually got through to Walter Monckton in London.

'I went on reading my book in the drawing room as I could not think anything *could* go wrong,' 'Fruity' Metcalfe later wrote to his wife, telling her that Edward and Wallis had appeared half an hour later to inform him that although Walter Monckton had offered to send a plane to carry them back to Britain, Edward had told him, 'We are *not* going,' and suggested that Metcalfe and Miss Arnold (a secretary) should make use of the plane.

'. . . I refuse to go *unless* we are invited to stay at Windsor

Castle,' Edward had continued petulantly, 'and the invitation and plane are sent personally by my brother.'[10]

It was one of the few occasions in their friendship that Metcalfe lost his temper with Edward and Wallis, as he later wrote to his wife:

> I just sat still, held my head & listened for about twenty minutes & then I started. I said *I'm* going to talk now. First of all I'll say that whatever I say is speaking as *your best* friend, I speak only for your good & for W[allis]'s, *understand that* . . . You *only* think of yourselves. You don't realize that there is at this moment a war going on that women & children are being bombed & killed while you talk of your *PRIDE*. What you've now said to Walter has just bitched up everything . . . You are just nuts. Do you really think for one instance they would send a plane out for me & Miss Arnold . . . if this plane *is* sent out to fetch you, which I doubt very much [now] then get into it & be b----y grateful. I went to bed then. It was after 3.15 a.m.'[11]

It was to be the start of many such trials and tribulations faced by the beleaguered British government as it attempted to negotiate, coax, and appeal to Edward's better nature, massaging his ego and gingerly steering him in the direction they wanted him to take.

In the end it took a personal visit and a considerable amount of persuasion by Walter Monckton, who flew precariously from London to the French Riviera in a fragile and minuscule RAF Leopard to inform Edward that his brother, King George VI, was adamant that they would not be able to stay at Windsor Castle, nor would he receive Wallis. Edward would, however, be offered the choice of two posts – either to be Deputy Regional Commissioner in Wales under Sir Wyndham Portal, or to be appointed as a Liaison Officer with the British Military Mission in Paris. Pacified by Monckton, Edward agreed to return to

Britain, and the ducal pair eventually set off for Cherbourg accompanied by Metcalfe and the cairn terriers in one car, whilst a second brought up the rear with their luggage.

At Cherbourg Edward was delighted to find that his cousin, Lord Louis Mountbatten RN, the Royal Navy's youngest captain, and his ship HMS *Kelly*, the navy's newest destroyer, had been specially dispatched to France to ferry them back across the English Channel. Edward had written to his long time ally and friend Winston Churchill, recently returned to his old post of First Lord of the Admiralty, prior to his departure from La Croë and requested that a Royal Navy destroyer be put at his disposal to ferry him, Wallis, and his personal entourage, back to British shores. However, it is evident that Edward had no idea that Churchill would use his new appointment to arrange for Mountbatten and the *Kelly* to perform the task, seeing it as a way to encourage and welcome his former king back to British shores. After years in the political wilderness, some of it undoubtedly due to his support for Edward during the abdication crisis, Churchill could sense that the political wind was changing; he was on a high, riding back to power, and he envisaged carrying Edward with him. Calling Edward's return 'an historic trip', he sent his son, Randolph Churchill, along for good measure with instructions to convey a personal message of welcome.

However, despite all the efforts in time of war, it was not long before Edward felt slighted once again. On landing back in a Portsmouth blacked-out as a precaution against air attack, on the very quayside from whence Edward had departed into exile, the Royal Marine band broke into 'God Save the King', and he inspected the guard of honour specially assembled as a mark of respect. Later, as he sat in the darkness next to Wallis as their car picked its way carefully out of the blacked-out docks, Edward had testily remarked, 'The short version, by God!'

'The short version of *what*, David?' Wallis had asked innocently, calling him by the name used by his family and friends.

'"God Save the King,"' Edward replied. 'The monarch gets the full treatment, other royalty only the first six bars. I'd rather become used to the full treatment.'[12]

Despite what Edward took to be a personal slight, the Windsors came out ahead by three cairn terriers. Completely flouting Britain's stringent quarantine laws they had brazenly brought their dogs into the country, bundling them into their car before driving off. Eventually the cairns' freedom was curtailed when someone reported them, and accordingly Pookie, Preezie and Detto were incarcerated in kennels until their master and mistress departed back to France a fortnight later.

If the ducal pair were depressed by the temporary loss of their dogs, however, General Sir Edmund Ironside, Chief of the British Imperial General Staff and Inspector-General of the Forces, was positively downcast with his lot in life. As Inspector-General of the Forces it was Ironside's responsibility to assess the fighting efficiency of the various forces at the Allies disposal, but he had a major problem – a lack information, not about the British army, but about the French forces. He had plenty of information about the British Expeditionary Force, its dispositions, strengths and weaknesses, what needed to be done to rectify any failings; but he knew virtually nothing about the condition or dispositions of the French forces. A major problem for British High Command in 1939 was that the French army resolutely refused to allow any British officers to inspect their lines, see their defences, or examine the Maginot Line. General Sir Edmund Ironside was not a man to be easily beaten.

At the beginning of September, a British Military Mission had been set up under the command of Major-General Howard-Vyse, ostensibly to liaise with General Gamelin at Vincennes. This small organ of the army, established in a villa at Nogent-sur-Marne with a staff of ten officers and thirty men, was ordered primarily to organize the transfer of information between London and the French High Command at Vincennes. Howard-Vyse's orders stated:

> The object of your mission is to act as the channel of communication between, on the one hand, CIGS and C-in-C, BEF in FRANCE and, on the other hand, General GAMELIN in his capacity as:
> (a) Chief of Staff of the French National Defence.
> (b) Commander-in-Chief of the French Land Forces.
> You will establish your headquarters close to General GAMELIN'S 'Cabinet Particulier'.
> You will collaborate with the British representatives of the Allied Military Committee and will have access, through the Anglo-French Liaison Section of the War Cabinet in FRANCE, to copies of the minutes of their meetings and to such other War Cabinet papers as are sent over.'[13]

Despite this clear brief, Major-General Richard Howard-Vyse (known as 'Wombat' to his friends because of his prominent ears and previous service in Australia) had also been given much more important *secret* orders to spy on the French lines, evaluate their fighting value, pinpoint their strengths and weaknesses, and report this information back to Ironside in London. But, with the French forbidding British Officers to even approach their lines, it was a task Howard-Vyse was finding impossible to accomplish. Therefore, when the suggestion was made in the second week of September that the Duke of Windsor might join the Military Mission, Ironside and Howard-Vyse looked upon the offer as a gift from the Gods, saw the wonderful possibilities the Duke presented and grabbed them with both hands.

On being told the news of the Duke's appointment by Howard-Vyse, Brigadier Davy who served with the Mission recalled, 'At last, we were given a heaven sent opportunity of visiting the French Front.'[14]

However, Ironside's needs were not going to be easily met, for by the time they had arrived in Britain, Edward and Wallis had already decided that of the two positions offered, the one of Deputy Regional Commissioner in Wales rather suited their needs best; albeit for the expedient reason that it would at last enable Edward to settle back to life in Britain, and in time possibly to recover much of his position and standing in British society. By the time that Edward met with George VI a few days later (it was the first time the two brothers had met since the night of the abdication) the Welsh post he had been offered whilst still at La Croë had been withdrawn and Edward was asked to take up the position with the Military Mission at Vincennes. It is almost certainly the case that having the former monarch resident on British soil was just too close for comfort for George VI, and the thought of having Edward in Britain for the duration was just unbearable, for he feared that Edward, as his elder brother, would compromise his position as king. George VI eventually summoned Hore-Belisha, the Secretary of State for War, to Buckingham Palace to urge that the Windsors should return to France with all haste, enumerating his unease at the situation by telling Hore-Belisha that all his ancestors had succeeded the throne after their predecessors had died, whereas 'mine is not only alive, but very much so.'[15]

Despite this obvious concern that Edward should not remain on British soil, the main reason for Edward's appointment to the Military Mission is almost certainly that Ironside and Howard-Vyse desperately needed an important personage, one the French would allow to inspect their lines under the guise of a goodwill tour. The initial plan by the Palace had been to banish Edward to some military backwater where he could make no gaffs, and make no headlines that might upset what George VI saw as his delicate position. What the Palace did not envisage, however, was that Ironside and Howard-Vyse would propel Edward into a high-profile tour of the French lines, during which an intelligence officer would accompany him, and together the two men would make a mental note of everything they saw. They would then return to Vincennes and write detailed reports on the French dispositions, strengths and weaknesses, for immediate dispatch back to London.

Having secured Edward's services, on 19 September Ironside and Howard-Vyse went to see General Lelong, the Military Attaché at the French Embassy, and put the next stage of their plan into operation. They gave Lelong the impression that the Duke of Windsor had been foisted upon them and the Military Mission, and Howard-Vyse went to great lengths to give the impression that the Duke would be an unwanted encumbrance, limiting his ability to do his job. The two men appealed to the Frenchman's better nature, asking if the French could help keep the Duke occupied and out of Howard-Vyse's way. Perhaps, they craftily suggested, it might be possible to keep the Duke busy by sending him on a morale-boosting tour of the French lines, visiting the troops – a sort of goodwill tour. After careful consideration and some misgivings, Lelong gave in and wrote to Gamelin to ask if such a tour might be possible, but he was obviously far from happy about it as is evident from the way he phrased his letter:

> The request is solely political. They do not really know what to do about this cumbersome person, especially in England and do not want him *croise les bras* [a uniquely French phrase

meaning: 'to stand about idly with one's arms crossed']. They
have therefore picked on the expedient Howard-Vyse, who is
not really proud of it. General Ironside has left it to him to sort
out with us the best way to employ him: [although] he
[Howard-Vyse] wishes to try this experiment, he tells me you'll
have to be very firm with him [the Duke]. The situation is
stupid and cannot be allowed to continue.[16]

Despite evident French reluctance, the dirty deed was done
and General Gamelin eventually agreed to let the Duke of
Windsor tour their lines. On 21 September, Howard-Vyse wrote
to Ironside: 'General Gamelin has no objection to the Duke of
Windsor going anywhere in the French zone, which is a great
relief to me.[17]

Already however, some Britons who remembered Edward's
affinity for Fascism and his praise for all things Aryan were
beginning to have feelings of unease. Edward made no secret of
the fact that he believed war with Germany a disaster of the first
magnitude and that a peace should be made, preserving the
strong Nazi barrier of Fascism against the Communist peril to
the east, even at the expense of Europe's smaller states. The Earl
of Crawford wrote in his diary on 14 September:

[The Duke of Windsor is] too irresponsible as a chatterbox to
be trusted with confidential information . . . I dined with Howe
[Francis Curzon, Fifth Earl of Hore] at the Club. He is working
at the Admiralty, and to his consternation saw the door of the
Secret Room open – the basement apartment where the
position of our fleet and the enemy is marked out by hour –
and lo! out came Churchill and the Duke of Windsor. Howe
. . . was horrified.[18]

With no invitation to stay at Windsor Castle, and treated like
'non-persons' by the vast majority of their former acquaintances,

Edward and Wallis stayed with the Metcalfes at their West Sussex home, South Hartfield House, during their time in Britain. Daily they sorted their affairs prior to the planned departure for France, taking time out to luncheon with those of their friends who had backbone enough not to shun them. They shopped, visited old haunts, and Edward arranged for the collection of his liqueurs still stored in the cellars of Buckingham Palace.

Before returning to France to take up his appointment, Edward entered into varied and lengthy negotiations with Hore-Belisha, which did little to enamour himself to the Government Minister or the War Office. When Edward was heir to the throne and then monarch, he had been given the honorary rank of Field-Marshal of the Army, but he had failed to discern the difference between those officers who had actually worked long and hard for their rank, and himself. His was purely an honorary title, and had little meaning other than the reality that senior military officers would pay deference to him on the parade ground or in the mess. But Edward actually thought his honorary rank meant something, that he was and could remain a field-marshal. Consequently, at his first meeting with Hore-Belisha, Edward made it clear he wanted to keep his rank and was not prepared to relinquish his field-marshal's baton. Hore-Belisha had the painful and difficult task of disillusioning the Duke; it would not be possible for him to remain a field-marshal, and carry out the duties of a lesser rank under the command of a real major-general, (making a mockery of the whole rank system) in this case Howard-Vyse. The best the War Office could do would be to offer Edward the honorary rank of Major-General, which was no less than Howard-Vyse, but Howard-Vyse would be the senior commanding officer. Edward was greatly disappointed with this outcome for he immensely enjoyed dressing up in his various uniforms. Apart from high army rank, he was also an honorary Air Marshal of the Royal Air Force, Admiral of the

Fleet, and a whole host of other ranks and orders, permitting him to wear virtually any sort of uniform, depending on the function or whatever took his fancy.

Next, Edward declared that it might be a good idea if he were to conduct a whirlwind tour of the Commands in Britain before departing for France, so that he might get the feel of soldiering and be in contact with the troops once again, adding wistfully that he would like Wallis to accompany him. It was a move designed to raise his and Wallis' profile within Britain, and the request was seen for what it was. When Hore-Belisha told George VI of Edward's request he recorded in his diary that:

[The King] was in a very distressed state. He thought that if the Duchess went to the Commands, she might have a hostile reception, particularly in Scotland. He did not want the Duke to go to the Commands in England [and] said the Duke had never had any discipline in his life.[19]

In a last effort to gain some concessions Edward made a second visit to Hore-Belisha, this time to state that he did not want to be paid for his services and asked that his generous gesture be announced to the press. Uncertain of his ground, Hore-Belisha called in his Military Secretary to discuss the issue, but the Military Secretary quickly disappointed Edward by informing him that no member of the royal family ever accepted payment for their services in the army anyway, so his gesture was hardly unique. Next, Edward asked if he might be given an Honorary Colonelcy in the Welsh Guards, to which Hore-Belisha responded that he did not appoint Honorary Colonels, and that the Duke would have to ask the King.

It was hardly the most appropriate time for Edward to pester Britain's Secretary of State for War with trivial requests. Not only was Poland being obliterated by Hitler's blitzkrieg, but Hore-

Belisha had just received intelligence information that Russian troops amassed on the Russo–Polish frontier were intending to attack Poland within the next twenty-four hours. He had also been visited by Mr Kirkpatrick, Head of the Central European Section of the Foreign Office, who informed the Secretary of State that the pro-Fascist Iron Guard of Romania were plotting an imminent coup to oust the legitimate government and throw in their lot with Germany. (The coup actually took place on 21 September when Romanian Premier Armand Calinescu was murdered.) As a result of these pressures Hore-Belisha had rather more important things on his mind that morning than Edward's frivolous demands; Europe was being blown apart before his very eyes, and his valuable time was being wasted by a disconsolate Duke who pestered him with banal trivialities. Finally, Hore-Belisha gave in on Edward's last two requests; he wanted to wear his decorations on his battledress, and he asked if he could have 'Fruity' Metcalfe as his equerry. Knowing decorations, medals and orders to be handed out between royalty like so much candy at Christmas, Hore-Belisha obviously saw no harm in massaging the Duke's ego a little, and in addition he agreed to Edward's request to have Metcalfe appointed as his equerry.

Eventually, and finally having run out of any more excuses not to return to France, Edward and Wallis together with the cairns (newly sprung from quarantine), and 'Fruity' Metcalfe (appointed equerry for the duration), departed Britain's shores on the windy morning of 29 September aboard HMS *Express*. With them travelled Captain Purvis, a British army translator who had been cleared by the French to accompany the Duke, despite the fact that after living in France for nearly two years Edward had a good working knowledge of the language. The Windsors reached Paris late that night, and booked into the Trianon Palace Hotel in Versailles having decided not, for the moment, to reopen their Boulevard Suchet home.

On the following morning, 30 September, Edward reported to the No.1 Military Mission, in La Faisanderie at Nogent-sur-Marne, a building where tame pheasants had once been bred. That morning Howard-Vyse briefed the Duke about his duties and informed him he was to conduct an investigative mission during which he would tour the French lines, evaluate their strengths and pinpoint any weaknesses in the French lines. Edward was delighted, for having envisaged a war career out of the limelight and forgotten in some backwater, the reality of being able to do something interesting was of great appeal. As it turned out the Duke of Windsor (who had a copious memory) was particularly well-suited for intelligence gathering. As a child he'd been trained for his future role as monarch by being introduced to large rooms filled with his parents' guests, and then taken into an ante-room, asked to remember all their names, what they'd worn, and where they'd stood. It was just the sort of training to produce the perfect spy, reminiscent of Rudyard Kipling's *Kim*. Unfortunately for Britain's government and her High Command, they failed to discern that Edward was capable of working towards a completely different agenda.

Three days after joining the Military Mission, on the night of Tuesday, 3 October, the Duke and Duchess of Windsor dined with Charles and Fern Bedaux, at Bedaux's Paris Ritz suite. It had been nearly two years since the defunct trip to the United States had been abandoned, and the two couples had apparently not met since. After recovering his mental equilibrium at the Reichenhall clinic in Munich, Bedaux threw the weight of his abilities and contacts behind the Nazi political machine – aimed at creating a Greater Reich through economic and political power, manipulation, assassination and outright coup. In addition to being a high-flying industrialist and political manipulator, he returned to his old career of economic and industrial espionage – travelling between states and gathering data on industrial plants so that when conflict came, as it inevitably would, Germany knew what was worth bombing, what was worth saving, and what was worth removal back to the Reich.

Through Bedaux's association with Armand Grégoire, Wallis Simpson's lawyer, Bedaux had become intimately involved with the right-wing Cagoularde plot, which attempted to overthrow the legitimate government of France and replace it with a French version of Franco-style dictatorship. That plot had ended in failure, but since that time Bedaux had been very busy indeed. He had travelled throughout Europe, primarily to countries the Nazis knew they ultimately wanted to conquer, gathering and compiling detailed packages of information on those countries' industries. In the years immediately after German conquest, Bedaux's work would pay enormous dividends to Germany as she conducted the economic rape of the occupied territories.

When the Duke and Duchess of Windsor returned to Paris, it immediately came to Bedaux's attention that Edward had been given a job of some importance with the British Military Mission. How he knew this has never been discovered, but given Bedaux's thirst for information and his passion for intelligence gathering, it cannot be beyond the realms of possibility to make a calculated guess that he had a plant in the Windsor retinue; after all, several of Candé's former staff were now in the Windsor's employ. (Indeed, it is known that one of the Duchess' maids had the German code name 'Miss Fox'. In the summer of 1940 she would travel back to occupied Paris and report to Otto Abetz, Bedaux's long-time friend, Gauleiter of Paris, and former Paris representative of Dienstelle Ribbentrop.) Going through 'Fruity' Metcalfe, Bedaux promptly invited the Duke and Duchess to dine with him at his private suite in the Ritz. However, Metcalfe obviously had some misgivings about the association, for he was to write to his wife: 'He [Bedaux] is like a will-o-wisp. He is never in the same place, town or *country* for more than six hours at a time. I can't make him out. He knows *too* much.'[20]

Nevertheless, Metcalfe arranged for the Windsors and Bedaux to dine together that night, writing to his wife the following day:

Last night I fixed a dinner in a private room here [the Ritz] for Charles B[edaux] to meet them. He, Charles, had much to say. He knows *too* much – about *every* country in Europe & also our Colonies. It is *terrifying* ... He has left at dawn for an unknown destination. He hinted at *Berlin* being one of the places! This meeting I arranged was the *first* time they had all met since the disaster of the 'Battle of Germany' & 'the USA' in 1937 – it was very funny in a way...[21]

For Bedaux to have declared he was travelling to Berlin the following day was an astonishingly frank statement to make, even between friends during those tense early days of the Second World War, particularly one would have thought, to the former British King who was now serving as a major-general with the British Army in France.

It is not known in exact detail what Edward and Bedaux discussed over that particular dinner, but it was obviously about the outbreak of war and the chances of Britain and France making peace moves before Europe descended into turmoil. It was certainly intimated that a war in Western Europe would be both a catastrophy and a tragedy, and that Germany should be allowed to expand eastward if it wanted to. Edward probably informed Bedaux what his new 'job' with the Military Mission really entailed, for it was too good a piece of gossip for Edward to have resisted telling an old friend. Edward and Bedaux also probably discussed the horrors of the First World War, of the terrible waste and casualties that had been inflicted on both sides during the pointless stalemate that lasted for four years. It is not unreasonable to suppose that Bedaux probably 'embellished' – or even made up – his wartime adventures to impart to his friend, for at this time he was still maintaining tales of his fictional World War One career – just as he had to Mrs Margantin his landlady in Grand Rapids way back in 1915.

Bearing in mind the Duke's loathing and fear of Bolshevism, he probably articulated on the folly of declaring war on Germany, draining her military strength as Europe's bastion against Russia, as well as the dangers of disintegration that would happen to the British Empire if she committed the vast quantity of men, materials and money necessary to defeat Germany. In 1943 Bedaux was asked what were the Duke of Windsor's political views at this time. He replied that the Duke had told him:

> That Capital is dead. The British Empire is holding together by a miracle and miracles do not last for ever, that a new order must come where the human being will have and enjoy without consideration of class, in that he will find order and decency . . .

'Are those ends to be accomplished politically?' Bedaux was asked.

'I think, [by] revolution,' he replied.

Bedaux was then asked if he had put 'influence upon the Duke of Windsor,' to which he retorted:

> No, the Duke of Windsor is fond of German ways. He likes Germans. He is three-fourths German. He likes German food in preference to British. He does not like French food at all. He will have messengers go into Germany and Austria to learn certain German dishes that he is fond of, and that he did not learn from me . . .[22]

Whilst this might seem a very prevaricating reply, it must be remembered that Bedaux was trying desperately to absolve himself of any culpability in pro-German activity, and he repeatedly prevaricated and digressed from the questions placed to him over the course of three days, hoping to minimize the charges that would be placed against him.

Despite this, it is unlikely that Bedaux told Edward where he had been just a few weeks before – for in the week prior to war, during those last heady days of August when Hitler had hesitated, not only had Charles Bedaux been in Germany, but he had been taking part in a sophisticated planning session with non other than Joachim von Ribbentrop, visiting the German Foreign Minister at his Salzberg château. The principal topic of these discussions was an idea advanced by Ribbentrop who wanted to find a way of establishing a standard currency for use throughout Europe once it came under the rule of the Greater Reich – a European currency, in fact. However, what Germany required for a conquered Europe had rather special needs, and Ribbentrop suggested they would require a monetary system based on something other than the gold standard – something immovable, like a unit of measurement based on human energy – Bedaux's discovery and hence the reason for his being there. This new currency, based on an extraordinarily complicated computation, would be equivalent to a unit of energy (be it the energy expended by a man during work, or the amount of energy used to produce a product) and was to be called the Bex. Bedaux recalled that:

During the meeting Ribbentrop got away from the conversation and began a tirade in English, reciting that twelve times he had gone to England to ask for an understanding, and twelve times he had been refused, and made threats ... during this tirade, a secretary-man with a slip of paper came in and Mr Ribbentrop ignored it and I noticed. I was more interested in the secretary than I was in Ribbentrop, because I could see it was something of importance. When he finally took the paper, he changed colour and said, 'This may change the entire thing,' without telling us what was on the paper. He excused himself and left. I remained to lunch with his wife, but he was no longer there. The paper, I found out later, was his order to go to Moscow to sign the treaty with Molotov. This happened during that conversation and ended the meeting. He [Ribbentrop] might have stayed to lunch but he left immediately and on his order I was returned to Berlin in his plane, while he went in the plane of Hitler or somebody.[23]

Bedaux's confidence in Ribbentrop's enthusiasm for his new currency had taken a sharp knock, however, when following his return to Berlin he had taken Dr Hjalmar Schacht, Head of the Reichsbank, out to lunch at a popular restaurant. Bedaux had been burbling on happily about his meeting with Ribbentrop and the proposed new currency when Schacht had interrupted him, saying testily, 'Mr Bedaux, are you an engineer, an economist, or a fool? You may be sure of one thing – if Ribbentrop could lay his hands on the money in Fort Knox, the money, German money, would rest on gold, and not on your unit of energy.' It was to be a bizarre fact that during the Second World War, those countries invaded by Germany paid for the privilege out of their own national gold reserves, for cash-strapped Nazi Germany funded its war by looting other nations' gold reserves to pay the vast costs involved in conquest. Thus the Nazis were looking for an alternative to the gold standard on which to base their new European empire, and a prime candidate had their plans succeeded would have been the Bex.

With all the facts to hand about the Duke of Windsor's and Bedaux's politics, and understanding their personalities, it is not too great a leap to conclude that they must have also discussed what could or *must* be done to stop such a conflict.

After a life at the centre of the stage, Edward had never really accepted that his opinions and strongly held political beliefs were no longer of consequence. He still saw himself as the ousted rightful British head of state, and it was his duty to stop this conflict before irreparable damage was done both to Germany and Britain, the peoples of 'Hun origin' as he liked to call them. He was convinced that the only victor from such a conflict would be Stalin and Bolshevism. He had already made his feelings known on the Peace Movement, and he saw himself as the rightful leader of that faction, very aware as he was of the possibilities of using it as his ticket back onto the world stage. What he was to say in private amongst friends in September and October 1939, he would make public and declare quite frankly and openly to friends, politicians, and the British government in 1940.

However, the Duke of Windsor's was not the only voice expressing fears for the survival of the British Empire, the spread of Communism, in the early autumn of 1939. Unknown to him, similar detailed exchanges of information, opinion, and negotiation were already being conducted in Switzerland between a representative of the British Air Ministry, and a member of the German Diplomatic Corp.

Since de Ropp had last cropped up in the mid 1930s his career within the Air Ministry had reached dizzying heights, and his contact and long-time friend F.W. Winterbotham, Head of the Air Intelligence Section of the Secret Intelligence Service (SIS), now wielded great power in intelligence circles and within the Air Ministry, although he would soon be transferred to Bletchley Park to run the code-breaking system, Ultra.

On 23 September, Reichsleiter Rosenberg, now Head of the Nazi Party's Foreign Affairs Office, had received a postcard from de Ropp in Switzerland, who had asked that they meet. Rosenberg had then written to Ribbentrop:

> I received by the roundabout channel of a private address a card from Switzerland from Baronet [sic] de Ropp, now Squadron Leader (Fliegermajor), in which he asked whether at the end of September there might take place a visit to Switzerland from ... a person known to him personally. There would be involved here a private exchange of views, which would have the purpose of setting forth in very broad outlines the views of the Führer with regard to England and France, and countered on the other hand with the views ... of the [British] Air Ministry, now become of extreme importance as a result of the war situation ...[24]

On 5 October, Reichsleiter Alfred Rosenberg reported to his Foreign Ministry that 'in accordance with instructions a member of the Aussenpolitisches Amt [foreign policy department] of the NSDAP [Nationalsozialistische Deutsche Arbeiterpartei] went to Montreux to invite Baron W. de Ropp to Berlin'. He then went on to report that de Ropp had informed the German contact that:

> Because of the war psychology prevailing in England and the weak position of Chamberlain it was [currently] beyond the power of the [Air] Ministry at the moment to make use, in the desired direction of a termination of hostilities ... It considered that this moment would only come about through considerable losses on the part of the British air forces and the related effects on the unity of the Empire. It believed that then the views represented by the Air Ministry would have to be taken into account, since the Empire could not permit its air strength to be reduced beyond a certain point.[25] [The reason being that by this time it was thought that the RAF could be used to control and subjugate any moves to break away from the British Empire.]

On 10 October, de Ropp, claiming to speak on behalf of the British Air Ministry, met with the German representative to discuss the futility of a European war, the economic and political damage that Britain and Germany would sustain if the conflict were to be a long, drawn out affair – 'The decline of the West, of the Aryan race, and the era of the Bolshevization of Europe, including England.' He then astounded the German who reported to Ribbentrop that de Ropp had told him that the British Air Ministry did not support its own government in its policy of war with Germany. Further, de Ropp revealed that there was little point in 'convincing Chamberlain alone', that the Air Ministry was 'convinced that the war would be decided by the Luftwaffe', and it would 'therefore depend on the Air Ministry to explain to the British government that, in view of the losses it had sustained, it no longer found itself in a position of being able to continue the war'. The Germans were further extremely interested to hear de Ropp suggest it might be 'necessary first to await the first clash and the resulting losses. He hoped that in the interest of the Aryan race, Germany's Luftwaffe would be so victorious as to create this basis . . .'

It was the first intimation the Germans received that a swift defeat, or military misadventure at the hands of the German army, might result in a swiftly negotiated end to the hostilities, and it is possible this intimation first germinated the idea and plan that was to follow in the months ahead. In the meantime, German interest was guaranteed to be focused on this development because:

It was arranged that if B[aron] d[e] R[opp] considered a new discussion of the situation expedient, he should write to the previously used address about Ausflugen [excursions]. If Fred[dy Winterbotham] wired him, however, that the Air Ministry now felt strong enough to be justified in hoping that it would prevail and the conditions were therefore created for his going to Berlin, he would write about Schnee [snow] . . .

He also advised that German propaganda should hit Britain in her weakest spot. The representative of the Aussenpolitisches Amt concluded his report by informing his superiors that de Ropp had also told him:

> You may be right, indeed, in saying that this war of the rootless elements against Germany is in reality not at all a war between Britain and German interests. I too believe now that the question is still whether or not the British Empire can be preserved in the interest of the Aryan race.[26]

The Germans were delighted by what they heard, and after de Ropp had referred back to Britain for further instructions, the code word 'Schnee' – Snow – was sent, indicating that 'Fred'[dy] had told him that the Air Ministry was sufficiently confident about the situation, and the possibilities of stalling the escalating conflict, for talks to continue. Another meeting took place towards the end of October:

> B[aron] d[e] R[opp] stated that our first talk has been a complete success. As a result of his subsequent efforts, the English circles which want an early peace because of their concern for the Empire, have brought it about that henceforth no official organ will proclaim the overthrow of the German regime as a war aim. He repeatedly stressed that the implications of that success were utterly incalculable.
>
> The thing now was to proceed to the second stage. These circles have to be mindful of the sentiments of the English people and therefore must in one way or another save appearances for England's commitment to the Poles . . . The Poles as such were of no further interest to them . . . [However, de Ropp] still believed that heavy armed clashes would unfortu-

nately be necessary ... [because] the British as a whole were still too sure of victory over Germany.

To my question as to the sources of these statements, that is, whether they might come from the Air Ministry (Fred)[dy Winterbotham], B. d. R. replied that the City, too, which as is well known, is very powerful, had now to be counted among the 'English Party'. I had the impression that he is currently in touch with Sir Ralph Glynn, an exponent of the City who, he asserts, has very close personal connections with Chamberlain. The City is motivated by anxiety about the value of British currency, which typifies the power of the British Empire. As an additional success of the 'English Party' he cited the fact that differences have already arisen in the inner circle of the present Government, between Churchill-Eden on the one side, and Halifax, not to speak of Chamberlain, on the other.[27]

Thus, the impression given to the Germans by Baron de Ropp in Switzerland *and* Edward, Duke of Windsor (via Bedaux's reports back to the Nazis) in Paris, was that a military stalemate must *not* be allowed to take place. If the French were defeated, and the British suffered a major defeat early in the war – a short sharp shock – Chamberlain would crumble, look towards the survival and future stability of the British Empire, and sue for peace. Hitler would then be able to swing his forces about-face to the East, pursue his policy of Lebensraum unmolested, and attack the real menace – Soviet Russia.

The only flaw in this plan was that when the time came to put the operation into effect in May 1940, the Germans were not faced with the weak vacillating and indeterminate leadership of Neville Chamberlain, but were faced with the stoicism and strength of Winston Churchill, and he was a completely different proposition. He would never give up, ever. Even if it meant the destruction and fall of Britain, and carrying on the fight from foreign shores.

Years later, in an attempt to explain his part in the complexities of 1939, Winterbotham was to say that the Nazis:

> ... saw much closer than ourselves the tyranny of Communism, the massacre of farmers and intellectuals, the police state in which families were made to spy on each other and where murder was the reward for one word out of place. They felt that we should welcome the destruction of the Bolsheviks. Some of them even felt that we should help in this anti-Russian drive; or, if we would not offer positive help, then the least that we could do was to stay neutral and well out of the way while the Nazis got on with the job.
>
> It seems that whereas history credits Hitler with wanting a quick victory in the West prior to launching his attack on Russia, in reality, he would have preferred to attack Russia without first engaging the Western Allies ...[28]

During an interview conducted in 1981, Freddy Winterbotham was asked: 'How well connected were you to de Ropp in the autumn of 1939? Were you, for instance, the "Fred" he referred to in the Rosenberg correspondence?' Winterbotham had hesitated for a few seconds before replying with a wistful smile:

> Bill [de Ropp] and I and were good friends, we had known each other for over twenty years. As to your question whether I was the Fred referred to in the German documents, let's just say I knew Bill was in Switzerland, and [we] were chatting on a personal and private basis when he came to back this country ...[29]

Events were now to take a turn for the worse, as mere blustering, intrigue and conspiracy – talk of how a war could be diverted or stopped – turned to actual 'physical action' that would in reality change the course of the war.

On Wednesday, 4 October, the day following his dinner at the Ritz with Bedaux, Edward was taken to lunch at General Gamelin's headquarters by Howard-Vyse. Here, accompanied by his new equerry, 'Fruity' Metcalfe, and Purvis, his official translator, Edward met Gamelin's right-hand man, Petibon, and also Marshal Jamet. It was a successful social encounter, the French accepted the Duke, everyone was put at their ease, and plans for the Duke's morale-boosting tours proceeded with startling speed. So much so that later that afternoon Howard-Vyse wrote to General Ironside to confirm that:

> The Duke of Windsor will leave here on Friday for a tour of General Billotte's first Group of Armies, starting from the left, i.e. the immediate right of the sector of the British Field Force. After visiting General Billotte, at Bohain, he will probably go to see the C.-in-C. As to this, I have written privately to the C.G.S. The details of the programme are being sent to me this evening by General George's Staff.[30]

On the following morning Edward's tours took an ominous turn for the French when they were informed that Captain Purvis had been involved in a serious car accident, and therefore would not be able to accompany the Duke. No evidence exists to show that Purvis had any accident at all, indeed, the incident seems to have been a ploy to enable a certain Captain John de Salis to act as his replacement. The French accepted the exchange of personnel without engaging in the formalities that Purvis had had to undergo, and the necessary passes and documents were issued to allow de Salis, instead of Purvis, to accompany the Duke to their more sensitive areas. Captain de Salis, however, apart from actually being fluent in French, was in reality no mere translator.

Captain Count John de Salis, of the Irish Guards, was an experienced line officer with an expertise in intelligence. Prior to the declaration of war, he had been a serving service diplomat of long standing. By a curious fluke (which meant that his appointment to the Duke was almost certainly not coincidence) he had once been well acquainted with Wallis Simpson when she had been Mrs Earl Winfield Spencer, and he a young diplomat attached to the British Embassy in Washington in the 1920s. He would tour with the Duke, act as his interpreter (despite Edward being able to speak French), and together they would compile the series of reports for General Ironside and the High Command back in London. Prior to acting as Purvis' replacement, de Salis had served on the staff of the august Supreme War Council at the headquarters of the Allied War Committee. The headquarters of the Allied War Committee was where General Ironside was based, and being on the staff of the Supreme War Council also meant that de Salis worked directly under Ironside, so the whole package was tied up very neatly. To be appointed as a mere translator to the Duke of Windsor was hardly the career move a professional British army officer like de Salis would make voluntarily, but the real 'job' he was to undertake was considered one of the utmost importance.

That Edward had not the slightest foreknowledge that Purvis would be replaced by de Salis is not in doubt, for on the journey back from Gamelin's headquarters, he yet again showed complete insensitivity to 'Fruity' Metcalfe's feelings by suggesting he travel without his 'man' to leave more room for the Duke's knick-knacks. As Metcalfe was later to recount to his wife:

> Coming back in the car we were talking about going 'somewhere interesting' on Friday for 3 or 4 days [and] *he* kept on saying how essential it was to be *really comfortable, etc, etc* & then I'm d-----d if he didn't say, 'Oh, Fruity, if you can do without your man it will leave us more room. You see there will be my man and Purvis's.' I said, 'What on earth can we

put in two motor cars?' (His own car plus a 5-seater French car with driver.) He said, 'Oh, if Thomas doesn't go I'll have more room for some of my little extra things.' [Amongst which was what the Duke called *kettly*, his personal tea-pot] ... At times, Babs, I see a *very vivid red*.[31]

On Friday, 6 October, Edward, Duke of Windsor, set off on his first tour (see Map I) 'along those sections of the line which ran from the British sector around Lille to the virtual gap in the defences in the Ardennes mountains'. Edward's entourage was a compact party made up of Metcalfe, de Salis, two batmen, the Duke's valet, and two drivers. After first going to the British Headquarters at Arras, Edward headed off to tour the French First Army under General Blanchard, situated on the right flank of the British Expeditionary Force and faced onto Belgian territory with its right wing faced to the western edge of the Ardennes. Here they stayed for two days, seeing all the French First Army's best equipment and men, visited the large fortifications, looked over the anti-tank defences, and met the various divisional commanders. Next Edward toured the French Ninth Army under General Corap which lay on the right flank of the First Army between Fourmies and Charleville, covering the last stretch of the Belgian frontier up to the Ardennes – the weak point the German Panzers would target with pinpoint accuracy a mere eight months later. The tour went very well, the Duke trying hard to be a social success with everyone he met, but all the time he and de Salis looked, watched – and remembered.

HRH was all through absolutely delightful company [Metcalfe wrote to his wife, telling her about his travels]. How we laughed at many incidents & at some of the French Generals I'm afraid ... The only few minutes I hated & when he went all wrong was when I had to get the hotel bills & get them paid. Then he was *frightful*.[32]

Back at La Faisanderie, however, Edward and de Salis wrote an entirely more serious and detailed account of all they had seen and heard, for despite the camaraderie and the social niceties of the visit, the two men had missed nothing. Within two days, Edward and de Salis had compiled an extremely detailed, six-page, secret report entitled: 'Report on Visit to the First French Army and Detachments D'Armée des Ardennes by His Royal Highness the Duke of Windsor, October, 1939'.

This was no mere social or vague appraisal of Britain's ally, but a thoroughly detailed intelligence assessment of the French defences in the First French Army's sector, as the following excerpts demonstrate:

The general principle on which the front line facing the Belgian frontier is defended consists of a belt of 1,500 to 2,000 yards in depth. This is known as the *'position de résistance'*. What we would call the support line is known as the *'ligne d'arrêt'*. There are a series of blockhouses, rather like Martelle towers, arranged chess-board fashion and connected by anti-tank obstructions, covered by enfilade fire.

The [Blockhouses] are built of very strong concrete with a sloped bank of earth towards the line of attack, and therefore they have only lateral fire with a very narrow traverse ... Owing to the very restricted space, changing the anti-tank gun from one loop-hole to the other cannot be effected with rapidity, probably more than a quarter of an hour being required to get the gun in action again.

There is a periscope for observation, the top of which projects through a movable steel cupola which appeared vulnerable and was very conspicuous. No anti-gas arrangements as regards the loop-holes were visible.

At Rocroi, Edward reported he had viewed a:

... blockhouse of the Boussios type. There is nothing of particular interest about it except a curious arrangement whereby
bombs could be dropped through the wall from the inside
down a kind of machicoulis channel cut in the wall, the point
of exit on the outside being some two feet from the ground.
This was designed so as to repel attackers endeavouring to
force the door at very close quarters ...

Of the valley of the Meuse, it was noted that:

The main features are the high and very heavily wooded ridges
which form the valley of the Meuse. It was difficult to ascertain
what was the general system of defence. A very large quantity
of wire entanglement has been constructed running in all
directions through the woods. These entanglements are covered
by machine gun fire, but in almost every case there is a very
narrow field of fire, and the entanglements could easily be
approached up to within a few yards under cover of the trees
and very thick undergrowth. There are no anti-tank defences,
as the woods are quite impassable to tanks without preliminary
clearing work.

Edward concluded his report by saying:

During this tour, which covered approximately fifty miles of
front-line sector, it was very noticeable that there was very little
military activity of any kind, and very few troops indeed to be
seen, only one Company of Infantry on the march being passed.
Two batteries of Anti-Aircraft Guns were seen, and in this case
very skilful precautions against observation had been taken.
The camouflage could only be described as excellent.[33]

He appended a personal letter to General Ironside with his
first report, commenting that he had found the staff at the

Military Mission 'helpful and pleasant to work with', and that he thought the French were, 'determined, if possible, to give the Germans battle in Belgium'. He added impertinently, 'Of course they will burrow like rabbits at the sound of the first shell, but French logic says never die unless you have to.'

Howard-Vyse was delighted by the success of Edward's first tour. It was all he had hoped for and more. He wrote a quick letter to Ironside to accompany the report, marking it too, as 'Secret':

> From 6–8 October, HRH the Duke of Windsor accompanied by Captain Count de Salis, paid a visit to the front of the French First Army, on the immediate right of the Sector of the BEF and of the Detachment d'Armée des Ardennes. He has produced a valuable report on the defences, of which three copies are coming over today . . . It will be realized that to give the French any sort of inkling of the source of this information would probably compromise the value of any missions which I may ask HRH to undertake subsequently . . .[34]

However, had Howard-Vyse known what was happening even as he sat writing his letter, he would have looked upon the entire exercise, and the future of the Duke of Windsor, in a different light. On the very night the letter was being transmitted to Ironside, on 9 October 1939, Edward was again dining with Mr Bedaux, and they were plotting an entirely different stratagem for the future conduct of the war.

The following morning, Bedaux boarded a train at Gare du Nord, and travelled to The Hague in Holland. Here he made a beeline straight for the German Embassy and a meeting with an associate of long standing, the German ambassador Count Julius von Zech-Burkesroda.

CHAPTER FIVE

Betrayal

O N 5 OCTOBER 1939, Poland surrendered and what the
American press was to dub the 'Phoney War' began. It was
a time when the French and British armies, deeply entrenched
along the Franco-Belgian/German frontier awaited an attack that
did not come; a time when the Allied High Command postured
and developed wild and fantastic schemes to bring about the
defeat of Germany and the downfall of its Führer. One scheme
that was met with considerable enthusiasm by the Generals was
that Allied troops should flood into Belgium, race eastward to
cross the Rhine bridges to plunge deep into the heart of the Ruhr,
crippling with one fell swoop Germany's industrial might and
critically damaging her ability to wage war. In pursuit of this aim,
the Allied High Command adopted General Gamelin's Plan D,
which proposed that as soon as Germany began her offensive
against the west, the left-wing of the Allied front should sweep
into Belgium in a great clockwise arc, outflanking the Germans
and leaving the Allies in the ideal position poised to strike deep
into Germany's industrial heart. Five years later, Field-Marshal
B.L. Montgomery would resurrect this plan as 'Operation Market
Garden', with equally disastrous results.

In Germany meanwhile, the 'Phoney War' became known as
the 'Sitzkrieg', the 'Sitting War', as opposed to the 'Blitzkrieg',

the 'Lightning War', but Hitler had already begun to formulate the offensive that would take place in the West even before the Polish campaign was over. On 9 October, the Führer issued a directive to his army chiefs in which he made his case for the invasion of the West, setting forth his conclusions that a prolonged war with Britain and France must not be allowed to happen; that a Germany exhausted by a war of attrition would be vulnerable to attack from Russia. He feared that the Soviet-German Pact, signed by Ribbentrop and Molotov mere weeks before, would not protect Germany from Russian attack for one minute longer than it suited Stalin's purposes. This concern prompted him to attempt a forced peace out of France by an early attack, convinced that once France fell, Britain would swiftly come to terms.[1] He concluded his directive by stating that Germany should strike soon, before it was too late, declaring: 'In the present situation, time may be reckoned an ally of the Western Powers rather that of ours ... The attack is to be launched this autumn, if conditions are at all possible.'[2]

Germany's military leaders, particularly Field Marshal von Brauchitsch, the Commander-in-Chief of the army, whilst sharing his Führer's enthusiasm for the defeat of Poland was far less enamoured by the thought of a war against Britain and France. The Allies, he knew, had far superior forces to that of Poland, indeed, to that of Germany too, for whilst Germany had 98 divisions at her disposal, she was currently only fielding an army of 62 divisions, the remaining 36 divisions being Reserve and *Landwehr* Units that were ill-equipped, and mostly made up of elderly reservists who had seen action in the First World War. The Allies on the other hand, as well as having vast empires to draw on for reserves of men, material, and money, had in excess of 6 million trained men; the French had already mobilized 110 divisions, the British Expeditionary Force consisted of 13 divisions, and the so far neutral Belgians could field 23 divisions –

all having the sole purpose of defeating any German offensive. An attack on the West would not be another Poland. It would be wholesale slaughter and bitter fighting.

At a meeting at the Reich Chancellery in mid October, Hitler announced to Brauchitsch and General Halder, his Chief of Staff, that he had provisionally decided that the date of the offensive in the West was to be 12 November. The Generals were not at all pleased to hear of this new development, having deluded themselves that with the conquest of Poland behind him, Hitler would be prepared to sit tight and out-wait the Allies, who they believed would soon become tired of a sitting war and be tempted to initiate an offensive against Germany – an offensive the generals knew they would have little trouble in repulsing. However, Hitler's plans for the creation of the Greater Reich were running to a different timetable to that of his Generals, and he needed to be rid of this threat to Germany's soft underbelly before he could once again turn his eyes eastward.

The German Attack Plan for the West had originally been devised by the General Staff several years before, and was broadly similar to that of the Schlieffen Plan used in the First World War. The main weight of the offensive was to be concentrated on Germany's right-wing under Army Group A, who would thrust across the Belgian plain towards the coast, whilst Army Group C, on the left-wing, pinned down the French army occupying the Maginot Line. The much smaller Army Group B, in the middle, would face the Ardennes in a purely secondary role to prevent an Allied counter-attack. Once Army Group A had achieved its objective of crossing the Belgian plain, it would then pour down into France in a great southerly sweep, effectively cutting-off the French army and the Maginot Line from the rest of France. (See Map II.)

However, Hitler's generals, who had spent years playing this very war game, ever refining their tactics as they played out this scenario time and time again, were now not at all keen to put their plan to the test. They began to make numerous excuses to Hitler over the next few weeks why the attack should not take place on 12 November, citing logistical problems, lack of supplies, unsuitable weather, etc. etc. – delaying tactics that made an increasingly furious Hitler more determined than ever that the attack should take place on the 12th.

This intended western offensive by Germany on 12 November was no secret to the Allied High Command, for they had an eminently reliable intelligence source code-named 'Agent 54'. Early in 1936 Czech intelligence had been approached by a German named Paul Thummel, who offered to pass on information about Germany's plans for European expansion, particularly towards Czechoslovakia, which was on Hitler's immediate shopping list for conquest. The Czechs were very interested in Herr Thummel for they soon discovered he was an important officer within the Abwehr Berlin Headquarters, and therefore privy to some of Germany's most sensitive information. By 1939, Czechoslovakia had to all intents and purposes ceased to exist, and Paul Thummel, alias 'A54', now worked for British Intelligence, regularly updating London on Hitler's plans. Thus London was fully aware of the situation across the English Channel, and the dire risk of imminent attack faced by the Allies on 12 November.

During the latter half of October, the Duke of Windsor had continued to tour the Allied defences. On 17 October he visited General Gort at the British Expeditionary Force Headquarters in Arras, on the 18th he toured the BEF defences around Lille, and then from the 26–28 October, he had visited and inspected the French Fourth and Fifth Armies on the Vosges sector – the western extremity of the Maginot Line that faced the eastern Belgian border. In a few brief weeks of travel he had journeyed

900 miles, and seen more of the vulnerable French defences along their mid-western sector that any other Briton. It was a trust that would prove misplaced, for Edward was seeing Bedaux on a regular basis, and Bedaux was a hive of activity.

Throughout September and October Bedaux had been busy as well, doing everything possible to insinuate himself into the French Ministry of Armament. Eventually his efforts paid off and he 'installed in the bosom of this ministry an office of control directed by Mr Caudron, principal engineer of the Bedaux organization, to which a certain number of Bedaux's organization was attached'.[3] This office was charged with the sensitive task of inspecting and controlling the output of the French armament industry. By February of 1940, the Minister of Armament would become so suspicious of the numerous intelligence leaks from this organization, that he requested Colonel Manges of the Fifth Intelligence Bureau to thoroughly investigate this office, which was not as one might assume located in the Ministry of Armament building, but had actually been sanctioned to operate from Bedaux's own offices of Société Française Bedaux, based in the Hotel Claridge on the Champs-Elysées.

On investigating Bedaux's business it was discovered that his secretary, in charge of typing confidential reports on armament factories and production, had spent five years living in Berlin and was currently the mistress of a German officer in the Second Bureau – Amt II of the SD. Colonel Manges immediately had the woman arrested and she was sent to a detention camp until the French defeat in July 1940. It was reported that after the fall of France the woman was often 'seen in Paris in the company of German officers'.[4] In 1943 Bedaux would claim to be a member of the Abwehr, and personally acquainted with its head, Admiral Canaris,[5] which coincided at the time with a report by J. Edgar Hoover to the US Secretary of State, Adolf Berle that declared:

... the French Cabinet in authority prior to the fall of France looked upon Bedaux as being very pro-German. This opinion avowedly was based upon the active assistance rendered by Bedaux to the German government, as well as his close association with the Duke and Duchess of Windsor.[6]

Yet there was even more to this multi-faceted man than either Colonel Manges or Hoover realized at the time, for Bedaux had recently done a personal favour and service to none other than Adolf Hitler himself. During the First World War, Hitler had served in the German army as a corporal under a lieutenant named Rosenbush, 'a full blooded Jew' who Hitler, with a touching mark of sentimentality, now wished to protect from his own creation – Nazism. Whilst Bedaux had been staying at his Berchtesgaden mansion next door to Hitler's Berghof prior to the outbreak of war, he had been visited by Hitler's adjutant, Fritz Wiedmann. Wiedmann told him that 'my Master feels it would be best for Rosenbush to leave Germany', and asked Bedaux to find employment for Rosenbush somewhere safely outside the borders of the Reich. Bedaux, keen to please Hitler, quickly found Rosenbush a job with Bedaux Associates in Istanbul, Turkey.[7] This favour and service not only reasserted Bedaux's place within the inner sanctum of the Nazi hierarchy, but, although Hitler never really trusted anyone, it was a deed that firmly ensconced him within that small group of men whom Hitler called friend, and who were occasionally made privy to his inner thoughts, workings and plans – and those men were very, very few and far between.

It was as a direct result of Bedaux's close association with Adolf Hitler that made him the perfect man – the only man in fact – whom Edward, Duke of Windsor, could trust and use for the delicate task ahead.

*

Whilst Edward had been making his tours of France's secret defences against German invasion, Bedaux's frequent trips out of France had taken him not only to Belgium and Holland, where he had gone directly to the German Embassy in The Hague, but he had also been travelling to Cologne in Germany. At the beginning of November, however, Bedaux received information that was of such importance that it necessitated him taking another special German trip, not to Cologne but to Berlin. This time he would not be imparting his information to some Nazi minion, but would be giving a detailed briefing to the very pinnacle of the Nazi State – Adolf Hitler.

On the evening of 6 November, the Duke and Duchess of Windsor again dined with Charles and Fern Bedaux at their suite in the Paris Ritz. After dinner the Duke and Bedaux retired for a long private discussion whilst Wallis and Fern made small talk. At the end of their meeting the Duke handed Bedaux a letter to give to the man he was to pass the information to – a reference if you like – assuring the recipient of the information's import-ance. The letter, folded in half, and folded once again into a narrow strip some seven inches long by two wide, was probably tucked into some discreet spot upon Bedaux's person, possibly his coat lining, or maybe even folded in his hat band. Then the two men parted, perhaps with a murmured word of assurance and a handshake, for Edward must have been fully aware of the implications of his desperate gamble; the enormity of the step he was about to take.

Early on 7 November, Charles Bedaux took the morning express from Paris to Brussels, and from there an afternoon train carried him towards his next destination, Cologne. Here, he remained overnight in a hotel awaiting a flight the following morning by Luftwaffe transport to his final destination – Berlin. It is to be wondered whether when Bedaux went to bed that night he realized the importance of the next forty-eight hours of his life, for he was about to change the course of the Second World War, and inexorably alter the shape of Europe for the next fifty years.

However, whilst Bedaux slept in his hotel suite that night, in the early hours of 8 November 1939, someone else was also busily engaged in an attempt to change the course of history. In Munich a thirty-eight-year-old Wurttemberger named Georg Elser was preparing to leave town in a hurry having started the clockwork mechanism of a time-bomb he had planted in the Burgerbraukeller – the building where Hitler was due to speak that coming evening. It was to be one of those strange twists of fate that whilst Georg Elser – a man determined to kill Hitler – failed not only in his aim to kill the dictator but also to stop the impending war as well, Charles Bedaux – equally determined in his mission – would not only succeed, but actually inadvertently cause Elser's plot to fail. Yet these two men would remain totally unaware of the other's existence.

Twelve hours later, on 8 November, Adolf Hitler flew to Munich to attend the Burgerbraukeller, commemorating the sixteenth anniversary of the 1923 Beer-Hall Putsch, but it would only be a short visit, for he wanted to be back in Berlin early the following morning to meet Bedaux. Hans Baur, Hitler's personal pilot recounted:

> A little after landing, the Führer asked me if it was possible to be back in Berlin on the 9th by ten in the morning, since he had an important appointment he could not put off. I couldn't give him an absolute assurance because of fog, frequent in November, which might prevent our landing for several hours. Hitler then decided to return to Berlin by train.[8]

At 8 p.m. Hitler arrived at the Burgerbraukeller to a tumultuous welcome by three thousand enthusiastic followers, who had assembled to commemorate the memory of those comrades who had died in the failed 1923 uprising. After several minutes of applause the gathered devotees settled down at exactly 8.08 p.m. to listen to Hitler's animated and volatile oration on the evils of communism, the bravery of the fallen, the glorious futures of those gathered, and the wonders of National Socialism. From experience the audience knew they were in for two hours of pure Führer rhetoric, and they revelled in it, for to be in the Burgerbraukeller on any 8th of November was a great honour. As the men sat and listened to Hitler's dithyrambic oration, few noticed a member of his entourage, a man in SS uniform, discreetly place a note on his Führer's table. Hitler continued to loudly proclaim, 'Today I confine myself to giving you the assurance that our adversaries will be utterly unable to subjugate us either militarily or economically. There can be only one victor, namely ourselves!'[9]

During the ecstatic cheering and applause with the mandatory accompaniment of outstretched saluting arms, Hitler paused to read the note that told him, 'Hermann Göring asks the Führer to shorten his speech and to return to Berlin as anticipated by the quickest means possible. It is a matter of real importance.'[10]

To many in the audience it seemed that Hitler hurried through the rest of his speech, and by 8.58 p.m. he had finished, much to the surprise and astonishment of all those gathered. Hitler's Burgerbraukeller speeches normally lasted the full two hours, yet this had been only half its usual length. More to the point, the audience noted with disappointment that their Führer only lingered several minutes more while he shook a few hands, said his goodbyes, and put on his hat and coat. Every year up to now, Hitler had always stayed with his old comrades late into the night, and now it was obvious he was keen to be gone. At 9.09 p.m., with his entourage in tow, Hitler swept out of the Burgerbraukeller in a swirl of uniformed capes, overcoats and Nazi regalia, and boarded the motorcade that was to hurry him back to Munich's main rail station in time to catch the Reichsbahn Express 71 to Berlin, due to depart at 9.31 p.m.

At 9.20 p.m., whilst Hitler was travelling across central Munich to board his private lounge car which had been attached to the Reichsbahn express, the Burgerbraukeller was ripped apart by a powerful explosion – Georg Elser's bomb had been hidden in a pillar a mere six feet from where Hitler had stood giving his speech half an hour before.

One of Hitler's secretaries later recounted:

> I was with the Führer in the train which took us back to Berlin . . . He was witty and animated, as always after a successful meeting. With us was also Goebbels who enlivened the conversation with his caustic wit . . . The train stopped at Nuremberg for a few minutes to permit the receiving and sending of some urgent messages.[11]

It was here that Hitler first learned of the horrors that had taken place in the Burgerbraukeller, for in the carnage that immediately followed the explosion no one had thought to inform Hitler who was still in Munich awaiting the train's departure. That task was left to Goebbels, who told his Führer when he returned to the train.

> Hitler, incredulous, did not take it in at first but, finally, at [the] sight of Goebbel's haggard look, took it seriously . . . the Führer's expression froze into a hard, stubborn mask [and] in a peremptory voice harsh with emotion he exclaimed, 'Now I am completely reassured; the fact of having left the Burgerbrau-keller sooner than usual is the confirmation that Providence wants my destiny to be fulfilled.[12]

Hitler later told his secretary that, 'I felt within me an imperative need to cut this meeting short, to return to Berlin the same evening...'[13] It was to become the official party line promoted by Goebbels that the Germany's Führer had intuition – 'Providence' was on his side, and he was smiled upon by the gods. He was chosen.

But it was a lie, Hitler had always intended to return to Berlin early, for he had an appointment to keep the following morning at 10 a.m., and Hermann Göring's note was to tell him that the other half of his appointment, Charles Bedaux, had arrived. Emmy Göring later recounted that:

> On the evening of 8 November 1939 my husband told me that a German living abroad under a false name had come to bring him sensational news. The man had to leave by train on the following morning and had to see Adolf Hitler before then. At that moment an aide-de-camp burst into the room to announce that a bomb had just exploded in the Burgerbrau-keller. There were dead and injured. I was astonished at my husband's calm when the aide-de-camp added, 'What can have happened to the Führer?'
>
> 'Nothing at all,' Hermann had replied confidently. 'He is at present on his way to Berlin.'[14]

Another witness that supports the tenet that Hitler anticipated Bedaux's arrival with important news is Doris Mehner, a member of Himmler's personal staff who remembered that:

> The Reichsfuhrer told me on 8 November around three in the afternoon that the meeting at the Burgerbraukeller had been moved forward and would be shorter than expected. The Führer would not be returning to Berlin by plane but by train. A private carriage would be attached at eight in the evening to the regular train 71 for Berlin which left Munich at 9.31. Consequently I had to have Himmler's luggage and that of SS chiefs present transported at the hour stated. The Reichsführer

SS added, 'I prefer this solution. By train we are sure to arrive. By plane, with the November fogs . . .'[15]

As luck would have it 9 November dawned bright, crisp and clear, and Hans Baur could easily have landed his plane at the Templehof (in the unlikely event that Hitler could have survived being blown to bits at the Burgerbraukeller bombing, had he remained at the meeting). As it was, Bedaux, seated next to Hermann Göring in his chauffeur-driven supercharged Mercedes Benz, motored into Berlin on a bright, sunny autumn morning, passing under the Brandenburg Gate on their way to the Reich Chancellery.

They entered the imposing entrance foyer of the Reich Chancellery with its sixty-feet high ceilings, passing along corridors richly adorned with crisp cold marble, the neo-empire style furniture specially commisioned to epitomize the superiority of the new Germany – the nucleus of Hitler's Reich. The two men lingered for a few minutes in the Great Gallery before Hitler was ready to see them, Bedaux 'ill at ease in a tight fitting suit',[16] probably nervous, yet at the same time undoubtedly exhilarated by the magnitude of the information he had brought. It was a far cry from those first early years as a lodger on Eureka Avenue, Grand Rapids, photographing factory plans with a second-hand camera, and it was dizzying stuff for a man who, although eminently successful, had originated from a humble background.

At 10 a.m. Charles Bedaux and Hermann Göring were shown through the huge double doors into the Führer's private office, passing beneath the portrait of Bismarck that hung above. The doors were shut, the order given that they were not to be disturbed, and then the meeting that would change the course of the Second World War and the future of Europe began.

The exact phraseology and the wording that passed between

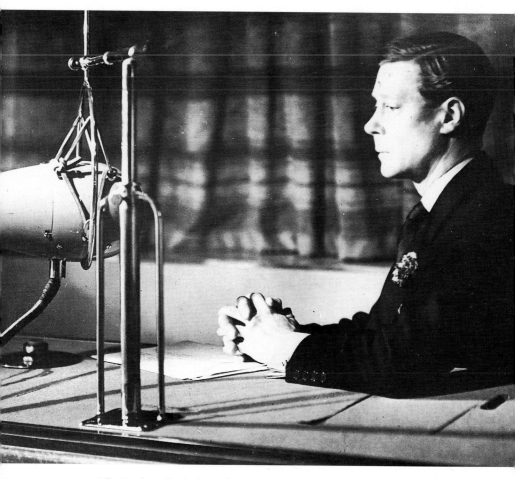
The Duke of Windsor delivers his abdication speech.

The Duke and Duchess of Windsor pose for photographs after their wedding at Candé, accompanied by Herman Rogers (left) and 'Fruity' Metcalfe (right).

The Duke of Windsor chats with Arthur Goerlitzer, Deputy Political Leader of Berlin, at Friedrichstrasse train station

The Duke of Windsor tours the Osram works with Dr Robert Ley.

The Duke of Windsor inspects the Guard of Honour on arriving at the SS training camp, Crossinsee.

Charles Bedaux arrives in New York aboard the SS *Europa* to organize the Duke of Windsor's American tour.

Adolf Hitler greets the Duke and Duchess of Windsor on the steps of his Alpine home at Berchtesgaden.

The Duke of Windsor with Lord Gort, the Duke of Gloucester, General Alexander, Lt. General Sir John Aird, Major General Howard-Vyse, and Brigadier Beckwith Smith at Bachy on the Franco-Belgian frontier in October 1939.

The Duke of Windsor pauses to chat with two Generals during his tour of the French lines in November 1939.

Adolf Hitler pauses to be photographed during his tour of Paris on 23 June 1940.
He is accompanied by Albert Speer on his right and Arno Breker on his left.

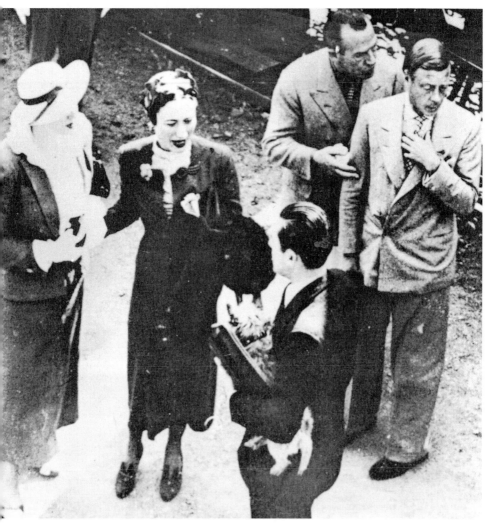

A very rare photograph of the Duke of Windsor with Charles Bedaux, taken in Hungary 1937. The Duchess is seen here with Fern Bedaux and Dudley Forwood.

Paris
4 November 1935

Lieber Herr Hitler,

Ich kehrte kürzlich von einer Reise im Norden zurück und habe sehr interessante Sichten wahrgenommen. Ich habe meine Ferien in grossen Einzelheiten Ihnen Bekannten, Mr B dargelegt. Ich kann kaum die Wichtigkeit dieser Information betonen, desalb habe ich unseren Freund in grossen Einzelheiten berichtet.

Ihre Vorschläge für die Zukunft finde ich erfreulich und bin ganz und gar derselben Meinung. Obgleich die Sache die zukünftigen Beziehungen zwischen unseren Nationen erleichtern würde bin ich der Meinung das man mit grossen Vorsicht in ihrer Ausführung voran gehen sollte.

Man hat mir mitgeteilt wenn die Sache so bleibt wie sie ist, muss ich weitere Reisen unternehmen. Ich bin überzeugt, das ich mich die Hilfeleistung unseren Freund verlassen kann.

E.P.

The 'EP' letter from Edward to Hitler, 4 November 1939.
(For a translation of the letter see page 153.)

the three men will probably never be known, but what can be conjectured with substantial clarity is that the information that Bedaux conveyed verbally to the German Führer was presented in an expressive, educated, and visually stimulating way, for Bedaux was naturally a gifted speaker, able to animate any subject he chose to talk about. It is also possible to make some fairly concise deductions about what happened during the next hour in Hitler's office.

Firstly, Bedaux handed Hitler the letter entrusted to him, a communiqué not only designed to emphasize Edward's importance as the source of the information – the former Head of State who was determined to 'save' his people from themselves because he knew best, but also designed to emphasize to Hitler that the information Bedaux was about to impart was of the utmost importance. Hitler would have taken the letter over to his desk and put on his spectacles. (It is a little known fact that Hitler was remarkably long-sighted. It was only vanity and the use of extraordinarily large print in his speech notes that prevented the German people from ever seeing their Führer wearing his round-lensed, wire-framed spectacles, and looking uncannily like Himmler). And then he read the letter, which used vaguely coded language to protect the writer should Bedaux have been intercepted.

Paris
4 November 1939

Dear Herr Hitler,

I have recently returned from a trip to the north and have observed some very interesting views.

I have described my holiday in great detail to your acquaintance, Mr B.

I am hardly able to stress the importance of the information, which is why I have gone into such great detail in explaining to our friend.

I find your suggestions for the future welcoming, and I am of the same opinion.

Even though the matter would ease future relations between our two nations, I am of the opinion that one should be very careful in the implementation.

I have been informed that I have to undertake more journeys if the matter remains as it is.

I am convinced that I can rely on the help of our friend.

EP*

If one looks beyond the letter's double-speak, it is possible to deduce several clear facts not only about the relationship between Edward, Bedaux and Hitler, but also what was going on behind the scenes, for the letter seems to imply he was replying to certain points that had recently been put to him. The first and second sentences clearly refer to the trips Edward had made to the north of Paris – his tours of the British Expeditionary Force and French defences – he makes clear that what he '*saw*' was of sufficient importance to necessitate Bedaux's trip to Berlin, and that Bedaux had been carefully briefed on what he had seen. In the third sentence it is evident that Edward was very concerned to emphasize the importance of his information, using a fifth of his letter to reinforce his first two sentences.

It is obvious that Edward is replying to some suggestion he had received, couriered either by Bedaux or a third party, and it was of sufficient significance and importance to warrant a response directly to the German leader. Whatever the suggestion made to Edward was, it could not possibly have been some trivial item sent by a minion, but necessarily demanded a direct reply to the originator.

There were very few options available to anyone in 1939 that would have eased relations between Britain and Germany, little

* See Appendix on page 306.

short of Hitler agreeing to order Germany's withdrawal from Poland (the only solution as far as Britain's politicians were concerned), unless the solution was to change the British government and Head of State. There are certain clues that point to this being the solution, for it must be remembered that Edward envisaged himself as a leader of what had become known as the 'Peace Movement' – that group of people for whom another European war on the plains of France and Belgium was a horrifying déjà vu – the nightmare second coming of the wholesale slaughter of the First World War. It must also be remembered that, regardless of reality, Edward *believed* himself to be the ousted rightful British Head of State, and if he ever wavered in that conviction Wallis undoubtedly reasserted it without a moment's hesitation.

Therefore the only suggestion for easing Anglo-German relations that could have been of interest to Edward was the intimation that he might somehow benefit from the situation to regain influence and power in Britain. That is not to say that Edward was advocating the wholesale destruction of Britain, invasion by Germany, and a puppet throne for himself. That, despite his undoubted feelings of betrayal is unlikely to have appealed to him, nor for that matter to Hitler either who initially saw the Reich's future of world domination as a German-heavy partnership between a vast Third Reich dominating continental Europe, and a smaller British Empire controlling her Commonwealth over the seas.

An insight into Hitler's attitude to this came a fortnight later when, over dinner in the Reich Chancellery with Walter Schellenberg (a man who would also become involved with Edward in July 1940), Hitler told the young SD officer:

'. . . I wanted to collaborate with Great Britain. But she rejected all my advances. It is true that there is nothing worse than a family quarrel and, from a racial point of view, the English are in a way our relatives ... It is extremely regrettable that we are engaged in this struggle to the death whilst our real enemies, to the east, wait tranquilly for Europe to be exhausted. It is for that reason that I don't want to destroy England and will never destroy her. But they must be brought to understand, and Churchill first of all, that Germany has also the right to live. And I shall fight England till she gets off her pedestal. The day will come when she will show herself disposed to envisage an accord between us. That is my real aim. Do you understand?'

'Yes, my Führer,' Schellenberg had replied, 'I follow your thought. But a war like this is comparable to an avalanche. And who would venture to plot the course of an avalanche?'

'My dear boy,' Hitler responded indulgently, 'those are my worries, leave them to me.'[17]

The most likely scenario suggested to Edward – initially spawned by de Ropp in Switzerland, who germinated the idea in German minds by informing them that the British Air Ministry was not fully behind its government, and that a swiftly executed 'bloody nose' on the battlefield would cause the British to sue for terms. Thus, if Germany could inflict a humiliating rout of the French and British armies on the battlefield, the British would come to terms, its discredited government under Chamberlain would fall, swiftly followed by the Monarch who had appointed and permitted his government to engage in such wholesale ineptitude in the first place. The net result of this would have been the installation of a moderate/appeasement peace-oriented government with possible right-wing inclinations, and a demand by the British people for the return of their beloved King Edward VIII – Edward the peaceful, Edward the honourable, and last but not least, Edward the romantic who had given up his throne for love.

Over the course of the next hour in the Chancellery, Bedaux gave a very detailed strategic briefing to Adolf Hitler and Hermann Göring in which he described all that Edward had seen in his October tours of the Allied lines; for Edward had covered a vast segment of the Allied frontier defences, from the BEF at Lille through to the French at Estreux, Boussois, Trelon, Rocroi, the Valley of the Meuse, covering Hiraumont, Revin, and Les Mazures, and onto Sedan and the front that faced the Ardennes. It was a very comprehensive brief, for Edward had been shown all of importance, and Bedaux was able to give very detailed information to the German leader, ranging from details of what the French called their 'position de résistance' and 'ligne d'arrêt' – consisting of wire entanglement, defence towers and anti-tank obstructions, to blockhouses that were poorly designed and limited by the efficiency of the anti-tank guns within. The observation and artillery posts had been poorly sited, the anti-tank ditches were ineffective and could be easily crossed, and the wire entanglements were 'very shallow and very narrow, usually twelve feet, and the stakes no larger than broomsticks of poor quality'.[18] More importantly, Bedaux was able to reveal to the Führer that whilst the French and British were prepared for conventional German attack with strong eastern defences in the form of the Maginot Line, the plan for an immediate move into Belgium should Germany attempt an outflanking manoeuvre across the Belgian plains was critically flawed. The Allies had little defence and minimal troops at the 'hinge' of their march into Belgium – the area immediately to the west of Sedan facing the Belgian border, for they did not believe it possible for an attacking army to come through the Ardennes.

Shortly after 11 a.m., Bedaux was ready to make his hasty departure back to France, and it is known that, 'the mysterious German – not identified – did in fact leave Berlin by air at noon, after having talked with Hitler for more than an hour in Göring's presence'.[19]

It is possible that Bedaux was given a message to take back with him – an expression of thanks, an assurance that the information imparted would only be used to force a swift peace in the West. But Hitler was ever adept at lying. The undoing of the Allies, France, and western Europe had taken barely an hour.

However, there is always a price to pay for perfidy, and Bedaux's penalty was to be seen coming out of the Chancellery by a Dutch diplomat who recognized him, and who passed the information on to his Intelligence Service, the Dutch GS III. Although the Dutch did not realize the significance of what their diplomat had seen, believing Bedaux to be merely an unsavoury pro-Nazi American, a member of the British Intelligence Service in Holland was given the information second-hand from a contact he had in the GS, reporting back to London that:

> ... the most interesting piece of information that Beck divulged to me is that on 9 November, their M.[ilitary]A.[ttaché] to Berlin was delivering a note from de With [the Dutch Ambassador] to the Reich Chancellery, when he recognized Bedaux coming out of the building. He approached B[edaux], who he's met before, intending to speak, but B[edaux] ignored him, got into an official car (a Luftwaffe vehicle) and was driven off.[20]

However, the wheels of officialdom in Britain were ever slow, and this vital clue to the disaster that was unfolding, targeted directly to the correct individuals within British Intelligence, remained unacted upon. Within a very short time the effects of Bedaux's visit to Berlin would be felt when the Allies received information from 'Agent 54' (Paul Thummel) telling them that the offensive of 12 November had been postponed.

A sense of the priorities of the time, the expediency of justice or morality under the circumstances, is amply demonstrated by a series of Civil Servant comments in the notation page of a British government document about Bedaux:

The only possible effect of an attempt on our part to blacken Mr B[edaux], would be to arouse natural resentment against us on the part of the business world.

T. North Whitehead 17.4

And in view of his widely known close friendship with the Duke of Windsor, the motives might be misunderstood.

F.B. Brans 18.4

I hope nevertheless we shall be able to get at such double-edged enemies of this country in due course.

L.E.S. 21.4[21]

Several days after Bedaux left Berlin, Walter Schellenberg commanded a skilful SD kidnap operation on the German Dutch frontier at Venlo. The target for Schellenberg's operation was the SIS station chief in The Hague, Major Richard Stevens, and his monocled acquaintance Captain Sigismund Best, a member of the 'Z' network – a quasi-independent branch of British Intelligence. It would be interesting to speculate that the operation was connected to Bedaux's activities, but, alas no, it was yet another example of Britain's Intelligence Service's incompetent and amateurish attempts to appease the Germans from their warlike actions, rather than properly stop Hitler's aggressive expansionist aims by threatening him with a Total War scenario.

Stevens and Best, two very important intelligence operatives in Holland, had initially been hooked in a successful sting operation that had started in the early part of October. Conned by the SD into believing that there was an anti-Nazi faction within the Wehrmacht, they had instigated negotiations aimed at the removal of Hitler and a return to European peace. Ultimate responsibility for Stevens' and Best's actions lay with Downing Street, for Chamberlain had made it known he was keen to exploit any divisions within the German hierarchy and would approve any operation that would result in German compliance of Britain's demands.

After the Venlo débâcle (in which Schellenberg's men had dashed across the German–Dutch frontier, bundled Stevens and Best into a car and made off with them) the whole seedy operation came to light, and Churchill was furious, for it did indeed smack strongly of appeasement. Not only had the 'negotiations' failed to demand Hitler's removal from power, but British Intelligence had ludicrously suggested that if the plotted coup had taken place, Hitler might have been permitted to remain Führer in a purely ceremonial position. This semi-appeasement was trivial, however, when compared to Churchill's great fear that Germany would leak details of these negotiations to the French, utterly shattering French confidence in Britain's will to stand firm, causing the Alliance to crumble, and assuring overall victory to the German cause. The whole affair was to further deepen the enmity between Chamberlain and Churchill, and even resulted in Chamberlain ordering the Intelligence Services to initiate low-level surveillance of Churchill and his acquaintances.

During the 'negotiations', Schellenberg had been able to report to Heydrich that: 'The British officers [Stevens & Best] declared that His Majesties government took a great interest in our attempt which would contribute powerfully to prevent the spread of war ... They assured us they were in direct contact with the [British] Foreign Office and Downing Street.'[22]

As it was, the laugh was on everyone (except Stevens and Best who ended up in a concentration camp for the duration), for the order to kidnap the two men had come from none other than Adolf Hitler, who immediately, and incorrectly, suspected the two Englishmen of organizing the Burgerbraukeller bombing. The Venlo kidnapping took place on the afternoon of 9 November, at the very time Bedaux was flying from Berlin, and the repercussions of Hitler's misconceived interference were extensive and far reaching. On the German side, although they were not able to utilize the appeasement negotiations to break the Allied governments asunder, Stevens and Best were extensively interrogated enabling the Germans to largely destroy Britain's intelligence networks in France, Belgium and Holland in 1940. Britain was to lose out as well because Stevens, as SIS station head in The Hague, might have learned of the Bedaux information from Beck at the GS, had he hung around long enough to find out, and might have targeted the information more effectively than his replacement.

Whichever way the point is considered, had Georg Elser either never existed, or even succeeded in his task, history would have been very different indeed. As it was, all he did was effectively queer the pitch for everyone, particularly the Allies.

Back in Paris Edward had pressing concerns of his own – his old friend 'Fruity' Metcalfe . . .

> I can't figger things out ['Fruity' Metcalfe wrote to his wife on the 22nd of October]. She [Wallis] & he [Edward] knows every d—n thing. She will know whom I dined or lunched with or have spoken to & *even seen*. I believe she has spies out & they work well. Anyhow it's terrifying . . . I'm fed up with Paris & this war – whichever you like. I don't like my job (anyhow today) & I never feel secure & safe when working for HRH.[23]

Metcalfe had begun to suspect that the Windsors were having him watched, and for the life of him, he could not figure out why. It has been alleged that Metcalfe, 'was contacted on the orders of the King and instructed that he was to remain at the

Duke's side, act as his ADC, and report what was going on to the Palace. If this is true it tends to suggest that 'Fruity' was employed by the King to spy on his brother – which explains many of the things that were to happen later'.[24] It is therefore entirely possible that 'Fruity' Metcalfe *was* being watched as well. However, it is unlikely he was under surveillance by British Intelligence, for they would not have revealed their hand to Edward as he would undoubtedly have been the cause of their activity. That leaves only two other possibilities, which were in effect one and the same, either Edward's entourage, including 'Fruity', were being watched by the Abwehr or the Sicherheitsdienst and they were informing Bedaux, or Bedaux himself, concerned that Metcalfe might be observing Edward and that his and Edward's activities might be discovered, had instigated the surveillance of Metcalfe to give him ample forewarning to make his escape should things become unstuck. This senario might well explain why Edward abandoned his friend 'Fruity' in Paris of 1940, directly in the path of the conquering Germans, and it is interesting to note that when Metcalfe did eventually manage to escape back to Britain he joined Scotland Yard where he remained for the rest of the war.

Meanwhile, Metcalfe's problems continued, and he wrote to his wife:

We started off, HRH, De Salis & myself . . . The atmosphere was chilly. *We* are under suspicion & must be made to feel it. But by slow degrees as we progress further & further from Paris & the environs of Suchet we *begin* to thaw gradually, slowly, as another mile is put between us & Suchet! It is extraordinary . . . (Slight lapses when a bill has to be paid!).[25]

A week later Edward and his entourage returned to Paris and Metcalfe wrote:

I am well but fed up as I always am when stuck in this infernal town. Saw the Windsors (the couple) yesterday afternoon ... Re HRH's funny methods of doing things – We do this last tour. He then, with de Salis ... make out his report for the CGS. I would naturally love to read it & hear what he did say but, oh no, I'm told nothing. Again when we start off one of these tours instructions come from French HQ a day or so ahead. Do you think I ever am told one word where we go or what the programme is? Certainly not.[26]

To gauge the level of professionalism to which Bedaux took his espionage work at this time can be discerned to some extent from papers he was caught with when he was finally arrested in North Africa three years later, for, in the art of spying, Bedaux was no amateur. He was not merely instructed to go here or there, 'and if you come across something interesting, let us know', nor did he decide for himself what work he'd engage upon, rather he was given a detailed brief on what to look for. It can't be proven that this was the case in 1939, but, considering that he had been engaged in espionage since 1913, it is unlikely that he worked on a freelance basis plotting his own intelligence coups, and thinking up for himself what he would discover next.

In 1942 Bedaux was captured with his instructions upon him, secreted within a Pathelith photographic paper box that proclaimed the contents to be light sensitive, but which in reality proved to be most enlightening to those investigating him. Clearly laid out in black and white that left no room for denial, Bedaux had instructions to spy on British-controlled West Africa (Germany was seriously contemplating an invasion of this area) and make particular note of 'military formation', 'armaments', 'troop movements', and 'the acquisition of military codes.'[27] What also interested the investigating Securitaire Militaire Offi-cers, OSS, and FBI men, was that as well as his detailed brief, Mr Charles Eugene Bedaux also had in his possession two German passports, numbers D3808 and D2912, proclaiming him to be a German citizen, and sheets of paper ruled into squares with random letters placed into each box – a pad for sending coded messages. Bedaux's only failure was that by 1942 he felt invulnerable, and had the misfortune to be caught behind the Allied lines by the swift moving front of Operation Torch. In 1939, however, he was active, virtually untouchable because of his eminently important patron, Edward, Duke of Windsor, and ultimately the most dangerous man in Western Europe, save one – and that was the man who was giving him the Allies' most important secrets.

Whilst Bedaux had been in Berlin, Edward had also been busy, prompting Oliver Harvey of the Foreign Office to record that:

> ... the Duke has sent a message to [Walter] Monckton from France to say that he is flying over during the weekend in a private aeroplane and wants to see Winston [Churchill] but that the King is not to know! Monckton, after taking Charles [Peakes] advice, has warned Winston, who is saying that he has to visit [the] fleet over this weekend and is telling Hardinge about it. He is also telling Belisha and will ring up the Duke tonight to tell him he cannot come.[28]

The reasons why Edward wanted to surreptitiously dash in and out of Britain without King George VI knowing can only be speculated at, but it could hardly have been a personal or trivial matter, nor is it likely to have been a coincidence that it was at the same time as Bedaux's trip to Berlin. If the reason was connected to Bedaux, it is possible to speculate that Edward had ideas of sounding out his closest friends, and wished to gauge what the political mood would be to various military scenarios adopted by Britain.

Bedaux meanwhile, reappeared in Paris about midweek and

on the following Sunday, 19 November, again dined with the Windsors, for as Metcalfe duly recorded:

> I dined at Suchet last night. The Bedaux's were there – it went very easily & I *seem* to be in very good books. I was welcomed as a sheep returning to the fold. I take it all with a couple of pinches of salt ... [For he had recently discovered that] one seems to be always competing against some d—n thing. The latest here is that I am told by one of the fellows at the Mission who arranges about pay, etc. that the W[ar] O[ffice] have got *no authority* to pay me at all ...

Metcalfe confronted Edward over the matter, writing:

> ... the *little tiny man* said – nothing – He then looked at me & said, 'Didn't they tell you at the WO that you wouldn't get any pay.' I said, 'Good God, no.' He looked just fishy ... What beats me is that HRH is quite prepared to do nothing for me at all. I really think I can't stay on with him without *any* authority or *pay*. In lots of ways I won't be sorry.[29]

On Thursday, 23 November, Hitler summoned his army chiefs to a conference in Berlin. By this time, Hitler had been digesting the information that Bedaux had brought for nearly a fortnight, and it must have been evident to him that he had been given a gift from the gods. General Rohricht, Head of the Training Department of the General Staff later recounted that: 'The Führer spent two hours in a lengthy review of the situation aimed at convincing the army Command that an offensive in the West was a necessity. He answered most sharply the objections which Field-Marshal von Brauchitsch had made beforehand.'[30]

Brauchitsch and Halder 'argued that the German army was not strong enough – it was the only argument that could have any chance of deterring the Führer. But he insisted that his will must prevail. After the conference many new formations were raised, to increase the army's strength. This was as far as the Führer would meet the opposing views.'[31]

Hitler then went on to assess the overview that was remarkably close to the thinking of the British and French High Command, undoubtedly passed on to him by Bedaux.

'We have an Achilles' Heel,' he told his Generals, 'the Ruhr ... If Britain and France push through Belgium and Holland into the Ruhr, we shall be in the greatest danger. That could lead to a paralysis of German resistance.' It was a choice he announced, 'between victory and destruction' and he ended on a prophetic note. 'I shall stand or fall in this struggle. I shall never survive the defeat of my people ...'[32]

The eventual success of Germany's brilliant new strategy – which was to force France to capitulate in just six weeks and drive the British army off the European Continent at Dunkirk – has gone down in history as the 'Manstein Plan', after General Fritz Erich von Manstein. Manstein certainly took a concept and turned it into a workable military strategy of which Hitler was incapable, but this strategy, nevertheless, convinced Germany of Hitler's own military genius, thereby reinforcing the success of his remilitarization of the Rhineland.

The innovative strategy that had become obvious to Hitler after he had digested the information Bedaux had brought him was nothing less than to pierce the French lines at Sedan, after making a surprise crossing of the heavily wooded Ardennes region in southern Belgium, and then strike across the plains of Northern France pushing a powerful armoured force straight through to the English Channel, cutting off the élite British and French forces who, as Hitler now knew, would advance into Belgium as far as the River Dyle, Albert Canal and River Scheldt as soon as the German offensive began.

That was the basic concept of Hitler's idea, crude and without definite objective. It was an eminently effective trap that would capture an entire army.

That Manstein developed the idea for this strategy from Hitler is evident from the private diaries of Frau Schmundt, wife of Colonel Schmundt, Hitler's chief military adjutant. Colonel Gerhardt Engel, Hitler's army adjutant noted; 'Schmundt was very excited and told me he had found M[anstein] expressing precisely the same opinion ... as the Führer is constantly expressing.'[33] Hitler thereupon instructed Schmundt to send for Manstein secretly, without informing either Brauchitsch or Halder in advance. Afterwards, Manstein scribbled in his diary, 'What an extraordinary conformity of my views.' According to Colonel-General Walther Warlimont, Hitler saw his General off with the words, 'Manstein is the only person to see what I'm getting at.'[34]

Once Manstein had developed Hitler's plan, turned it into a workable strategy with all the logistical planning and military organization necessary for the efficient running of a successful campaign, his services were no longer required, and by early February he would be shuffled off to Stettin on the Baltic coast; his presence and ability as a military planner was not to be allowed to detract from the Führer's 'intuition'.

By early December, Edward was still deeply engrossed in his French tours, although to his dismay he had not been allowed near the lines again for some time. His acquaintance with Bedaux had now blossomed into a weekly friendship during which time he and Wallis dined with Charles and Fern, mostly at Bedaux's private suite at the Ritz. What they discussed after dinner can only be speculated on, but it was probably not to the Allies' benefit.

By this time Edward had other problems, which though trivial considering Europe's situation, needed his urgent attention, for the war had now impinged upon his personal comfort and he selfishly determined to use his influence to try to resolve it. Early in the autumn the Windsors' chef, an eminently qualified French gentleman who could produce culinary delights at the drop of a hat, had been called up for service in the French army. Edward now won himself few friends and not a little criticism for using his time at the Military Mission, with its remit as liaison to General Gamelin, to badger the French High Command for the return of his cook. Metcalfe was to caustically comment:

> They [the Windsors] are now arranging to get their chef sent to them for his *Mess* [i.e. The Windsors' Suchet home]. This is a joke. The chef had been mobilized & sent to some unit in the S. of France – but they've been upsetting the whole ruddy army to get him and today when I saw HRH for a few seconds he also looked a bit sour & unsteady & said there had been some stupid misunderstanding with the French about the chef & he must go to the Mission to put it straight. It was not a major-general's job but if people under that rank couldn't do certain things he as a major-general would have to do it personally. They say that the Germans are bombing the Maginot Line and that the French are replying. Losses are taking place on both sides but the battle of HRH's chef is making more noise than all that shelling.[35]

Edward's interference in the French chain of command in an effort to get his chef returned eventually won him a stern rebuke from Howard-Vyse, who had more important matters on his mind than whether Edward and Wallis had gourmet delicacies of sufficient quality for their table at weekend parties (such as their chef's famous white grapes stuffed with soft cheese).

On 17 December, Howard-Vyse received a communication from a Mr James of the Field Security Police in London, indicating that the intelligence reports from Holland were at last hitting their mark, and that at least someone in the British security services had become aware of the danger that Bedaux posed.

> Further to my communication at the beginning of the month, I would request that you inform Major-General HRH the Duke of Windsor that it has come to our notice that his acquaintance, Mr C.E. Bedaux is believed to be engaged in conduct incompatible with his status as a citizen of a neutral state. HRH is therefore requested to cease all activity and contact with this gentleman immediately.
>
> Our F[ield] S[ecurity] P[olice] office with the B[ritish] E[xpeditionary] F[orce], who has been following the gentleman currently reports he is not in the country at the moment. He made a sudden departure on the night of 10 December, and we do not know where he has gone. If anyone at your M[ilitary] M[ission] should hear of him, please inform me or our office at Arras immediately.[36]

The letter also reveals that Howard-Vyse had received a prior warning about Bedaux and the Duke at the beginning of the month, but of this there is no trace, presumably because it might have been too sensitive to have been allowed to remain in existance. It might however have explained why Edward was disgruntled at not being allowed to conduct more tours and see more French defences.

What is evident from the few British documents that remain in existance concerning the Duke of Windsor and Bedaux is that a substantial proportion of the disaster that was to come was as a result of sheer incompetence, not mere complacency as a result of the Duke's importance or even an ulterior motive of manipulating the situation to protect the Duke; that came later. The documents that survive tell a chilling tale, for not only do the intelligence submissions back to London show that the men in Holland were virtually saying, 'Stop Bedaux', but also that they then completely failed to understand why London would not give them the go ahead to stop him themselves. It is also clear that they were aware Bedaux was receiving his information from a Briton, although they misunderstood and believed the Briton to be with the BEF proper. The other fact that becomes evident is that the British Field Security Police were also aware there was a security leak within the BEF, but failed to associate it with the Duke, and one suspects that they were being prompted to write to Howard-Vyse and order the Duke to stop seeing Bedaux by an intelligence organ back in London, who either did not want to reveal their hand by showing an interest, or were too afraid of outrightly accusing their former king of betraying Allied secrets.

Despite the FSP communication of 17 December to Howard-Vyse, telling him to order Edward to stop seeing Bedaux, Edward took no notice whatsoever.

As 1939 began to draw to a close and Christmas approached, the Windsors entered into a new subliminal phase of public relations, promoting their personalities in the newspapers with visits to the French troops, smiling, waving, and handing out parcels, which amongst other things contained mufflers knitted by the Duke himself. The Windsors also began to receive Christmas greetings from their various friends and well-wishers, including many officers of the French army he had visited, who had no inkling of what Britain's ex-king intended for their country in the new decade of the 1940s:

Grand Quartier General des Armées Francanses
Avec les voeux très respectueux du, Colonel Petibon.
Noël 1939

Curiously Edward would retain these cards in a scrap book, which he kept amongst his private papers, long after the war was over.

War apart, and despite the fact that a million men under arms were enduring a bitter miserable Christmas watching each other across the Franco-German frontier, the Windsors saw no reason why such misery should impinge upon their Christmas celebrations:

Paris has more people than ever [Wallis wrote to her Aunt Bessie]. Quite a lot of people came over from London on one pretext or another though not many women ... Elsie is still going strong – parties every weekend at Versailles – and I think she is going to remain in Paris for the rest of the winter – her first. We never dress at night – that is no evening clothes – only dinner or afternoon frocks and dark suits on those who have no uniforms.[37]

On Christmas Eve, the Windsors' Boulevard Suchet home glittered like a Christmas tree, and with every light ablaze the house echoed to the sound of laughter, the tinkling of a piano, the groan and whine of bagpipes, as Edward and Wallis gave a party to thirty select guests. Edward amused everyone with a loud rendition of something nobody could identify on his bagpipes, and Noël Coward entertained all with his perennial and ever popular *Mad Dogs and Englishmen*. Despite the depression and the dangers of war, the party was recognized by everyone as a stunning success.

After celebrating a quiet but cultured Christmas Day surrounded by a few intimates, Edward and Wallis felt duty bound to put on another party. A few days before Christmas they had attended the dour Christmas celebrations of the Free Polish Forces in France, at the invitation of General Sikorski, and now reciprocated the occasion with an invitation to Sikorski to attend a party at Suchet. Also invited were a select number of the Duke's new acquaintances, French and British officers. The party was to be a notable event for many reasons, the main being that Edward now showed a complete disregard for Howard-Vyse's orders not to see Bedaux. In reality Edward had been seeing Bedaux throughout December anyway, but this was to be the first time he flaunted the friendship completely in the face of his superior officer's instructions. The second notable occurrence was that for the first time the way Bedaux operated was witnessed by a member of the Military Mission's staff – Purvis (the man who had ostensibly suffered a serious car accident, but who had since quietly reappeared on the Military Mission's staff). Purvis was horrified at Bedaux's brazenness, and realizing the implications of what Bedaux was saying and doing, excused himself from the celebrations and promptly reported back to Howard-Vyse the following morning.

Having received an instruction from the Field Security Police to order the Duke of Windsor to stop seeing Bedaux, Howard-Vyse instantly reported what Purvis had told him, passing the information to his superior officer and long-time friend, General Ironside.

His report to his old friend had implications on several levels; firstly, he undoubtedly hoped Ironside would handle the situation tactfully, and he kept the information on an informal footing by addressing his letter 'Dear Dick', and secondly, he was obviously concerned enough, (perhaps feeling the need to cover his own back should anything go wrong) to send a formally laid out and typed letter (the norm was informal handwritten notes between the two men), officially heading it 'SECRET & CONFIDENTIAL'. He reported that:

I fear I may have something of a problem here with HRH's ability to keep important matters confidential ... Purvis came to see me this morning to tell me that HRH had put on a Christmas do yesterday to which he had been invited. It was apparently quite a lavish affair, with even General Sikorski in

attendance as well as a member of [General] Petibon's staff –
[General] Blonc. HRH chatted and mingled superbly as he
always does, and introduced Purvis to that man Bedeaux[sic].
Bedeaux asked him what he thought of Fort Vaux. Apparently
he'd served there in the World War, and thought it had
been too badly damaged ever to be of use again. Purvis
was horrified, and for a moment thought [General] Blonc
had heard what Bedeaux was saying. He excused himself and
beat a hasty retreat, lest the Yank compromise all our hard
work.

But, surely the point is, how did Bedeaux know Purvis &
HRH had been to Vaux – unless HRH told him? This begs the
serious question, is HRH's value to us outweighed by his
inability to keep a confidence? Do you want me to inform
James [of the FSP] that we've come across this American, or
shall I leave you to do it? Please let me know by the next
plane.[38]

We now come to one of the most curious episodes in this whole
tale, for apart from the chicanery that appears to have been
undertaken on the British side, the Germans themselves had been
far from idle. Throughout December, Manstein had worked on
the bare bones of his Führer's concept. Hitler, however, was never
a man to waste anything, for his chief of staff, General Halder,
had worked long and hard to create the original attack plan.
Hitler therefore saw no good reason just to throw this aside, and
used it in a way that Halder would never have contemplated in
his wildest dreams – he gave it to the Allies.

Throughout most of the autumn and winter of 1939 the
German Luftwaffe had been overflying Belgian territory and the
Maginot Line region on an almost daily basis, busily gathering
intelligence material for assessment by the High Command, and
there had been numerous diplomatic protests from Belgium.
Immediately after Christmas these reconnaissance overflights

increased dramatically, often with several such incursions happening on one day, particularly in the Eastern Belgian region.

At 11.25 a.m. on 10 January 1940, Belgian soldiers on duty at a guard post near Mechelen-sur-Meuse saw an aircraft trip lightly out of the sky, swoop low over them, and drop out of sight behind some trees. Next they heard a crash, the sound of twisting metal and breaking glass as the aircraft hit the ground, followed by the sudden silence as its engine stopped. Unslinging their rifles, the six Belgian soldiers ran to the crash sight, for they correctly recognized the black crosses on the monoplane as indicating it was a German aircraft, an ME108 Taifun (Typhoon) of the Luftflotte II. Crossing the winter-hardened ground, their boots pounding into the frost stiffened grass 'the soldiers needed to jump across a ditch to get to the field. One [soldier] jumped to the far bank and then held out his rifle for the others to hang onto. As they passed him they scrambled up the bank and through some bushes out of sight. I could see the tail of the plane sticking up over the bushes . . .'[39]

On gaining the field and passing through the bushes, the Belgian soldiers were confronted by a Luftwaffe officer in a leather jacket who waved to them to show his friendly intentions, but who kept looking furtively over his shoulder in the direction of some bushes. Then the soldiers noticed a flicker of fire from behind the hedge and, realizing there was another German on the loose, immediately rushed across and stopped him burning any more papers. The soldiers had just participated in the celebrated Mechelen Incident, which in early 1940 incredibly gave the Allies a virtually complete set of the German attack plans that much of the future Allied defence strategy would be based upon.

It was of course too good to be true, and the Allied High Command should have realized that the incredibly good fortune of having their enemy's attack plans literally drop out of the sky into their lap could only have more sinister connotations.

The Mechelen Incident is a curious tale, for it is the story of a light Luftwaffe aircraft on a routine flight from Munster to Bonn which became lost, blown off course by atrocious weather, the pilot accidentally strayed over the German border into Belgium, and then, completely disorientated, put his aircraft down on Belgian territory by accident. The official reason for the flight was to courier a set of the German attack plans from Munster to the High Command Headquarters in Bonn. But far from being an accidental crash, it was a carefully stage-managed incident with the Machiavellian plotting of which only the Nazis were capable – a careful manipulation of circumstances to give the effect of a wonderful piece of luck for the Allies.

The German side of the tale is almost as interesting as the Belgians', for the two pilots (taken into custody for violating Belgian sovereignty) Majors Reinberger and Hoenmanns, were interviewed in Brussels a few days later by the German Military Attaché, the Assistant Air Attaché, and a German Lieutenant General. The interview was necessarily tainted for even if German Embassy staff had been aware of the real purpose of the crash, it was noted in Ambassador von Bulow-Schwate's report to his Foreign Ministry that 'it was taken for granted that the conversation was being overheard with listening devices'. During the interview Major Reinberger, General Student's liaison officer to the Luftflotte II and the man charged with responsibility for the documents, reported that, 'After an emergency landing, [Major Reinberger] took the courier pouches behind some bushes in order to burn them out of sight of approaching Belgian soldiers, whose attention Major Hoenmenns engaged in order to gain time . . . [When] the light of the fire attracted the attention of the soldiers . . . the fire was forcibly extinguished.'[40]

It is important to note the behaviour of the German leadership, for one would have thought that the loss to their enemies of a 'complete operational plan for the attack in the West' would have been considered a total disaster and the undoing of years of careful planning. General Student noted that, 'Hitler remained quite calm and self possessed',[41] for as has been clearly shown, he already had another plan, the final details of which were being sorted out by Manstein. Despite Reinberger's 'attempt' to burn the documents, he did not make a very good job of it, for 'the documents which the German staff officer was carrying were not burned, and copies of them were promptly passed on by the Belgians to the French and British governments – revealing clearly the outline of the German plan.'[42]

Anyone who has ever tried to burn paper in the open air can immediately see how Reinberger's 'attempts' were doomed to failure, for paper is exceedingly hard to contain and incinerate properly in the face of any but the lightest of breezes. If he had really intended to burn the papers why did he not use the easiest item to hand, the ME108? – for there is little that is quite as inflammable as a downed aircraft with tanks half-filled with gasolene and the void above filled with explosive gasoline vapour. A careless match would have resulted in an instantaneous inferno that the Belgians could not have extinguished, and would have easily resulted in the total obliteration of every scrap of Germany's secret attack plan.

To understand clearly what occurred that morning, it is important to look at what else was happening in the region at the same time that day; the weather, the aircraft and pilots, where they came from and where they were headed for. (See Map III.)

Firstly, far from the weather that day being atrocious, it was actually a very good day by January standards, good enough for other Luftwaffe aircraft to be sent on reconnaissance missions into Eastern Belgium. The weather records of the Institut Royal Météorologique de Belgique show that:

The 10th of January, 1940 was a rather cold but very sunny day in Eastern Belgium. The maximum temperature stayed well below 0°C with a value of −3.0°C, while the minimum temperature reached about −12°C. The predominant wind direction was ENE-ly, mean windspeed about 15–20km/h [9–12mph]. There was no precipitations [rain, sleet or snow, etc.] recorded in the period 9–14 January 1940.[43]

Although it was undoubtedly cold, visibility that day was very good and the weather easily within the flying capability of any competent pilot, let alone two highly qualified and experienced Luftwaffe Majors. In fact these two Majors were actually *over-qualified* for the mundane courier task allotted to them; however, they were eminently qualified once the real purpose of their mission is understood. In addition, these two men explained their straying over Belgian airspace as a result of being blown off-course by strong winds; unable to work out their position they had made a forced landing in Belgium by accident. Another discrepancy immediately becomes apparent when one realizes that the wind that day was a 9–12 knot East-North-Easterly, which means that although the ME108 did not fly against the wind to get to Belgium, flying as they were with a crosswind, the two pilots overflew first the mile-wide Rhine on a crisp cold clear day (a hard enough task to miss even in the dark) with little more than a breeze to assist them, but that they then also overflew part of Holland to get to where they crashed – for Mechelen-sur-Meuse is near the Belgian–Dutch border, *not* the German one. On that day in January 1940, Majors Reinberger and Hoenmanns were given an extraordinarily easy task for two experienced pilots. Flying from Munster to Bonn, a distance of only 80 miles, all they had to do was fly for 40 miles before sighting the Rhine, and then follow it straight to Bonn.

Next it is important to note that the two Majors did not fly into Belgian airspace in a bag of cloth and string with an engine attached, which was typical of most light transport planes of the late 1930s, but were aboard an eminently good aircraft, an ME108. The ME108 was a military-derived cabin monoplane descended from the earlier and very advanced BF108, designed by Willi Messerschmidt in the mid-1930s. This was a solid aircraft, not easily displaced by any but the strongest of air disturbances, and its powerful engine could propel it along at a very respectable speed. Its squared-off wings and distinctive shape would become renowned during the Second World War, for not only had the BF108 spawned the military derivative two-seater ME108, but it was also such a good aircraft that a slight alteration to its fuselage and an increased engine size turned this fast modern aircraft into the renowned single-seater ME109, a virtual all-weather capability fighter plane that saw service from the frozen wastes of Russia to the heat-blanched deserts of North Africa.

It is therefore inconsistent and absurd to suggest that this highly technical and superb plane, piloted by an extremely qualified officer, was blown off-course across the Rhine, the German–Dutch frontier, across part of Holland, then the Dutch–Belgian border, by a 9–12 mile per hour ENE breeze on a clear and sunny day. In the almost impossible event that this should be the case, it certainly does not explain why Major Hoenemann, mere minutes flying time from German airspace, piloting an ME108 equipped with advanced navigational equipment to give the direction, felt so disorientated that he felt the need to crash-land on Belgian soil.

On the same morning as the crash, the German Luftwaffe had two other operations active in the same region, and there must be some level of speculation that they were connected to the Mechelen Incident. Firstly, at 10.15 a.m. a Heinkel III took off from a military airfield near Cologne and flew south-west on a reconnaissance trip over eastern Belgium. It flew in low and was spotted by the Belgians at Houffalize (10.36 a.m.), St Hubert (10.40 a.m.), Jemelle (10.43 a.m.), Dinant (10.45 a.m.), flew back to Jemelle (10.51 a.m.), Namur (10.59 a.m.), Laroche (11.11 a.m.), and was last seen at Fauvillers (11.15 a.m.).[44] (See Map III.)

The flight by the Heinkel III is important because firstly it demonstrates that competent and exact reconnaissance flying was possible in the region on that day, and, secondly, it must be noted that the Heinkel was flying in the same region of Belgium as the ME108 was to crash. Five minutes after the Heinkel was last seen at Fauvillers, the ME108 of the High Command Transport Division crashed amidst a welter of flung dirt, weeds and noise, not in some remote wetland or deserted farmland region, but literally within a hundred yards of the main Lindenheuvel to Maastricht road, and within easy sight of a manned guard post.

An hour later, a Junkers 88 took off from the Luftwaffe airbase at Wesseling and headed off to eastern Belgium. It was identified at Fauvillers (1.07 p.m.), flying in the opposite direction to the Heinkel III spotted earlier that day, and proceeded to fly on to Laroche, Marche, and Huy (1.27 p.m.), then Aywaille, Veviers, and Vis (1.44 p.m.).[45] (See Map III.) Its course at that time was northward, which would have taken it directly to Mechelen, fifteen miles and a mere three minutes flying-time away.

There is one final item of interest to this whole event that should, if nothing else, have caused the Allies to wonder at their good luck: German High Command regulations strictly forbade the carrying of any secret papers by aircraft in order to avoid exactly this eventuality. In *all* cases of courier transfer of sensitive military material the information was carried overland by car or, more often, by train.

Of course, the incredible coincidence that on the *only* occasion such a transfer was made by air, firstly, the courier was not only carrying a complete set of attack plans, secondly, the plane crashed, thirdly, the plane crashed in enemy territory, and, fourthly, the plans fell into Allied hands, was no coincidence at all.

Even with the limited information available to him at the time, tactical expert and military historian, Captain Basil Liddell Hart, writing in 1948 of the Mechelen plane crash, was dubious enough of the whole incident to write, 'It is natural to ask whether it really was an accident.'[46]

Whether the information was ever doubted or not, the Allies were so desperate for any advantage that fate gave them that they instantly grasped at what the Germans had given them. Little thought was given as to whether the accident was real or not, or for that matter whether the Germans would change their attack plan. Indeed, General Ironside wrote in his diary on 13 January:

> In the night we began to get news from Belgium that the Germans intended to attack through Holland and Belgium . . . It seems pretty definite . . . We rang up the French, who reported that they were more sure than ever that something was about to start. It is freezing hard and the conditions are good for an advance through the Low Countries . . .[47]

However, the Belgians, concerned that if they allowed the Allied armies onto their territory it would show a breach of neutrality to the Germans and thereby give the Germans an excuse to invade, declined to permit any French or British troops into their country. Ironside, despite the misjudgement of sending the Duke of Windsor to Howard-Vyse, was in reality a good, professional, high-ranking officer, who saw all too clearly that the French government was more in tune with the needs of the time than his own government. Whilst the French leaders received daily briefings about what was happening on their Northern border, consulted their military leaders, listened to those specialists qualified in matters of defence, Ironside outed his frustrations into his diary on 13 January by commenting bitterly:

> The Prime Minister was down at Chequers and telephoned a bit, but he did not seem taken with the military value of speed and wanted a full Cabinet to decide. They have always prated so much of a Cabinet being able to assemble so quickly that it disgusted me to find that it couldn't be assembled.

A few days later he commented that:

> Old Chamberlain may be a wise old thing, but he is not seized with the military position. He is never in close touch with his military advisers. Daladier is . . . The difference between Chamberlain and Churchill during this little crisis is most marked. Churchill, fully seized with the military value of going to Belgium, is enthusiastic and full of energy. Chamberlain is negative and angry at Belgium making conditions.[48]

Back in Paris on 20 January, Metcalfe wrote, 'I dined at Suchet last night. They [Edward & Wallis] were in splendid form – I've never seen either of them better – I enjoyed myself a lot . . .'[49]

It was to be no wonder, for everything was now going perfectly and the Windsors were riding on a high – everything was going to be all right. As for Edward's orders not to see

Bedaux again ... he simply took no notice at all, and they even took to playing golf together.

The information gleaned from the captured Mechelene documents was considered of utmost importance by the Allies, for they believed that at long last they had an insight into the projected German offensive in the West. Having gained the knowledge that the Germans intended their thrust across the Belgian plains (which had been suspected anyway), plans were now put into place to counter that eventuality, a strategy for the deployment of the BEF and French once the Germans attacked – Gamelin's Plan D. As a result, the Allied War Council entered into a special meeting in London a few days later, but, as unbelievable as it might sound, things were about to get even worse, for Edward, Duke of Windsor was in town.

Edward stayed at Claridges for three nights, and though his presence in London is well documented, whilst in London Edward did more than just attend Military conferences and meet with Churchill, for he attempted to influence the government into opening up a line of communication with the Nazis to discuss terms and a swift end to the war. One evening Edward met with Chamberlain's loyal supporter Lord Beaverbrook, at the home of his faithful adviser and go-between to the Palace – Walter Monckton. Monckton was ever a loyal friend and counsellor, but what he heard his former monarch uttering greatly disquietened him, and a few days later he met with Charles Peake of the Foreign Office to disclose that he had been present at:

... a frightful interview between the D[uke] of W[indsor] & the Beaver two days ago ... [The two men] found themselves in agreement that the war should be ended at once by a peace offer to Germany. The Beaver suggested that the Duke should get out of uniform, come home & after enlisting powerful City support, stump the country in which case he predicted that the Duke would have a tremendous success.[50]

As soon as Beaverbrook was gone, Monckton tried as tactfully as possible to point out to Edward that he had been 'speaking high treason'.[51]

On 27 January, Count Julius von Zech-Burkersroda, the German Ambassador to Holland, wrote to Ernst Weizsacker, State Secretary at the Auswärtiges Amt, the Foreign Ministry, to report on the information he had gleaned from his latest meeting with Charles Bedaux, saying:

As of course you know, W[indsor] is a member of the British Military Mission with the French army. He does not, however, feel entirely satisfied with this position and seeks a field of activity in which he would not have merely a representative character and which would permit him a more active role. In order to attain this objective he was recently in London. There, however, he achieved nothing and is supposed to be disgruntled over it. He has expressed himself in especially uncomplimentary terms about Chamberlain, whom he particularly dislikes and who, he thinks, is responsible for his being frozen out.[52]

The correspondence continued a few weeks later with Zech-Burkersroda writing:

The Duke of W[indsor], about whom I wrote to you in my letter of the 27th of last month, has said that the Allied War Council devoted an exhaustive discussion at its last meeting to the situation that would arise if Germany invaded Belgium. On the military side, it was held that the best plan would be to make the main resistance effort in the line behind the Belgian–French border, even at the risk that Belgium would be occupied by us. The political authorities are said to have at first opposed this plan: after the humiliation suffered in Poland, it would be impossible to surrender Belgium and the Netherlands also to the Germans. In the end, however, the political authorities became more yielding.

Heil Hitler!

Zech[53]

Unknown to Bedaux, Zech-Burkersroda, Edward, Howard-Vyse, or even Ironside, there was yet another hand playing in this multi-faceted game of military poker, for in Holland, in The Hague, in the very embassy that Bedaux was visiting to speak to Zeck-Burkesroda, there was a man named Walbach, and Walbach was a spy *too*, only he worked for the British. Wilhelm Heottle, formerly of Amt VI of the RSHA, and later Assistant Chief of Amt VI-B of the SS secret service (the SD) later confirmed that Walbach had been a very clever spy who evaded capture at the last minute, only to appear in Britain working for British Intelligence.[54] In February 1940, however, Walbach would prove to be an invaluable source of information to the British, except that somewhere in the British higher echelons of Whitehall, Walbach's valuable information was side-tracked and not acted upon for it conflicted with perceived notions of duty to one's former monarch.

On 21 February 1940, Major Langford, an intelligence officer based in The Hague, sent a cyphered message to a Colonel Vivian in London headed, 'IMMEDIATE & URGENT'.

Saw Walbach again this evening. He informed me that Bedeaux[sic] is visiting Z[ech]-B[urkesroda] on an almost fortnightly basis and that he is also crossing the frontier, travelling by train to Cologne, just as often. W[albach] has had an opportunity to see the transcribed information that

B[edaux] brings verbally, and says it is of the best quality –
defence material, strengths, weaknesses and so on.

Davis [not identified, but probably another British opera-
tive] suggests stopping B[edaux] permanently, but, if we do
that, will the leak find another courier, one we do not know
of? At the moment, we know of B[edaux]'s ... existence, and
to some extent can keep tabs on him. Suggest we contact the
F[ield] S[ecurity] P[olice] at Arras, and ask them to observe
who B[edaux] is associating with in Paris. I do not know if we
dare inform Ronin at the D[euxieme] B[ureau], for there is
little doubt from what W[albach] has told me that B[edaux]'s
source is with the BEF for he recently was in London to attend
an A[llied] W[ar] C[ouncil] meeting . . .[55]

Although this devastating piece of information never seems
to have been acted upon, for no one stopped Bedaux despite the
crystal clear evidence of his activity, this message must have
struck a sensitive spot in London, for the document is clearly
marked as having been forwarded to 'PM' and 'Cadogan'. It is
also interesting that some unknown hand from 1940 wrote on it:
'I recommend WC see this.' It can be speculated whether 'WC'
(possibly Winston Churchill), saw this *before* or *after* the PM
(Chamberlain), for as a close acquaintance of Edward he may
also have met Bedaux on some occasion. For this communication
from The Hague to have reached those so high up in the British
government is surely indicative of, firstly, its sensitivity, but,
secondly, and more importantly, that the men in power must
have had more than a vague inkling *who* Bedaux's source was.

Events were now building a momentum of their own, and
on 2 March State Secretary Weizsacker again wrote to Zech-
Burkesroda.

I still owe you an answer to your two letters dated 27 January
and 19 February, regarding the Duke of W[indsor].

I referred both your letters to the Foreign Minister, who also showed your second letter to the Führer. (However I myself added a remark to the last two lines of your letter dated 19 February, i.e.: Surrender of the Coast.)

Should you ... receive further information of this sort, I would be grateful to receive these, preferably in Report Form to my personal address. The Foreign Minister would also prefer this format.[56]

The reference made by Weizacker to the 'Surrender of the Coast' is a curious notation in his referral to Zech-Burkesroda's letter of 19 February, and it is possible that Zech-Burkesroda was referring to Bedaux's most recent information – that the Duke of Windsor had recently toured the French Seventh Army in the Dunkirk sector from 9–12 February. It would go a long way to explaining the curious form of the German offensive in the last days in the battle for France, for Hitler ordered his panzers to halt for several days allowing the Allies to escape to Dunkirk – it was almost as if the Allies were *herded* into a situation that the Germans wanted. It would not be unfair to say that the Germans manipulated their enemy throughout the battle for Belgium and France, and it was as if the Germans *knew* the Allies next move before it had even been taken – which is exactly what happened.

If Zech-Burkesroda's letter *did* refer to Edward's latest tour, then an idea of what information Bedaux could have passed on to him may be gleaned from what Edward officially reported back to Ironside, for he informed him that:

The defences of the VIIth Army and – to the north of it in the coastal sector – the 68th Division, which is under Admiralty command, and has the dual role of defending the DUNKIRK sector and co-operating with the navy in defence of the coast takes two forms:

1. Flooded areas, containing at some point within it a canal forming and anti-tank obstacle.
2. On the flanks of the flooded areas, two or three Defensive Systems – Front, Intermediate and Rear – each from one to two kilometres deep, and three to five kilometres apart.

The Duke then went on to expand on his assessment of the Dunkirk and environs defences by revealing:

It is anticipated that areas selected for flooding will take a minimum of six days, and a maximum of fifteen (in summer) to fill to a depth of two feet.

By flooding Les Moeres, and an area immediately west of it, the Anti-tank ditch with blockhouses lining the west side of Les Moeres would be isolated by water. Whether Les Moeres, or the area west of it, or both areas, should eventually be flooded, does not seem to be decided.

In the area of XVI Corps the Front System follows the line of heights from Mont Noir to Steenvoorde, thence north and bearing west; the Intermediate System passes in front of Hazebrouck and continues north roughly parallel to the Front System; the Rear System in part the Cassel Defences, pass immediately east of Cassel, then bear west as far as Clairmarais.

In the area of the 68th Division the Front System consists, in the south, of the flooded area of Les Moeres with blockhouses at intervals in the ditch running SW from Ghyveld, and forming the western boundary of the area. This ditch is now being converted into an anti-tank obstacle.

From Ghyveld to the sea the Front System is of the normal land pattern and extends in depth from the Belgian frontier to the line Ghyveld-Bray Dunes (2–3 km). A second system with its left on Fort des Dunes was spoken of but no work was seen.

On the ... front visited ... [tank obstacles] appeared to be about 9ft deep, 3–4ft wide at bottom, and 12–15ft wide at top, the side facing the enemy vertical, and revetted with fascines.

These dimensions would generally be greater where advantage had been taken of converting drainage canals. Experiments with tanks have shown that while in the heavy land South of Bergues, tanks were stopped, in the sandy country to the north the second tank was able to clear the obstacle.

The comprehensive twelve-page report was concluded with the comments that:

> However strong this sector, as well as the rest of the Front System may be, it cannot be said that the Intermediate or Rear Systems on this front are yet ready to withstand attack by armoured vehicles. The Ghyveld-North Sea Front System of the 68th Division was spoken of as being impregnable to any attack, except a long prepared operation. No doubt, the fact that 26,000 men are available in the sector lends strength to the conviction, but with the present state of the defences everything must depend of time being available for flooding.[57]

Despite these highly detailed reports by the Duke to Ironside, worse still was yet to come for the British, for in early April another Walbach revelation came winging its way to London, only this one would leave no doubt as to Bedaux's source, and would be read with consternation and horror by the very highest men in the land.

On 4 April 1940, a Colonel Finch received the latest of Major Langford's desperate communiqués regarding Bedaux. Major Langford's messages had begun to take on a frantic quality, for he could not understand why his vitally important information was never acted upon, and why he was prevented from acting against a man he knew to be a danger of the first order:

> Received an urgent message from Walbach requesting a meeting at the usual place. He informed me that Z[ech]-

B[urkesroda]'s agent Bedeaux[sic] is still bringing information of great importance, and asked why we have not stopped him. I think that W[albach] fears that B[edaux] might one day bring information exposing him. The Abwehr have placed a man named Protze in the embassy, and W[albach] fears P[rotze]'s purpose is to tighten security.

W[albach] has said that Z[ech]-B[urkesroda] accidentally referred to B[edaux]'s source as 'Willi', and thinks this might be part of the man's name. Also Z[ech]-B[urkesroda] has on more than one occasion hinted that B[edaux]'s source is an important person with the BEF!! B[edaux] has got to be stopped. Please refer to my message of 12 March [Missing from the archives] and advise.[58]

If ever a doubt lingered in the British establishment who Bedaux's source was, this document ended that, for it must have been known that 'Willi' was the German code name for the Duke of Windsor. Yet apparently those in the highest echelons again did nothing, for who really had the courage to utter the words 'Treason' and 'Betrayal' when referring to their own former king?

The 'Walbach' documents are incomplete for it is known there were once at least three cyphered telegrams sent back to London. A message of 12 March was referred to, but this no longer seems to exist. It is fair to assume therefore that the Walbach messages, together with the vast majority of similar documents that could cause embarrassment to the British government / establishment, or those that refer to the Duke of Windsor have long since been 'pulled' from any archive. All too frequently any documents that refer to the Duke of Windsor during this period are missing from archives around the world with notations such as 'Withheld until . . .', 'Lost', or, more frequently, missing completely with no notation at all.

*

However much influence the Duke's perfidy was to have, the entire blame for the ensuing disaster of the Battle for France cannot be placed completely at his door, for there was great complacency and incompetence right through the British political and military command structure. Simply, these men could not believe they were facing a military machine that had been honed to a fine edge and that would destroy them within a mere month of blitzkrieg. And so the sitzkrieg drew to a close and the ever increasing German activity that would result in a well planned victory began to pick up speed. The new attack plans were disseminated to the various army and Division Commanders, troops were moved, the vast logistical nightmare of supplying an army on the attack was sorted out.

Under the new attack plan, now named Falle Gelb, 'Plan Yellow' (see Map IV), Army Group B facing the Ardennes became a pivotal centre of attack. Army Group B was under the command of the advocate of high-speed warfare, General Heinz Guderian, and he had twenty divisions transferred to him from Army Group A. Included in the transfer to Guderian was an extra seven armoured and three motorized divisions to provide him with ample equipment and men to power the punch through the ineffectual Allied lines at Sedan, enabling him to sustain his thrust deep into France and behind the Allied Armies.

If complacency among the Allied commanders was not a deciding factor, it was certainly a substantial cause of their defeat. On 1 May Agent 54, alias Paul Thummel, notified Allied intelligence that Hitler's armies were imminently about to attack and roll Westward on 10 May. His information was exact, comprehensive, and accurate – yet the Allies did nothing. Two days later, the Allies were given a second chance to act, for Thummel's Commanding Officer, General Oster, Second-in-Command of the whole Abwehr organization and a staunch but secret anti-Nazi, confirmed Thummel's information to the Allies – and *still* his information was ignored. On 7 May, an RAF reconnaissance Spitfire spotted a vast column of 400 Panzer tanks moving in on the Ardennes near Luxembourg, the clouds of dust and noise made by the vehicles could be seen for miles around. The RAF pilot risked his life to overfly the column several times to be sure of his report and photos, knowing his information to be of vital importance.

On 8 May the War Office issued an Intelligence Assessment that declared there was 'No Sign Of An Imminent Invasion' – yet with the information and records to hand, it is inconceivable how they came to this conclusion.

This is a sorry story of personal risk and often ultimate sacrifice by such men as Agent 54, the RAF reconnaissance pilot, and by the soldiers on the ground who were flung with irresponsible abandon into the death-embrace of a blitzkrieg attack, to which the Germans knew all the game moves even before the Allies took them. The tale would not be complete without the comment that, incredibly, not only were most of the RAF and Army Headquarters records from this period destroyed during the fall back and defeat to come, but, astonishingly, very few documents from Whitehall were permitted to survive either.

One could almost say that this was a period that needed to be expunged for ever from the nation's archives and the national memory – there was, quite frankly, just too much that needed to be forgotten.

At 3.30 a.m. on 10 May 1940, Field Marshal H.G. von Mackensen, the German Ambassador to Italy received a courier from Ribbentrop at his office in the Rome Embassy. The courier handed him a letter from Hitler to Mussolini, a large package of papers, and a letter of instruction from Ribbentrop which told him to 'Call on Count Ciano at 5.45 a.m., German Summer Time', and arrange a meeting with Mussolini at 6 a.m. at the latest. Count Ciano, the Italian Foreign Minister, later recorded that:

> In the middle of the night, von Mackensen telephoned me to say that within three-quarters of an hour he would come to see me, and together we would go to the Duce, as he had orders to confer with him at exactly 5 a.m. He would say nothing over the telephone about the reasons for the meeting. When he arrived ... he had with him a large package of papers which certainly could not have arrived by telephone. He muttered with embarrassment an excuse about a diplomatic courier who had remained at the hotel until instructions to proceed had come from Berlin ...[59]

On arriving, Mussolini 'read Hitler's note, which listed the reasons for the invasion of Belgium and Holland ...' "Duce: When you receive this letter I shall already have crossed the Rubicon."'

After briefly explaining how events had been brought to a head, and that he feared imminent Allied action, Hitler went on to say:

> An attempt to attack the German Western Front from the Rhine to the frontier of Luxembourg is likewise out of the question. Any similar attempt would be drowned in a sea of blood ...
>
> Nor would it be possible to end the war in the Allies favour by cutting Germany off from her sources of petroleum supplies since, as a result of our domestic measures directed towards autarky and our Four Year Plan, we shall already be in a position to supply our own requirements in the course of the year.
>
> The only possibility for France and England to hope for

192

success would be to destroy the Ruhr or at least paralyze production there. From the beginning, all Anglo–French military plans have been directed toward this objective.

As, judging from the situation, we have been threatened since yesterday by immediate danger, I have therefore decided today to give the order to attack on the Western Front at 5.35 a.m. tomorrow to ensure the neutrality of Belgium and Holland, above all by military measures.

I beg you, Duce, apart from any feelings, to understand the force of the circumstances which compel me to act.

After a few further sentences of persuasion and Nazi rhetoric, the letter ended, 'With the greetings of an old comrade. Yours, A. Hitler.'[60]

Once he had finished Hitler's letter '. . . the Duce examined the accompanying papers for a long time. Finally, after almost two hours, he told Mackensen that he had been convinced that France and Great Britain were preparing to attack Germany through Belgium and Holland.'

There is no sign of the extensive package of papers that Mackensen presented to Mussolini for his perusal, and even Hitler's letter to Mussolini had to be translated from an Italian copy after the war. It would be interesting to speculate what it was that Mussolini was shown, for although the documents were probably massaged by the Nazis, it is important to remember that well into 1940 Germany continued to supply anti-aircraft guns, military aircraft and ordnance to Belgium and Holland under existing contracts.

It is entirely possible that the Nazis' information with regard to Belgian and Dutch neutrality was supplemented by the information brought to them by Bedaux who, as we have seen, was eminently well connected to the very highest echelons of the

Allied command structure, and Hitler undoubtedly learned of Gamelin's Plan D and the Ruhr attack by this means. Additionally, Bedaux was connected to all avenues of industry, ministries of supply, and the French Ministry of Armament. The information he imparted could have been quite dazzling.

At the start of the offensive on Holland and Belgium, Adolf Hitler issued Military Protocol orders that were quite specific – there were to be minimal attacks on Dutch and Belgian cities, and no targeting of civilians. The German army was passing through on its way to the Allies, for Hitler had an appointment to keep and a promise to meet, but that promise was about to be broken.

CHAPTER SIX

Disaster

PREPARING FOR THE Falle Gelb offensive against the West, the German army had spent most of the late spring of 1940 moving ever closer to its new dispersal points. The infantry and panzer Divisions of Army Groups A, B, and C, located in positions from which they would storm across the Dutch, Belgian and Luxembourg frontiers on Y-Day (the German version of D-Day), attacked on 10 May with great speed, effectively rolling-up the defending armies before them like a carpet. Preparing for the offensive, the German High Command had made great use of their intelligence resources, and whilst Hitler was careful never to expose *his* source for fear of losing that man's potential in the future, the army received intelligence on their objectives that was of remarkable clarity. The months of sitzkrieg had not been spent in idle contemplation and by May 1940 the High Command knew which areas were likely to be difficult to overcome, and which areas would quite literally be a walkover. The might of the German war-machine was on the move again, a mere seven months after the defeat of Poland.

In the days immediately preceeding the 10 May attack on the West, Hitler had been keen to formalize the niceties of war, notifying the Dutch, Belgian, and Luxembourg governments of Germany's intent in letters skilfully termed 'Memorandum'. No one was fooled, these were formal declarations of war, yet hidden behind the official wording Hitler was determined to carefully present Germany's case as a legitimate need to launch a pre-emptive strike to defend her borders against Allied attack, declaring:

> The Reich Government has for a long time had no doubts as to what was the chief aim of the British and French war policy. It consists in the spreading of the war to other countries and of the misuse of their peoples as auxiliary and mercenary troops for England and France.

The German communiqué then went on to enumerate eight points of contention with the Benelux countries and stated:

> Evidence in the hands of the German government shows that English and French preparations on Belgian and Netherlands territory for an attack against Germany are already well advanced. Thus for some time now obstacles on the Belgian border toward France which might hinder the entry of the English and French invasion army have been secretly removed. Airfields in Belgium and the Netherlands have been reconnoitred by English and French officers and extensions affected. Belgium has made transport facilities available at the frontier and recently advance parties of the headquarters personnel and the units of the French and English invasion army have arrived in various parts of Belgium and the Netherlands. These facts, together with further information which have accumulated in the last few days, furnish conclusive proof that the English and French attack against Germany is imminent, and that this attack will be directed against the Ruhr through Belgium and the Netherlands.[1]

Hitler's assertion that Germany was about to be attacked was of course a ploy, for although Gamelin's Plan D existed on paper and in the minds of the Allied High Command, the tactic was only designed for use should Germany attack according to the original plan, which had been reinforced in the minds of the Allied Generals by the documents captured in the Mechelene Incident. However, despite clear evidence that Germany intended to ignore Belgium's sovereignty, the Belgian government was reluctant to climb down from its precarious seat on the fence of neutrality, and refused to allow Allied forces onto her territory for fear of provoking German aggression. Belgian reluctance to commit themselves to the Allied cause had therefore caused months of great anxiety and frustration to the Allied High Command, and British and French governments alike. In the end, Germany was to show scant regard for Belgium's attempts at non-provocation, and the country found herself unwillingly caught in the middle of a titanic struggle for European supremacy.

'At 4 a.m. the invasion of Holland and Belgium took place,' General Ironside wrote in his diary on 10 May.

> We were summoned at 7 a.m. to the Admiralty to a Chiefs of Staff meeting. I had great difficulty in getting in from White-hall and then we sat for half an hour listening to rumours that were coming in, and they began telephoning to the French. Then I got away and could not get out [of the building] again. All the night watchmen [were] away and the day's men not there. Doors double and treble locked. I walked up to one of the windows, opened it and climbed out. So much for security.
>
> Now we go to war with the old Cabinet or a change ... We are not likely to get much news about the whole situation for some time. Meanwhile we still have this measly Cabinet which doesn't know if it is on its head or its heels.[2]

Action quickly followed from the Allied side, and that night the Allies took their first decisive step in the battle for the Low Countries, initiating Operation Royal Marine, sowing the Rhine with air-dropped mines in the hope of crippling Germany's ability to use her great inland waterway, breaking the line of communication between the Ruhr, the Western Front, and Germany's seaports.

On 11 May, Ironside wrote:

Winston is now Prime Minister, and was not able to come to our conference at 10.30 p.m. . . . Chamberlain made a most moving speech on the BBC last night . . . The news this morning seems to be good as far as the advance into Belgium is concerned. The air fighting has been very severe indeed . . . [the Germans are] attacking opposite Liege and the French are in contact in the south of Luxembourg.[3]

On all fronts, the attack seemed to be progressing as had been forecast by the Allied planners and experts – the attack on the Maginot Line being a diversion whilst the main thrust of the German offensive powered across the Low Countries to engage the French and BEF on the central Belgian plains, before attempting the anticipated push through the Allied lines and enter Northern France. The British Expeditionary Force and French First and Ninth Armies, following the Allied plan of defence drawn on the maps for months, began to move to the north and prepared to engage the enemy on the Belgian plains, but they were about to be wrong-footed – a feint the repercussions of which would affect the entire direction of the war.

Ironside, fully appraised of the situation, wrote later that day: 'The next few days will be critical days indeed and the fate of the Empire may well rest on the men now fighting in France. I wonder if the people know how serious things are. They have been kept in the dark for so long that they would be angry if they knew.'

The Germans initiated their attack in the West with a brilliantly conceived strategy using a newly developed force in warfare – the parachute trooper. During the earliest hours of the offensive, over 4,000 German paratroopers were dropped at various points in Holland and Belgium, critically damaging the ability of those countries to defend themselves. However, there was a more sinister purpose to these attacks than mere technical advantage, for they were a diversion conjured up by Hitler to distract Allied attention from the real target of the attack – the Ardennes. Rotterdam was descended upon by crack units of Germany's new-style airborne army, combined with a simultaneous assault on the Dutch-German frontier. This double-edged attack caused great confusion and alarm to the Dutch, and, combined with the overwhelming air superiority of Germany's Luftwaffe, stripped the Dutch of a significant proportion of their defence ability. Exploiting the mayhem that the paratrooper landings behind the lines caused, the panzer forces battered their way through the Dutch lines with blitzkrieg tactics, linking up with the paratroopers in just three days. As the French Seventh Army arrived on the outskirts of Rotterdam to help the Dutch city survive the onslaught, it was snatched from under their noses, and capitulated. Rotterdam's fall had taken a mere five days.

During the first week of the German offensive in the West the news for the Allies was nearly all bad, and it seemed to many that every radio report brought revelations of a fresh disaster that had befallen them; first came the alarming news of the multiple German paratrooper landings all over the Low Countries, Rotterdam fell, then came the news that Germany's steamroller advance was punching multiple holes in Allied lines struggling valiantly to hold their own against Hitler's blitzkrieg strategy. The sitzkrieg was over and it seemed as if there was no holding the German advance.

Throughout the earliest days of the attack in the West, Edward, Duke of Windsor, remained in Paris pottering about between his Boulevard Suchet home and the Military Mission at Vincennes, for Howard-Vyse had long since run out of any useful tasks to which he could put his former king. In early March Howard-Vyse had sent Ironside a letter in which he had made clear his efforts to economize the men and material his Mission was using, and pointed out that:

> ... in the interests of economy, I do not propose to fill the appointments of GSO2 [(being 1 General Staff Officer – de Salis) '1 batman, 1 car and 1 driver for HRH, the Duke of Windsor']⁴ ... at present, but to keep them for emergency only. I would also like to point out that the GSO2 provided for HRH, the Duke of Windsor is for his use only, and the occasional work I have had for him, apart from the reports of the Duke of Windsor's tours, has been so spasmodic and so little that it cannot be taken into account. All his [de Salis'] work amounts to is keeping himself and, indirectly, HRH in the picture sufficiently to enable the latter to talk intelligently when he does his tours of the French front.⁵

Within the Windsors' entourage there were murmurs of discontent as well, for whilst the peoples of Belgium, Holland, France, and Britain, together with Western democracy, struggled to survive the onslaught by fascist forces, the lesser mortals in Edward and Wallis' lives found themselves performing tasks whose only purpose seemed to be to indulge the ducal couples' narrow obsession with their own comfort and existence. Foremost amongst these was 'Fruity' Metcalfe – a decent, right-thinking man who could have served a useful purpose in the war effort – who came to perceive the situation in which he now found himself as insufferable. In a rare glimpse of emotion, he made his feelings felt to Mrs Clare Luce (wife of the American journalist and owner of *Time* magazine, Henry Luce) one evening in early May. Whilst pandemonium reigned supreme and Parisians fled their beautiful city, Metcalfe and Luce had found themselves thrust into each other's company one evening, and decided to dine at a small restaurant. Over dinner, the intimacy of the situation encouraged Metcalfe to unburden himself of the many slights the Duke had heaped upon him over the months, and it is clear that Metcalfe wished to be gone:

'You have to help me, Clare!' he had declared. 'The Duke has ordered me to take those bloody cairns to La Croë [in the South of France]. I was a *soldier*! When I resigned from my regiment in India to serve the Prince, it wasn't to be a valet to his God-damned dogs!'[6]

By this time the Windsors' spell seemed to break on others too, those who would once never have dared contradict or voice a contrary thought to that expounded by the egotistical Edward, now found his and the Duchess' views just too intolerable to remain silent.

Diana Cooper, wife of the British Minister of Information, visited the Windsors at home in Suchet and was outraged when the Duke cynically commented to her that the British must be mad not to see they were doomed. 'Well,' Diana Cooper had retorted, 'maybe we are, but I'd rather be mad than turned slave by fear or reason.'[7]

The Windsors' utter egocentricity and complete disregard for the sensibilities of others seemed to know no bounds, and they did themselves no good at all by voicing their outrageous opinions to anyone unlucky enough to find themselves forced to listen. At the start of the German offensive, Clare Luce had been invited to dinner at Boulevard Suchet one evening. As she had sat with the Windsors afterward, they had listened to the radio and heard that the Germans had been bombing London and the small towns and villages along the south coast of England:

'I've driven through many of those villages,' Mrs Luce had remarked to her hosts. 'I hate to see the British so wantonly attacked.'

'After what they did to me,' Wallis caustically retorted, 'I can't say I feel sorry for them – a whole nation against a lone woman!'

History does not record what Mrs Luce made of Wallis' monstrous comment. Yet within a few brief weeks of the Duchess making her comments about the air-warfare pitted against Britain, the Duke too would make unwholesome statements in the same vein, enabling Hoynigen-Heuene, the German Ambassador in Lisbon, to report that:

'The Duke [of Windsor] definitely believes that continued severe bombing would make England ready for peace.'[8]

With Neville Chamberlain's resignation on 10 May a miasma was shrugged off the country's shoulders, for no one could quite forget that his had been the voice that had appeased Hitler; his the hand that had waved the scrap of paper that proclaimed 'peace in our time', that was no peace at all. Winston Churchill's appointment as prime minister caused a change in the wind that could almost be tasted; no one could quite say what the taste was, but its repercussions were felt almost immediately as Churchill acted swiftly to destroy the very structure of those men who would negotiate an appeasement peace with the Nazis. Within days of Churchill's arrival a close friend of Edward's, the Duke of Buccleugh, was ousted from his influential position as Lord Steward of the Royal Household, Sir Oswald and Lady Mosley were arrested and imprisoned under newly implemented defence laws, and Vernon Kell, the Head of MI5, was dismissed for allegedly leaking official secrets to the Germans. Sir Samuel Hoare, the former Air Minister and boss of Freddy Winterbotham, confidant and friend of Edward, was shunted out of the country at high speed. Although, surprisingly, he was given an appointment that would become remarkably important to a Britain beleaguered in years to come by a fascist-conquered Europe – he was sent to become British Ambassador to Spain, and when Edward eventually ran, he ran to Sam Hoare.

'The quicker we get [the Hoares] out of the country the better,' Sir Alexander Cadogan commented in his diary at the time. 'But I'd sooner send them to a penal settlement. He'll be the Quisling of England when Germany conquers us and I am dead.'

Throughout 12–13 May the Germans pushed relentlessly at the Allied defences in the Low Countries, drawing ever more Allied troops northward into a great trap, sucking the strength out of the French and British forces, as ever increasing quantities of men and materials were thrown into Belgium in an effort to stem the German offensive. The matador's cloak was working, and with Allied attention firmly fixed upon the rapidly crumbling defences of Holland, the ever worsening situation in the Low Countries, Guderian's panzers began their thrust through the Ardennes. There followed thirty-six hours of frantic forest fighting as the understrength Allied troops on the ground faced overwhelming odds. The Germans battered their way forward until the panzers were at the virtually undefended French frontier. By 13 May Guderian's 19th Panzers were on the outskirts of Sedan, travelling the very roads of the Duke's First Tour, seeing now for themselves the inadequate defences, the 'little attempt at concealment', the 'weak' anti-tank ditches; faced the French gun crews who 'seemed to be insufficiently trained'.

Realizing with horror the implications of a German breakthrough at the little-defended front facing the Ardennes, the Allies began to take urgent measures to stop the rot before the whole Allied war effort was destroyed from within. In an effort to stem the German tide, the Allies drew upon their only source of instantly available defence – air power – and the RAF was thrown into an attack against Guderian's forces in an attempt to hold them. It was a desperate venture and Allied air losses were appalling as aircraft were thrown time and time again against the massed German mechanized armour pouring into France. They faced the overwhelming air superiority of the Luftwaffe that outnumbered the Allied machines two to one. Of the 109 Allied aircraft thrown piecemeal into the effort, 45 planes were lost. Losses at such a devastating level could not be maintained for very long without critical damage to the whole Allied air-defence structure as 'there would soon be no viable RAF left'.[9]

Early in the morning of 15 May Winston Churchill took an urgent call from the French Premier.

'We have been defeated,' Paul Reynaud intoned emotionally. 'The front is broken near Sedan; they [the Germans] are pouring through in great numbers with tanks and armoured cars.'

German tenacity, sheer weight of numbers, luck, and a little help from their friends, was winning through. The Allied line broke under the enormous weight of the attack, and Guderian's panzers flooded across the Meuse at Sedan, charging into the hinterland of northern France.

American Ambassador William C. Bullitt was with the French Defence Minister, Edouard Daladier, when the news broke. Receiving a telephone call from Gamelin, Bullitt had watched and listened as Daladier had suddenly leaned forward to grasp the edge of his desk.

'No!' the Defence Minister had gasped, 'that's not possible! You are mistaken!' He listened for a few moments longer before shouting, 'You must attack!'

'Attack? What with?' Gamelin had retorted. 'I have no more reserves.'

The following day Bullitt sent a telegram to Washington saying, 'It seems clear that without a miracle like the Battle of Marne, the French army will be completely crushed.'

By a curious link, Bullitt was at this time associating closely with the German's very own 'miracle' worker, for he had just issued Charles Bedaux with an American diplomatic passport and leased Château Candé from him (making the property an Annex of the American Embassy). Bedaux had continued to stay in Paris, basing himself at the Ritz throughout the late spring until the German offensive had started. Now he ordered the Ritz to look after his suite (furnished with his own possessions), and he and Fern withdrew to the security and comfort of Château Candé to await the result of his efforts. In 1943 he would state that at this time he, 'attended to the relief of stricken Americans. A number of them would, I know, testify on my behalf, but I have not retained their names.'[10] Bedaux's home, Candé, was to be a safe retreat and remained totally unscathed during the ensuing mayhem as France was conquered by Germany. Indeed, the locals of nearby Tours commented on how remarkable it was that although their town was almost completely flattened, and every building in the region suffered major damage of some form during the invasion, Candé, secluded within its own grounds, remained absolutely unscathed; an island of peace, tranquillity and safety in a sea of misery.

On 6 February, 1943, J. Edgar Hoover was to write a confidential memo to Major General George V. Strong of G2 of the War Department, to inform him that:

The Rogerses [Herman and Katherine] reported that when Tours, where the Château of Candé is located, was bombed by the Germans, the Bedaux chateau was the only place not levelled in the locality. Mr Rogers stated he received information from Max Brusset, Chief de Cabinet, advising that

when the Germans came to Tours, Bedaux met the Commanding German General and entertained him and his entire staff,
to the disgust of the French people.

Hoover supplemented this information with details of a letter
he had recently received from John Hall Wheeler, a publisher
from New York, who declared:

> In 1937, Mr Bedaux submitted a manuscript to Scribners. I had
> lunch and dinner with him on several occasions, and he talked
> to me very freely regarding his views. He told me that he was
> strongly in sympathy with the Nazi movement in Germany,
> and had been on their payroll as a sort of publicity man, that
> he knew Hitler personally and had spent some time with him
> at Berchtesgaden. I expressed my detestation of everything
> Fascist and Nazi, and he said he was sorry to hear this because
> both England and the United States were going to go Fascist
> and that people like myself would have a hard time. He
> intimated that the Duke of Windsor was a strong believer in
> the totalitarian philosophy . . . While it seems almost incredible
> that a man should speak so freely to a comparative stranger, I
> do not think Mr Bedaux was romancing and, in light of what
> he divulged to me, he is almost certainly a potential menace.[11]

After the German break-out at Sedan, consternation began to
grow in Paris that the German effort to overcome and defeat
France might actually succeed. The following day the Duke of
Windsor travelled to Vincennes to announce to Howard-Vyse
and the Military Mission that he would be taking a few days off
to settle the Duchess into safer surroundings at Biarritz. What
Howard-Vyse thought of the Duke's sense of priorities is not
recorded, but his feelings must have ran high for he was later
heard to say that he 'never wished to see that man again'.

Whilst the Military Mission faced the prospect of a hard battle, working in shifts to keep the liaison between the French and British Command functioning adequately, Edward, a major-general in the British army, swanned off to the French Atlantic coast near the Spanish frontier, driven by his loyal chauffeur, Ladbrooke, with several maids in tow, to settle Wallis during her self-imposed exile from Paris. On their way to Biarritz they travelled south out of Paris through Orleans, Poitiers and Bordeaux, passing within five miles of Bedaux's Château Candé at Tours. It is not known whether they paused in their journey to call on Bedaux socially, or perhaps to refresh themselves, but it is likely. They continued their journey onto Biarritz with Wallis clinging to the guide book she had used during her travels around France in the winter of 1936 and the spring of 1937, using it to attempt to find them overnight lodgings. The overnight stop was not as comfortable as Edward and Wallis might have hoped, for, with war raging, they were hard pressed to persuade the owner of a hotel filled to overflowing to even let them spend the night in his sitting room. There is no record where the maids and chauffeur slept.

Edward returned to Paris whilst Wallis settled comfortably into the splendid isolation and safety of the Hotel de Palais at Biarritz, far from the hustle, bustle, and danger of a Paris facing the distinct prospect of occupation. To Edward's embarrassment and Wallis' acute discomfort, the Duchess' abandonment of war-stricken Paris soon became a target of the German Propaganda Ministry, who not only reported over the radio that Wallis was staying in the safety of Biarritz, but even broadcast her address and room number as well. It must have felt like being bitten by a pet that one had nurtured, for Wallis was to comment that the Germans had 'played a most unchivalrous trick on me. Instantly,' she recalled, 'I became the most unpopular guest in the long history of the Hotel de Palais.'

Quite why Wallis was under the impression the Germans had played a trick on her is unclear, unless via Bedaux they had actually suggested the move. Alternatively if she and the Duke had called on Bedaux during their journey from Paris, the ever informative Bedaux might well have passed the information on. Perhaps the most telling comment made by Wallis was that she thought the Germans' radio broadcast of her location was unchivalrous. Why Wallis thought the Germans should have made an exception and behaved chivalrously towards her when they were not doing so to the rest of Europe is also a little hard to understand – they were after all busily engaged in total war: Poland and Holland had fallen, Belgium was overrun, France invaded, and the tens of thousands on the long trek to refugee status were being strafed in the highways of France by a Luftwaffe instructed to cause mayhem and block the Allied lines of communication. Unless, of course, Wallis was under the impression that the Germans owed her and the Duke something.

Meanwhile, on the Front, confusion and disaster reigned supreme. The gun emplacements which the French had placed so much hope in were obliterated by a combination of extremely accurate German anti-tank fire and dive-bomber. The artillery was similarly targeted remorselessly. Yet there was pitifully little Allied air-cover to be seen, and what there was suffered extremely bad losses. The French light artillery, called in to stiffen the line of resistance, was hopelessly entangled in the endless column of refugees that filled the roads to overflowing. It was hard enough to march against the flow of panic-stricken civilians – the elderly, men, women and children, horses and carts, and cars with a lifetime's possessions strapped on to the roof – but to face up to the numerous air attacks was especially hard, for the French light artillery of 1940 was still largely horse drawn and the unfortunate animals were easy and purposeful targets for any passing German aircraft intent on causing panic below.

Back at Allied Headquarters, the High Command listened to the hourly briefings with ever increasing consternation, for even ostensibly good news eventually turned out to be inaccurate, further complicating the situation. Gamelin had been reassured with the news that the Germans had been halted and contained at Sedan, little realizing that the French Seventh Armoured Battalion which was supposedly stalling the German advance had in reality been destroyed by the panzers. The theory expounded mere days before that the German advance would be stopped by the River Meuse, turned out to be only so much over-optimistic rhetoric, as the natural obstacle was swept over by Hitler's forces, and the penetration into France itself worsened.

Technically, the German forces were now at the most vulnerable point in the operation, for having passed on each side of Sedan (wisely knowing to leave the massive Vauban fortifications well alone, untouched, and cut off), they had pushed on into French territory and their lines of communication were becoming ever more susceptible to counter-attack. Had the Allies mounted a vigorous counter-stroke at this time, and utilized what remained of their air-power in an all-out assault on the two bridges over the river Meuse to stop the tanks crossing, the German troops would have found themselves in a nightmare position – trapped in enemy territory without armoured support, their retreat blocked by the River Meuse, their front and side flanks open to attack combined with the dangers of having left the enemy fortification of Vauban in their very midst. However, nothing happened. The Allied troops on the ground were pounded out of their defensive positions by ferocious air and artillery attack, found their ranks penetrated by the ever probing panzers, were chased across the countryside without the chance of digging-in a new defensive line, and the rumour began that the Allies were on the run.

This was not strictly true, for although morale had not been high at the start of the offensive (and it was certainly beginning to crumble under the constant bombardment and offensive), the majority of the difficulties lay in the officer corps' underestimation of the enemy they faced and a complete misinterpretation of the German attack plan. It was not by chance that Hitler had ordered his attack at this the Allies' most vulnerable point – what was to become known as the 'gap' – and the Allied Commanders continued to misunderstand the very concept of the German attack.

As the offensive proceeded, Guderian found his forces penetrating the inner core of the French defences, for having cracked the hard outer shell they were now flooding into the vulnerable interior of the French countryside with little opposition. This could not remain the situation for long, and, knowing that the French would do everything within their power to counter-attack, Guderian decided prompt and decisive action would be the order of the day. He swung the 1st and 2nd Panzer Divisions into a westward thrust along the rear of the French lines, cutting off their lines of communication and possibilities of retreat, hoping that his 3rd Panzer Division could move fast enough to fill the gap left by the departing 1st and 2nd before the well equipped 2nd French Army could act and fill the gap. It would be a monumental comment on the whole German strategy that the attack was so swift, so absolute, that the German infantry could hardly keep up with the panzers that swept all before them.

Yet another opportunity was missed by the Allies, for with French communications stretched to the limit, and with their men and machines in the field scattered to the four winds, a counter-attack was planned even though it became ever harder to organize such an action against a front that moved almost hourly. Despite the difficulties, General Georges, placed in overall charge of the devastated sector by Gamelin, decided a counter-attack *must* be attempted if the German penetration into France were to be stopped. However, such an attack could not be easily organized as the French tanks, regarded as competent and formidable machines by the Germans, had been thoroughly dispersed across the countryside. To launch an effective wedge into the German column, these tanks needed to be returned to their dispersal points, be organized, re-fuelled, and given exact orders for the planned operation. All this took time, something the Allies had pitifully little of. Despite the decision to act, in the end so few French tanks returned to their dispersal points that the attack was twice postponed before it was decided that the Front had moved sufficiently to have rendered the planned operation obsolete, and so the attack failed.

On the Front the two French infantry divisions took a terrible pounding from the relentless German offensive and began to disintegrate, the Allied defence of the West began to falter.

Ironside wrote in his diary on the 15th:

The war is coming nearer and nearer to us and it makes one think all the more. We are living a new phase of history the course of which no man can foresee. Nobody believed that we should be engaged in war, certainly not in a death struggle so soon. We made no preparations . . . and we cannot catch up. It is too late. The year may see us beaten.[12]

On 16 May, the German advance began to pick up momentum, sweeping all before it at a startling rate. Within twenty-four hours they penetrated a further fifty miles into French territory and reached the River Oise, a little under halfway from Sedan to the English Channel, and a mere forty miles from Arras. On reaching the Oise, the first of several strange orders reached the German commanders heading the attack – on the 17th, Guderian was ordered to stop. He was given the order by Field-Marshal von Kliest, who later related:

The order came when my leading elements had reached the Oise, between Guise and La Fere. I was told that it was a direct order from the Führer. But I don't think it was the direct consequence of the decision to replace the 12th Army by the 2nd as our backer-up.[13]

Hitler's inclination to pause, let the strategy of the 'bloody nose' (as expounded by de Ropp) on the battlefield take effect was not entirely successful, for having sent his panzers rolling, it was an entirely different matter to apply the brakes to an all-out offensive and attempt to politically manipulate the situation. Hitler was to discover this during the first artificial pause in the battle, for on receiving the High Command order to stop, Guderian, seeing little sense in a strategy that allowed time for the Allies to gather themselves together, promptly resigned his command and withdrew himself to the Army Group Head-quarters in a monumental huff. Here he was ordered to await General List, the commander of the 12th Army. No one wished to loose the genius for armoured command that was Heinz Guderian and he later related the encounter with his senior officer:

In the name of General von Rundstedt, he [List] cancelled my removal from command, and explained that the halt order came from the top, so that it had to be enforced. But he recognized my reasons for wishing to continue the advance and gave me permission on behalf of the Army Group to carry on strong reconnaisance.[14]

Guderian's interpretation of *strong reconnaissance* was some-thing quite different to that envisaged by the High Command, however, for him it was a means to maintain his effort by *strong reconnaissance* to reach the Channel. He later admitted that the halt to the attack was contrary to what he perceived to be the way to proceed, adding: 'It seemed unimaginable that Hitler ... might have lost his nerve and stopped the immediate advance.'[15] The offensive under Guderian continued, splitting the Allied forces in two – one half in France, the other trapped in Belgium.

The British Expeditionary Force's effort to maintain a defence against this unremitting German offensive was now beginning to fall into serious trouble as well, for the front moved so rapidly that it was almost impossible to supply and communicate with troops on a front that were hardly able to dig in, let alone hold a position. General Gort, Commander-in-Chief of the BEF began to think the impossible – unless he was able to extricate his forces from this dire situation, he would lose an entire army. Unfortunately, at the very start of the German offensive Gort had taken an impulsive decision that was to have devastating repercussions on the overall British ability to fight an effective war. Ever the soldier's Commander-in-Chief, General Gort had abandoned his highly effective and organized GHQ at Arras in favour of being near the action, and based himself in a small village near Lille. In the autumn of 1939 a great deal of effort had been expended in equipping the BEF GHQ at Arras with a complex and advanced communications system together with the necessary staff to run an army in the field. That was now rendered almost useless as Gort, with only a small contingent of staff officers to assist him, attempted to control all the complexities of a modern war on a grand scale from a small village near the Front, and communicated with his GHQ by the less than efficient French telephone system. Worse still, the reports that came in from the battle on the ever-worsening situation – the up-to-date intelligence – continued to arrive at the GHQ in Arras, and the officers of GHQ were only sporadically able to contact their Commander-in Chief on the failing civilian phone system. The result was that Gort was frequently left cut-off for long periods of time, unable to give an instant and necessary decision, and the orders that eventually got through to GHQ were often out of date as a result of the time it had taken to receive them. In this most modern of offensives, time was to prove of the essence.

By the 17th, after a week of disaster and retreat, Gort could see which way the battle was heading, and valiantly decided on a previously unimaginable course of action – to plan the evacuation of an army of several hundred thousand men from the European continent, and enable them to fight another day. Of immediate concern was the rapid German advance, and this needed to be checked if there was to be any hope of holding enough territory to evacuate *from*. Ordered by General Georges to assist in the defence of the Canal du Nord (a vital defensive position that was to act as an impenetrable tank barrier), Gort sent a brigade to assist only to discover that on arriving there was no one to assist; the 70th Brigade of the 23rd Northumberland Division were on their own, with their right flank exposed to attack and encirclement. There was no choice, however, the Canal had to be defended and so the troops were ordered to dig in.

Further to the north-east the BEF's 3rd Division under Major-General B. L. Montgomery was faring little better. They had been fighting a slow constant retreat, with heavy sporadic skirmishing and their supplies were now running low. The division had been split into separate fighting units all intent on one purpose – to slow the enemy advance – and many an heroic incident took place as the men fought to survive with equipment that was often inadequate for the purpose. Captain Mike Lonsdale, of the Duke of Cornwall's Light Infantry, established himself with a small group of men in an isolated copse with the enemy about to flood past on both sides. He was later to recount that as they'd waited:

A Panzer IV came growling towards us. We pulled back from the edge of the copse to settle ourselves into a position on the far side of a clearing and waited for it. As the tank crossed to the middle of the clearing, we fired a PIAT (Platoon Infantry Anti-Tank) at it, but the damn thing glanced off it with a loud bang. Then we opened up on it with a bren-gun and some rifles, but the bullets just bounced off. We might as well have been armed with pea-shooters, for all the good we could do ... We had no choice other than to fall back yet again, and in a hurry too.[16]

By this time, on 18 May, the Germans had sent in excess of 40,000 military vehicles, which poured through the gap at Sedan, flooding into northern France. Antwerp had fallen, and Amiens was facing the prospect of imminent attack by an almost automaton force that had appeared over the horizon. The German offensive continued to push towards the Channel with remarkable speed, effectively herding the Allied forces before them in an attack that was devastating in its implementation. Kliest was later to recount:

I was half-way to the sea when one of my staff brought me an extract from the French radio which said that the commander of their 6th Army on the Meuse had been sacked, and General Giraud appointed to take charge of the situation. Just as I was reading it, the door opened and a handsome French General was ushered in. He introduced himself with the words, 'I am General Giraud.' He told me how he had set out in an armoured car to look for his army, and had found himself in the midst of my [German] forces far ahead of where he had expected them to be. My first encounter with the British was when my tanks came upon, and overran, an infantry battalion whose men were equipped with dummy cartridges for field exercises ... He [Guderian] had already cut the BEF's communications with its bases; he was now aiming to cut it off from retreat to the sea.[17]

Guderian would wheel his forces northward within the next twenty-four hours in a move designed to catch the Allied forces in the bag and pull the draw-strings shut.

In an attempt to gauge a clearer picture of what was happening at the Front, Ironside travelled to France to view the situation for himself. On the evening of the 20th he caught the 9 p.m. train, and travelling via Boulogne arrived at Gort's Headquarters by 6 a.m. the following morning. By this time Arras was surrounded by German forces on three sides and just managing to hold on. The rear Allied sector was swamped by fleeing civilians, military traffic, and invaded by the all-pervasive crump and rumble of the desperate battle that was being fought just over the immediate horizon – an ever-present reminder of just how close the Germans really were. 'The roads [were] an indescribable mass of refugees,' Ironside commented, 'both Belgian and French, moving down in every kind of conveyance. Poor women pushing perambulators, horsed wagons with all the family and its goods in it ... Poor devils. It was a horrible sight.' On his arrival Ironside was appraised of the situation, and came to the conclusion that immediate action was necessary if there was any possibility of turning the present tide of the German incursion. He was later to record that:

> I told the C-in-C [Gort] that in my opinion only an attack with all his force, backed if it was possible by the French troops near him, in the direction of Amiens would release the BEF from their present encirclement. Did he agree? ... After some thought, Lord Gort did not agree. I asked him to try, but the C-in-C said no, he could not agree.[18]

The decision not to act upon Ironside's advice cannot be firmly laid at Gort's feet, however, for his forces were already heavily committed to the fighting in Belgium, desperately trying to hold the Escaut Line. To assemble an attacking force of any worthwhile substance was to deprive another area of its valuable commitment to the defence of that region. Ironside had brought the plan with him from London for all-out attack on Amiens, and the unrealistic expectation that such an offensive could turn the tide of the war to the Allies' favour 'can only be explained by the fact that the War Cabinet was totally out of touch with the position in France'.[19]

Eventually Gort agreed to attempt a limited counter-attack southward from the Arras area, and the operation code-named Frankforce, with two Battalions of the Durham Light Infantry supported by a mere 74 tanks, attempted a breakout on 21 May. This was minimal men and equipment for an operation of this kind, and of the 74 tanks available, 58 were the antiquated type Mk1's (armed with a single 7.9mm machine-gun) and 16 were Mk2's (armed with a 2 pound gun and 7.9mm machine-gun). The British tanks were slow, old-fashioned, and totally inadequate when put up against the ultra-modern, fast, well-equipped superior panzers of the German army. What was really required was an attack on a divisional basis with all the men, support and logistics that that entailed. Despite the limitations, however, the British counter-attack was pushed on with ferocious force in a last-ditch attempt to turn the tide at this late stage of the debacle, and they fought on desperately despite heavy losses. Rundstedt was later to admit that:

> A critical moment in the drive came just as my forces had reached the Channel . . . For a short time it was feared that our armoured divisions would be cut off before the infantry divisions could come up to support them. None of the French counter-attacks carried any serious threat as this one did.

However, as a drowning man's struggles to keep afloat become ever weaker, so the Allies had been critically damaged and the counter-attack failed. It would prove to be the Allies' last attempt to break the stranglehold that the Germans had on the forces trapped to the north, and now the drawstrings on the bag were drawn ever tighter as the Allies were forced into an ever-decreasing pocket – effectively herding them towards Dunkirk.

Up to this point in the offensive, Hitler's forces had enjoyed unprecedented success, for no one on the Allied side could reasonably have expected that Hitler would know that Gamelin's projected Plan D would disastrously leave the Allies' right flank uncovered, and that the Germans would unerringly hit the exact spot where the defensive line was fatally flawed – at the Ardennes and Sedan. Had the Germans not attacked at these Allied fault-lines with devastating accuracy, they would not have enjoyed the success they were to subsequently have. It is entirely likely that if Germany had attacked according to the *old* Plan, it is possible that Gamelin's strategy as expounded under his Plan D might well have worked, and the German attack in the West would have ground to an uncomfortable halt on the Belgian plains. General Blumentritt was to later endorse this by saying:

> The fact that Hitler's 'judgement' had been justified in [the] face of his generals intoxicated him, and made it much more difficult for them ever to argue with, or restrain him, again.[20]

Yet, as has been shown, Hitler's inspirational judgements usually had a firm foundation in fact and excellent intelligence. But his source of intelligence was just about to panic and run.

On 23 May another strange incident occurred in the German offensive in the West. After heavy fighting, and wheeling north-ward to cut off the Allied retreat, Guderian's forces came to the Canal du Nord – the line that the Allies had decided would be their last-ditch defence against the panzers. It was an ideal anti-tank defence, and, as Gort was to say, it was 'the only anti-tank obstacle [we had] on this flank'. If the Germans crossed it, there was nothing left to stop them from cutting the entire remainder of the BEF from the sea and any chance of escape – the Germans would capture an army of over 300,000 men in one fell swoop, and it was a very attractive prize, for with the capture of the army would come the prize of Britain, for these same men composed a major proportion of Britain's defence against invasion.

At this point, just as the German forces were winning the life and death struggle to take the canal bridges and had begun to pour their armour across, Field Marshal Kleist received a direct order from the Führer to stop. Further, in the face of overwhelming victory, he was now ordered to withdraw his forces back across the Canal. It was an order that made absolutely no sense, and Kleist later admitted, 'I decided to ignore it, and to push on across the Canal. My armoured cars actually entered Hazebrouck, and cut across the British lines of retreat . . . then came a more emphatic order that I was to withdraw behind the Canal. My tanks were kept halted for three days.' Guderian recounted that, 'Field-Marshal von Brauchitsch, whom I asked after the French campaign why he had agreed to stop the panzer-forces before Dunkirk, told me that it was by order of Hitler – and added that he had hoped somebody would be disobedient.' General Thoma of the General Staff repeatedly sent urgent requests to the OKH (Oberkommando des Heeres), demanding that the panzers be allowed to push on, but his requests were ignored. He was later to remark that, 'You can never talk to a fool. Hitler spoilt the chance of victory.'[21]

But Hitler was nobody's fool, and the obliteration of the British army had not been part of the bargain, just a 'bloody nose' – the short-sharp-shock – to let the British government taste defeat, and then a swiftly negotiated peace before he could once again turn eastward.

Things are not good [Ironside recorded on the 23 May]. Boulogne was isolated by German tanks this morning at 8 a.m. and I have only just got my three battalions of motorized infantry and the Tank Regiment into Calais in time . . . Meanwhile the BEF is short of food and ammunition. Damn bad.

We have sent complete discretion to Gort to move his army as he likes to try to save it . . . Gort is very nearly surrounded and there is just the possibility that he may be able to withdraw through Ypres to Dunkirk. I have directed some food there for him. That may help if he attempts to withdraw. I cannot see that we have much hope of getting any of the BEF out . . .[22]

Ironside was well aware of the defensive situation at Dunkirk for the Duke of Windsor had reported on all that he had seen just three months before, commenting on the:

. . . canal forming an anti-tank obstacle [and] Front System follow[ing] the line of heights from Mont Noir to Steenvoorde, thence north and bearing west; the Intermediate System passes in from of Hazebrouck and continues north roughly parallel to the Front System; the Rear System, in part of the Cassel Defences, pass immediately east of Cassel then bear west as far as Clairmarais . . . From Ghyveld to the sea the Front System is of normal land pattern and extends in depth from the Belgian frontier to the line Ghyveld – Bray Dunes (2–3 kilometres). A seconds system with its left of Fort des Dunes was spoken of but no work was seen.[23]

Little did Ironside realize it at the time, but Bray Dunes would be the final redoubt that the BEF would be herded into, and that the survival of the BEF would depend on there being enough time for rescue by a fleet of little ships.

The British were to learn that the Germans were holding back, however, for via Y Service (Britain's range of listening posts whose task it was to gather as many encoded German signals as possible for transfer to the code-breaking centre at Bletchley Park) operators were amazed to intercept a German transmission broadcast loud and clear in plain language that had not been encoded. At 11.42 a.m. on 24 May, the Germans broadcast a message that stated that the attack on the line of Dunkirk-Hazebrouck-Merville defences, some 30 miles long, was to be 'discontinued for the present'.

It was almost as if Hitler was waiting for something, and wanted the British to know he was holding back. The halt continued for the rest of the 24th, through the 25th, and into the 26th. To many in the German High Command, Hitler's orders seemed the utmost folly. Halder recorded in his diary on the 26 May:

> 0800 ... Our armoured forces have stopped as if paralyzed on the high ground between Bethune and St Omer in compliance with top level orders, and must not attack.
>
> 1100 ... All through the morning ObdH [Brauchitsch] is very nervy. I can sympathize with him, for these orders from the top make no sense. In one area they call for a head-on attack against a front retiring in orderly fashion, and elsewhere they freeze the troops on the spot where the enemy rear could be cut into at any time. Von Rundstedt, too, cannot stand it, and has gone up forward to Hoth and Kliest to look over the land for the next armoured moves.
>
> 1330 ... [Brauchitsch] summoned to Führer. Returns beaming. At last the Führer has given permission to move on Dunkirk to prevent evacuations.[24]

However it was too late, for if Hitler had expected the British government, now headed by the indomitable Winston Churchill rather than the ineffectual Neville Chamberlain, to open up peace negotiations he was sorely disappointed. Instead, Churchill initiated Operation Dynamo – the evacuation from Dunkirk of as many Allied soldiers as possible, removing them from the fascist-dominated continent to fight another day. Churchill had not used the pause in the German offensive to open up discussions.

On the same day the Belgian army cracked under the relentless pressure of attack by Army Group B under General Bock. Belgium was overrun by German columns that seemed to be able to move about at will, and the Belgian army was penned in to a narrow strip of coastline, its back against the sea. King Leopold had no choice, he could see the BEF being driven into the sea and in the process of evacuation back to British shores, the French army rendered impotent by the overwhelming superiority of German tactics in the field. Late in the afternoon the Belgian King requested an armistice of the Germans, and the country fell into an uneasy peace early the following morning.

The British withdrawal from continental Europe now became a race to get away before the German trap closed, causing the capture of a British army on the continent. Luckily Churchill, instinctively sensing that disaster was looming, had put plans in place over a week before for rescuing bits of the BEF from French inlets. At the time he had little concept that the plan would be used in seven days to evacuate a whole army, for there had been little expectation of saving much of the BEF, and the Admiralty had pessimistically forecast a rescue of only 45,000 men before the enclave fell to German conquest. As it was, Dunkirk struggled on, and the thousands of men trapped on Bray Dunes were exposed to air attack with little fighter cover as the RAF were only able to stay over the stronghold a few minutes at a time due to the long flight over the Channel. Over the next ten days, under constant and merciless attack by infantry, armour and air power, the Allies clung on desperately to the portion of France that was to be their escape ground, and by 4 June 338,000 troops (224,000 British and 114,000 French) had been evacuated across the

Channel to the relative safety of Britain, to continue the battle against Fascism. 'At the same time it is evident that the preservation of the BEF to fight another day would have been impossible without Hitler's action in halting Kleist's panzer forces outside Dunkirk.'[25]

During this time another chain of events had begun to take shape, indicative of an establishment that felt it necessary to cover its tracks for fear of ever admitting that anything had not been perfect. On 25 May, at the height of the battle for France, General Ironside was relieved of his command, and commented in his diary that 'I was told that I had to take over the command in England and organize that. I am to be made a field-marshal later. Not at once, because the public may think that I am being given a sop and turned out. An honour for me and a new and most important job, one much more to my liking than CIGS in every way'.[26] However, there was infinitely more to it than just that, for he was being quietly shuffled off to one side and would be forced to retire within the year, at a time when Britain needed its most capable military men. It is possible that Ironside's effective demotion was as a result of his use of the Duke of Windsor, for on the same day as Ironside was relieved of his command, Howard-Vyse was ordered to destroy all the documents at the Military Mission. This despite the fact that the battle for France was still raging, and the need to liaise with Gamelin's Headquarters was more important than ever. However, despite outward appearances, there was another excuse that existed to remove Ironside, and that came from the Field Security Police. Early in May, the Field Security Police reported that General Ironside's staff car was making frequent and lengthy visits to a house in Holland Park, and that on investigating, the FSP officer – Malcolm Muggeridge – reported that the house was occupied

223

by persons with 'dubious political association'. Ironside was reputed to have had Fascist associations in the past, and Muggeridge was inclined to think that Ironside's visits were 'personal rather than political'. On the day after Muggeridge's report, the evening papers carried the headline 'Ironside's Sacked'.[27] Whether Ironside ever really contemplated any activity that was detrimental to his country's interests has to be doubted for there was never any suggestion of disloyalty, and he was a capable and efficient staff officer. However, it can surely be no coincidence that his removal was based upon a report submitted by the Field Security Police – the same military organ that had spent months warning of Bedaux, and the Duke's association with him. Ironside was ultimately responsible for Edward's appointment to Howard-Vyse's Military Mission, and the FSP warnings to Howard-Vyse must have crossed Ironside's desk. If the FSP were exacting their pound of flesh for the disaster happening over the Channel, then it would be Ironside's head that would roll under the dubious excuse of his visits to the Holland Park house, for it could never be admitted publicly that Ironside was paying the price for appointing Windsor.

Meanwhile, in Paris events began to move swiftly as well. On 27 May, the Duke of Windsor was with 'Fruity' Metcalfe when he learned that Howard-Vyse had been ordered to destroy all the Mission's records. This, combined with the knowledge that Ironside was no longer CIGS was not in any way comforting. The Duke must have spent the afternoon pondering his situation, and later that evening, after he and Metcalfe had dined together at Suchet, the Duke must have come to certain conclusions about what was necessary to protect his own safety and position. Despite the fact that he was a serving major-general in the British army, attached to the Military Mission that was still conducting an important liaison with the French High Command, he came to a conclusion that not many men in his situation would have done. That evening, before Metcalfe departed he asked his ex-King, 'What are your orders for tomorrow, sir?'

'I don't know yet,' Edward had replied. 'Ring me at nine-thirty.'

Metcalfe departed home for his bed and a good night's sleep. The following morning, after dressing and a light breakfast and coffee, Metcalfe finally got around to telephoning Edward for his brief on the day's activity. The phone was answered by the concierge who informed him that, shortly after six o'clock that morning, the Duke, driven by Ladbrooke and accompanied by the remaining servants packed into two cars, had departed from Paris for the South of France. Astonished and thunderstruck Metcalfe had asked:

'Any instructions for me?'

'Nothing, sir,' the concierge had replied.

Metcalfe had been abandoned in Paris, and as he was not officially attached to any military authority his future looked extremely uncertain and grim if he were captured by the Germans. Edward had made a thorough job of abandoning his friend alone in Paris, for not only had he left taking two cars, the one remaining 'runabout' had been disabled, his own private store of gasoline had been poured down the drain, and 'Fruity' had been left with little chance of escape. There has never been a satisfactory reason given why the Duke of Windsor so callously abandoned his friend in the face of an advancing enemy, but it is possible that Edward was frightened that 'Fruity' Metcalfe knew too much about his meetings with Bedaux, for he was aware that Metcalfe had been asked to keep an eye on him by his younger brother, the King. Alternatively, it may simply be that Edward, with plenty to hide about his culpability in the disaster that was unfolding in the Allies lap, just didn't know how much 'Fruity' knew, and thought discretion the better part of valour. And so, Edward, Duke of Windsor, a serving major-general in the British army, packed his bags, his bits and pieces, his beloved 'kettly', and fled.

The ever resourceful 'Fruity' was not about to be bagged by the Germans, and by a mixture of a deviously purloined bicycle, hitchhiking, and many weary walks, he eventually fetched up at Cherbourg, and escaped back to Britain where he was to spend the remainder of the war working for Scotland Yard. When his wife, Lady Alexandra, eventually heard the story of her husband's abandonment and escape across chaotic France she told him, 'I don't want to see the Windsor's again, ever!'[28]

On 28 May, Winston Churchill convened a secret meeting at Downing Street. It was a gathering at which no minutes were taken, and during the discussion: 'It was agreed that the Windsors should be brought to Britain immediately, at the very least for interrogation by Cadogan and Vansittart on their peculiar role in Nazi collaboration.'[29]

Across the rest of France, the French were not quite so lucky as to be able to up sticks and flee. Calais swiftly succumbed to the panzers, and the German army, now occupying a belt of Northern France some one hundred miles long by forty miles wide, turned its attention increasingly to the French Seventh, Sixth and Second Armies to the South, crossing the Rivers Somme and Aisne to head for the interior of France and on to Paris. It seemed as if nothing could stop the German onward march, backed up by the might of fast-moving panzers and supported by heavy air cover.

In Paris Mrs Clare Luce, crossing the concourse at the Gare du Nord train station, was accosted by:

... an old Red Cross nurse, a Frenchwoman with a white face and staring eyes, [who] put down the bowl of broth she was ladling out to the refugees and came to me and took my arm in tense fingers.

'Madame,' she said, 'you are American?'

I said: 'Yes,' and she went on: 'Then you must tell me the truth: *qui nous a trahi?* Who has betrayed us?'

That was the first time I heard the word *trahi* in Paris. At first it was no more than a whisper, like the little winds that come in the dim days before a hurricane . . . And then the whisper became a great wail that swept through France, a great wail of the damned: *Trahi . . . trahi . . .*[30]

Throughout France vehicles of the retreating French army were seen bedaubed with hand-written slogans scrawled in chalk: *Vendu pas vaincu.* Betrayed not beaten.

CHAPTER SEVEN

Flight

FLEEING THE UNSAVOURY horrors of war, and discarding any responsibility he may have had to assist his countrymen through the ensuing debacle, Edward retraced his steps of a mere fortnight before, journeying south down the overflowing French highways towards Biarritz, and Wallis. Few men living through such calamitous events, particularly a major-general in the British army, could so easily have shrugged all responsibility from their shoulders, decided they'd had enough of military service, washed their hands of the whole catastrophe at the Front, packed their bags, and fled. There was a common phrase for such rare behaviour, but no one dared intimate it when referring to the Duke – at least not on record.

The Duke's hurried departure from Paris and his abandonment of the loyal Metcalfe could have been excused as a spur of the moment decision – a momentary lapse of self-control – were it not for the fact that on the day before his hasty departure he telephoned Wallis in Biarritz to announce that he'd be joining her the following day and that together they would be journeying on to La Croë. That he telephoned his intentions to Wallis *before* his evening meal with Metcalfe is clear as not only did the two men dine late, but Wallis also had time that day to write *and* post a letter to her Aunt Bessie in the United States saying: 'The

Duke telephoned he is arriving tomorrow. It will be nicer for me to be in my own house as hotels are never restful for me ... I will wire when I arrive at La Croë and will try and write often though there is nothing one can say except that morale is excellent ...' – a strange phrase, considering the Allies had been decimated and France all but defeated.

Whilst Edward collected his Duchess from sunny Biarritz, the 'WE' monogrammed luggage was loaded aboard their cars under a glaringly hot sky and servants were organized to ensure that their every need was pandered to, men of the French and British armies to the north fought for their very lives, playing a life and death game of hide-and-seek amongst the Bray Dunes. On the Dunkirk beaches, long lines of Allied soldiers queued neck-deep out into the sea whilst the Luftwaffe strafed at will, and the ships of Operation Dynamo struggled to evacuate a defeated army. France's once proud military machine, swelled by men and materials from her colonies, fell ever backward under the onslaught of Hitler's panzers and defeat loomed ever closer. Men, women, and children, innocent of any complicity in their situation, wandering the highways and byways of Western Europe, were injured, horribly maimed, and killed by the thousand. It was a disaster of the first magnitude, and Europe would never be the same again.

The luggage and servants loaded aboard their convoy of cars, Edward and Wallis settled comfortably into the back of their Buick limousine, whilst the faithful Ladbroke chauffeured them down to their luxury home, La Croë, on the French Riviera. 'The smell of catastrophe was in the air,' Wallis wrote in her memoirs. 'It occurred to me that we were breasting a tide; all the traffic was headed in the direction we had left, towards the coast. We alone were pointed towards the Italian frontier.'

Settled once again into the comforts at La Croë, the staff were issued with their charcoal-grey Riviera uniforms, and only the small number of guests present could intimate anything was amiss with the world. Edward and Wallis reactivated a minimalist form of social life, although the ever diminishing procession of visiting acquaintances and only the occasional dinner party made it hard to keep the illusion going. The rest of humanity was consumed with the disaster that was unfolding – Western democracy was in its death throes, obliterated by the Teuton hoards of Herr Hitler, and the Riviera residents had other things on their mind than to pander to the ritual exercise in servile flattery that was ever an element of a visit to the Duke and Duchess of Windsor. Amongst those that did call at La Croë was their close neighbour Maurice Chevalier, and a visiting couple, Mr and Mrs Edmund Pendleton Rogers, who noted that despite the desperate situation and the horrors of war, the Duke was still keen to show his collection of Adolf Hitler photographs to anyone who expressed an interest. However, the majority of well-to-do on the Riviera, those who would under normal circumstances have called on the Windsors, looked uneasily over their shoulders at the posturing taking place over the frontier in Italy, and fled before Mussolini felt confident enough to order his forces to carve off a slice of France as well.

To be fair, Edward did attach himself to the French command ranged along the Italian frontier and visited the army head-quarters at Nice. Though whether this was at the Duke's own instigation is unknown, as is whether his trips to inspect parading troops actually benefited anyone, except in the accepted sense of morale boosting. But it was a little too late for that, and even the most obdurate French élitist could see that their beloved Third Republic was facing imminent obliteration.

Yet still Edward would not free himself of the intrigue that perpetually surrounded him – of the unsavoury characters that were always within easy reach throughout this whole period. Amongst the Windsors' neighbours at La Croë was an old acquaintance of the Duke's, a friend who had been in Austria during his exile of winter 1936 and early 1937 – Captain George Wood. Captain Wood was a curious man, and in many respects could easily have been formed by the same mould that had created Charles Bedaux, they even had similar looks, were extravagant, held some very strange views, and thus were attracted to the Duke of Windsor like a bee to a honey pot. Britain's civil servants were not quite so enamoured of Captain Wood, however, prompting someone known only as MS to write to Churchill's Private Secretary:

> I saw in the papers that a certain Captain George Wood – and his wife – have attached themselves to the Duke of Windsor's party. A nasty bit of work, if he is the man I am thinking of: lived for years in Vienna married to a Hungarian, daughter married a Hohenberg [Prince Ernst Hohenberg, son of the ill-fated Archduke Franz Ferdinand, whose assassination in 1914 at Sarajevo had ignited the First World War] last year, poses as a notch big-game shot, 'a white hunter' – very unEnglish au frond [sic], though exaggeratedly English in appearance and façon d'être. I should suspect him of holding utterly defeatist views, and being a bad influence.[1]

On 31 May Churchill flew to Paris to assess the crumbling situation for himself, intending to instil some confidence into the faltering French leadership, to see if there was anything more that could be done to halt the overwhelming tide of Germans flooding across France. Clearly, the French told him, we need better and increased air cover to have any hope of changing the situation – but that was something Churchill was no longer prepared to do. Britain's airforce had suffered a severe mauling at the hands of the Luftwaffe, and Churchill decided that it was now the time to look towards one's own survival, and what remained of the RAF must be held back for Britain's defence. Everywhere Churchill went he saw dejection and panic in men's eyes, but what impressed the situation most clearly upon him was the sight of staff at the French Foreign Ministry burning their papers and records on the Quai d'Orsay – the fear of imminent defeat lurked deep within these men's hearts. On his return from Paris, Churchill was disturbed and angered when he saw signs of the same crumbling confidence and erupting panic in Britain too. When he was asked if the nation's paintings should be dispatched with haste to Canada, he had retorted, 'No,' in his renowned growl. 'Bury them in caves. None must go. We are going to beat them.'

His confidence was a deep-seated belief in his own ability to strengthen men's hearts, and that the very force of his personality could turn the situation and change Britain's defeat into victory, but it would be a hard struggle, the outcome not assured, and the dangers far greater than they appear in hindsight.

On 4 June, Churchill gave one of his most rousing speeches, making use of rhetoric to galvanize the country into a force to be reckoned with, saying:

Even though large tracts of Europe have fallen under the grip of the Gestapo, and all the odious apparatus of Nazi rule, we shall not flag or fail. We shall go on to the end. We shall fight in France. We shall fight on the seas and oceans. We shall fight with growing confidence and growing strength in the air. We shall defend our island whatever the cost may be. We shall fight on the beaches. We shall fight on the landing grounds. We shall fight in the streets and fields. We shall fight in the hills. We shall never surrender. And even if, which I do not for a moment believe, this island, or a large part of it, were subjugated and starving, then our Empire beyond the oceans, armed and guarded by the British fleet, will carry on the struggle until in God's good time the New World with all its power and might sets forth to the rescue and the liberation of the old.[2]

It was a speech of intent not only aimed at the British population, clearly establishing for them his determination to eventually win through against the struggle ahead, but it was also a statement of determination aimed at the French government which teetered painfully between continuing the struggle or capitulating. If there was any doubt remaining to Hitler that Chamberlain's resignation had utterly deflected his plans (the tactic of Short-Sharp-Shock as advocated by de Ropp a mere nine months before) he now realized his well-laid plans risked being dashed into a million glittering shards. Churchill would never give up, ever. He would carry on the struggle to his dying breath, and his obsession to see the destruction of Nazism sounded the death-knell of Hitler's aims to quickly knock out the Allies before swinging eastward.

By this time Hitler had become desperate to disengage his forces from the conflict in the West, to end what risked becoming a protracted war with Britain, for there were now disturbing noises coming from the Soviet Union, and he clearly understood the danger from Stalin risked overtaking his own ability to manipulate events. Russia, having already occupied Lithuania, Latvia, and Estonia, now turned towards Romania, and that caused paramount concern to Hitler, for Romania was Germany's main source of oil. The previous August Ribbentrop had travelled to Moscow to sign the Russo-German Non-Aggression Pact with Molotov, and to Hitler's fury he now discovered that his foreign minister had been outwitted by the wily Russians. He was informed that despite prior assurances from the Russians that they would avoid a conflict with Romania over the Bessarabian region (which Russia claimed), Stalin was now resolved to use force to settle the problem. This bombshell was bad enough, but to Hitler's consternation he now learned that Stalin was also claiming the neighbouring region of Bukovina, a province that had never been Russian, had a high proportion of ethnic Germans in its population, and straddled the main supply route of Romanian oil to Germany. The turning of this region into a Russian sphere of influence thus threatened Germany's precious supply of fuels, and that could not be allowed. Without Romanian oil, Germany would grind to a halt.

Summoning Ribbentrop to brief him on the finer points of the Non-Aggression Pact, Hitler was dismayed to find that Ribbentrop had also been outfoxed by Molotov, for deep within the Secret Protocol of the Pact negotiated between the two Foreign Ministers was a direct reference to the Bessarabia region that concluded, 'The German party declares its total disinterest in these regions.' The reference was in the plural, thus clearly indicating that Germany could not intervene diplomatically in the occupation of Bukovina by Russia without resorting to force of arms. It was obvious to Hitler that Stalin had finely timed his action against Romania to coincide with Germany's heavy military commitments to a war in the West.

The need to prevent any form of stalemate or war of attrition developing between Britain and Germany now became of paramount importance to Hitler. Yes, he had won an incredible and resounding victory over the Allies; yes, Germany now occupied Belgium, Luxembourg, Holland and France; yes, luck, fortune, and what Hitler liked to call his 'destiny', had been on the German side, but now it was time to be gone – for a war that could not wait beckoned in the East. The gamble that he could quickly knock out the West, before having to return his forces to the East had paid off – almost – but only if he could now disentangle his armies from the Allies and return them to face the threat of Stalin and Russian Bolshevism. Something had to be done, and quickly. In the weeks ahead German efforts to cultivate a man whose ego knew no bounds would redouble.

On 16 June, General Vigon, Head of the Spanish Supreme Army Defence Council, an important man within Franco's new Junta Government in Spain, visited Hitler. During their conversation, Hitler informed General Vigon that the Duke of Windsor would shortly be travelling to Spain, and suggested to the Spaniard that Germany would have a substantial interest if the Spanish government could use its influence to have the Duke and his wife delayed long enough for contact to be established 'once more'.[3] Hitler, it would seem, had not only been kept abreast of the Duke of Windsor's movements, including where he and the Duchess were currently residing, but he also seemed to have access to better information regarding their future plans than the British government possessed, for the Duke had not yet made his plans to travel to Spain known to his own government. It is not known if Edward intentionally made provision to keep the Nazis informed of his future plans, but it does imply that the Windsors were surrounded by a hotbed of intrigue, and that anybody – from acquaintance, to maid, to gardener – could well have been an agent specifically placed to keep tabs on someone whom Hitler clearly regarded as a valuable asset, should he have need of him again. It must also be remembered that the Windsors rarely strayed far from their former acquaintances, and that nearly everyone to enter their lives came by reference or referral.

On 17 June the Duke's ADC, Major Gray Phillips, appeared at La Croë after what he readily described as a horrible journey lasting four days during which he had hitch-hiked, ridden in lorries, ambulances, and thumbed lifts on carts. The Duke's evident pleasure at the return of his comptroller turned to delight when Phillips delved deeply into his pocket to produce his master's beloved George II silver cruet set, which he had nurtured carefully all the way from Paris. The servants quickly produced a meal for him which he fell upon hungrily, eating and drinking whilst he informed the Duke and Duchess of the chaos and mayhem he had seen as he'd travelled southward.

On the same day as Gray Phillips arrived at La Croë, Paul Reynaud, the French Premier, utterly dejected and distraught at the fall of France, resigned, and his place was taken by the eighty-four-year-old Marshal Pétain, the hero of Verdun, who promptly initiated moves to sign an armistice with the attacking Germans. One of Reynaud's Cabinet supporters later commented, 'by what mystery and by what aberration the President of the Republic and the President of the Council, both hostile to the armistice, called to power the man whose first move they knew would be to ask for an armistice.'[4] The last nails were being hammered into the coffin of the Third Republic. Pétain would in short order appoint Pierre Laval (a long time acquaintance of both the Duke and Bedaux) to his government, and both men would ultimately be condemned to death after the war for collaboration. Charles Bedaux undoubtedly celebrated the news of Pétain's succession, for he had long been an acquaintance of the great man; indeed, in the late 1920s he had even suggested to Pétain that a fitting monument for his past services should be erected, and offered to pay for a great equestrian statue of the ancient French soldier out of his own pocket. J. Edgar Hoover was to write to Adolf Berle, the Assistant Secretary of State that:

> ... the French Cabinet in authority prior to the fall of France looked upon Bedaux as being very pro-German. This opinion

avowedly was based upon the active assistance rendered by
Bedaux to the German government, as well as his close association with the Duke and Duchess of Windsor.[5]

In the early years of the occupation, Bedaux would make
great use of his contacts at the very pinnacle of the Vichy
government. In Bedaux's eyes it was the opening overture of the
new world order – one he had worked long and hard to spawn.
An OSS report recorded that:

> Bedaux has not only been pro-Nazi and pro-Fascist since the
> collapse of France, but was very much so in his sentiments for
> a number of years before Munich. His pro-Nazi sentiments can
> perhaps best be described as those of a conscientious believer
> in Hitler's 'New Order' in Europe . . . France was only half-
> hearted in the acceptance of his labor plan, the United States
> labor leaders contested him, but in Germany he found fertile
> soil. The Germans . . . readily accepted his labor-saving systems,
> and when Hitler and his followers not only endorsed what he
> was doing but made him their personal friend, he was much
> more inclined to believe that Nazism was what the world
> needed.[6]

In the Duke's case there must have been a certain amount of
goodwill towards Laval as well, for he had known the man for a
good many years, had been involved with him during the failed
Hoare–Laval Pact, dined often with him throughout 1938 and
1939, and their thoughts on the future of Europe were not
dissimilar.

A certain amount of concern now began to mount back in
London, for no one quite knew what Edward would do next.
What were his intentions? Where would he go? Would he allow
himself to be 'captured' by the Germans? Would he suddenly
appear in a neutral country? Would his unfettered wanderings on

a continent aflame with war compromise Britain's struggle to survive? There was clearly an urgent desire to know his whereabouts, and Sir Alexander Hardinge sent coded memos to Bordeaux, Nice and Marseilles:

> Immediate.
> Please send me any information you have or can get from Consular Offices under your supervision regarding Duke of Windsor's whereabouts & do anything you can to facilitate his return to this country.[7]

The Duke and Duchess had remained at La Croë until 19 June, having been engaged in discussions with the Consul General at Nice, Hugh Dodds – Churchill's uncle by marriage. Dodds had had a difficult time persuading the Windsors that they could not remain at La Croë, where the Duke had evidently thought that he could stay, immune from the horrors of war, his Riviera home an island of peace in a sea of woe. Dodds later reported on his encounter with the Duke that:

> [The Duke of Windsor] was obviously reluctant to leave Antibes where he and the Duchess were in residence. I expressed the very definite opinion that he should leave France without delay, as with the rapid advance of German troops he might find himself cut off ... I suggested that he might take passage in one of the cargo ships that were coming into Cannes. This he positively refused to do. I then suggested that he should go through Spain and I offered to accompany him and facilitate his journey. He approved of this plan and promised to be ready to leave on the morning of 19 June.
>
> On my arrival at Antibes to accompany His Royal Highness, I received the impression that he was once again inclined to remain at his villa. Again I urged the necessity for departure and I promised to proceed him to Perpignan to prepare the way for him to cross the frontier.[8]

Having persuaded the Duke that it was impossible for him and the Duchess to remain at La Croë, isolated in a country about to be occupied, and perhaps finally comprehending that his and the Duchess' persons were not inviolable, that his hand would be strengthened by his continued independence and freedom of movement, Edward opted to up sticks and move to the safety of a neutral country. He rejected Dodds' suggestion that he and the Duchess should escape from the Riviera aboard a merchant ship bound for Gibraltar. This was not a welcome suggestion on two counts; firstly, the thought that he and Wallis should seek passage on a vessel little better than a coal boat was abhorrent, and, secondly, and more importantly, he did not want to go to this little colony where he would be placing himself firmly in the hands of the British establishment who could control his future actions and movement. That was not at all what he had in mind. Thus Spain was the obvious destination, knowing he would be welcomed and treated with the respect he and Wallis were due, and such a move would have the very real advantage of allowing him to visit and seek the council of Sir Sam Hoare on a face to face basis.

Loading up three vehicles, the Duke and Duchess headed the small convoy, driven by Ladbroke, followed by George Wood (now installed as the Duke's equerry) and his wife, Gray Phillips, and the Duchess' maid, with a small lorry bringing up the rear with the indispensable possessions and paraphernalia of royalty on the move. They had an uncomfortable journey, undergoing the same difficulties as the rest of humanity and the not insubstantial danger of air attack. At every town they encountered road blocks, to which the Duke called out: '*Je suis le Prince de Galles. Laissez-moi passer, s'il vous plait.*' The old touch of authority had not left him, and on each occasion the barricades were swiftly moved to allow the ducal convoy to pass. However, they still encountered the many frustrating problems of negotiating heavy traffic, dealt with the numerous delays, eventually managing to cross a Spanish frontier overwhelmed with a constant stream of refugees fleeing the fighting to the north.

Despite the concerns of the journey, the difficulties in crossing the Spanish frontier, the Duke also had to contend with the worries about what was going to happen to his possessions that he was leaving behind, and fretted constantly that *his* goods should remain inviolable to the effects of war. The more valuable items from La Croë had been taken and hidden in various cellars in the region, his possessions would be safe in the face of Italian conquest. As for his home in Paris, Edward need not have worried, for that was protected from looting, break-in or violation, by a certificate placed upon the front door that stated that the property was a possession of, and protected by the German Reich.[9] For much of the war Edward's Boulevard Suchet home would have German soldiers on sentry duty at its front door, and the only loss the Duke suffered was the theft of a pair of riding boots – which were miraculously returned several days later as they were so small in the foot, no one else could get into them.

The Duke and Duchess eventually arrived safely in a Madrid still pock-marked from the all too recent civil war. Everywhere there was noticeable poverty, not perceived poverty but real grinding poverty, with the Spanish citizens who queued for food literally wearing rags. The ducal convoy swept into the Plaza de la Lealtad, and the Windsors booked into a suite at the Madrid Ritz. They were entering the final phases of their extraordinary and unwholesome adventure, and the Duke's life would never be quite the same again, for although perceived by the general populace as the romantic of the century, the higher echelons of the British government knew the sum of the Duke's metal, and they did not like what they had found.

One might think that Hugh Dodds' efforts to place Edward out of reach of the invading fascist hands would be met with praise, but Churchill was not at all pleased by this development, for he would have sooner had the Windsors make the hazardous sea journey to the safety and security of British sovereignty at Gibraltar. Spain was an obvious destination for one trying to escape a war-torn France to the safety of a neutral state – except that Spain was very much more than just a neutral state.

Spain was ruled by a Fascist military junta headed by Generalissimo Francisco Franco, and he owed a great debt to Hitler and Mussolini for the support they had given him during the civil war. As such, Spain was a state much attuned to Nazi Germany's philosophy on the future of Europe, and Franco himself was not dissimilar to Benito Mussolini in his methods of rule. Hitler harboured great hopes that Spain would join the Axis powers and help create the new world order, except that, despite the debt he owed, the wily Franco resolutely kept his country out of the war. However, he did permit Spain to act as a major conduit for key materials to Germany over the next five years, supplying iron, mercury, coal, and incredibly, oil from the United States, shipped via the Canary Islands, through Spain, occupied France, and into the heartland of the Reich.

The other concern of the British government was that the Duke of Windsor had a great many friends and relatives amongst the aristocracy in Spain, particularly the Infante Alfonso, the second son of King Alfonso XIII, a General in the Spanish Air Force, and a man who had wholly embraced the new doctrines of his Generalissimo, Francisco Franco. Upon becoming King, Edward had granted Alfonso a five-year rent-free tenancy of one of the royal properties in Kew. That tenancy was now coming up for renewal, and Alfonso had high hopes that the exiled Duke still retained enough influence to perpetuate his rent-free status, so amongst many other things the two men had much to discuss and favours to swap.

These facts, known to the higher echelons of the British government, culminated to create the very real concern that if Edward became too settled – too comfortable – it might well prove near impossible to winkle him out of the luxuries and comfortable heat of Spain – a country that could well join the Axis at any moment. In the weeks ahead the Spanish junta would offer many inducements to Edward and Wallis, including rent-free use of a summer palace for the war's duration. It must have been very tempting to remain in a neutral country, near his royal relatives, respected and appreciated, Wallis addressed as 'Highness', amongst people whose politics he found himself in accord with. Edward seemed oblivious to the fact that Franco might feel sufficiently beholden to Hitler and Mussolini to do more than remain a friendly neutral. In fact the situation in Spain was so delicate that the new British Ambassador, Sir Samuel Hoare, had only been in his job a few days before nervously cabling Sir Archibald Sinclair, the Air Minister:

> I think I ought to bring this question to your urgent attention. It may well be that things go badly in Spain and that we have to leave at very short notice and in very difficult conditions. May I rely on you to send me out a machine to bring us back in these circumstances. We have to face facts in the world today and we can not exclude the possibilities of a coup organized by German gunmen . . .[10]

Yet beyond these good reasons why it disturbed the British government to think of their ex-king remaining at large in Europe, particularly in Spain, there was a far greater concern for Britain's leaders that the Duke should have opted to go to

Madrid – and that was the capability of German intelligence in that city.

Sir Sam Hoare had been in the embassy barely a week when, on 1 June, he submitted his 'Annual Report on Spain' (most of which had been written prior to his arrival) to the Foreign Office, that stated the British government should:

> ... withstand the persistent provocations of a German con-
> trolled press, a Gestapo run police, a miserably incompetent
> and corrupt regime in constant terror of the Germans ...[11]

Coming from Sir Sam Hoare this report was condemnation indeed, although it must be said that his actions were not indicative of a man who was pro-Fascist, rather a man who had failed to fully comprehend the dangers of Fascism, seeing it like many others in the 1930s as the bastion against Bolshevism. And now that Churchill had, perhaps with a caustic touch of malice, sent him to live in the midst of a Fascist country, Hoare was beginning at last to see the realities of what the future held for this particular brand of government. These sentiments, if they were coming to the fore, would not help him, however, for when confronted with his former King and Emperor, Hoare was little better than putty in the Duke's small but manipulative hands. On the day following Hoare's report to the Foreign Office, the Naval Attaché, Captain A.H. Hillgarth, reported to his new ambassador that he was extremely concerned at the level of morale in the Embassy, writing:

> ... in effect the Embassy your Excellency has come to com-
> mand is defeatist. This is not only patent in private conver-
> sation but is evident in the general interpretation of policy. As
> it is Spain with whom we have to deal and the Spanish
> viewpoint is very largely influenced by German and Italian

propaganda, our belief in ourselves, which must betray itself in our words and actions is of supreme importance . . .[12]

It is important to understand the level of German activity in Madrid at that time not only to comprehend the importance the Nazis placed in manipulating the embryonic Fascist Spanish state, but also to realize the level of British concern lest the Duke should throw himself willingly into their midst. In 1940 Madrid the German diplomatic presence was exceedingly impressive, for they had no small legation in this dusty outpost of south-west Europe, but a massive establishment in the centre of the city bedecked with all the imposing Teutonic art for which the Nazis would become renowned, complete with multiple swastika banners, two dozen embassy staff cars, and an outlandishly huge staff of 391 diplomatic personnel. The danger of this presence is amplified when it is understood that of these 391 people, only 171 were real diplomats, and the remaining 220 people were secret service personnel engaged in intelligence work, divided between the Abwehr on the one hand, and the Sicherheitsdienst – the SD – on the other. Both these agencies were morbidly jealous of each other, almost to the extent that one would have thought they worked for different powers, but then that was typical of the rivalry between these two intelligence organs of the Wehrmacht and the SS. By 1940 the Abwehr was firmly entrenched in Spain and complimenting themselves that they had the upper hand over the rival SD men. They were fortunate, for the Head of the Abwehr, Admiral Canaris, took a particular interest in Spain as he liked the country, spoke Spanish fluently, and found he could easily cultivate the help of his old friend General Campos Martinez – the Chief of the Spanish Secret Service.

It is therefore surprising and more than a little puzzling that

Sam Hoare was to suspend all operations and activity by British intelligence operatives working in Madrid as soon as the Duke and Duchess of Windsor arrived. The men of British Intelligence would remain inactive and unable to keep tabs on what was happening for exactly seven days – the length of the Duke's stay in Madrid.

What exactly happened during the course of the Windsors' month-long stay in the Iberian peninsular has always been the subject of much speculation, and to discern the truth about what happened is not easy as the majority of documents are still withheld and will stay State secrets until the year 2016. The remaining documents and information regarding what happened can, however, go a long way to indicate the direction that events took, during this time of the most delicate and secret negotiations.

The first thing that happened upon the Duke's arrival in Madrid was, as we have seen, that Sam Hoare immediately suspended all activities by Britain's intelligence services in that city. The implication was clear, the Duke would have no interference or impediment placed in his path – whatever he wanted to do. The Duke had been corresponding with Sam Hoare for some time prior to his arrival. Those letters have never been seen even by the British government, for until the end of his days Edward himself kept the secret correspondence from Sir Samuel Hoare, together with a dossier headed 'German Documents', the contents of which also can only be speculated on. Throughout the Second World War the Duke of Windsor kept those dossiers locked in his metal dispatch case, to which he had the only key, and after his wartime travels ended in 1945 with his return home to Paris, the Duke locked both dossiers securely away in his private safe.

On 22 June, Sam Hoare sent a cyphered message to London,

marked 'Limited Distribution' which stated: 'Duke of Windsor has telegraphed asking me to facilitate his passage across the frontier. I am doing so and propose to show His Royal Highness the usual courtesies.'

He then went on to add a curious second paragraph, which in view of what has been discovered about the Duke's activities and associates is rather explicit, if still prone to speculation: 'In view of press articles saying that it is intended to *arrest him on arrival in England* [author's italics], please confirm that I am acting correctly.'[13]

Hoare was clearly asking for guidance on what he should do, and requesting official confirmation or denial of the rumour that the Duke had done something of such enormity that it warranted his arrest. The reply to Hoare's request (Foreign Office document H/XLI/9) is closed to public scrutiny until 2016.

There now began a lengthy correspondence between Churchill and the Duke by cyphered telegram, and the messages that passed between them were most strange; Churchill, often gently chiding, behaved almost like a parent persuading a petulant child to come away from a cliff top; the Duke, ever evasive, finding reasons and excuses why he could not comply. Churchill, undoubtedly aware of the Duke's weakness and predilection for banner-waving Fascism, was anxious not to threaten his former king too much in case he tipped the scales and drove the petulant Duke into the arms of the all too welcoming Nazis. However, it is important to remember that Churchill had other things on his mind, too, like defending Britain against invasion by Germany, and at that time he didn't need the asinine complication of the Duke of Windsor. On 22 June Churchill sent the following message to the Duke: 'We should like Your Royal Highness to come home as soon as possible. Arrangement will be made through His Majesty's Ambassador at Madrid with whom you should communicate.'[14]

The following message, either a supplemental or a reply, is closed until 2016.

At some point over the next forty-eight hours, however, the Duke sent a private message to Churchill, possibly explaining his position, or perhaps sounding out his former staunch ally to determine what was likely to happen to him in view of the rumours about his impending arrest. Churchill did not reply and so Sam Hoare sent the following cyphered message: '*Following for Prime Minister from Ambassador*. Duke of Windsor is most anxious to have a reply to his personal wire before leaving here . . . I hope you can help him with a friendly answer as soon as possible.'[15]

Again, the reply is closed until 2016.

Late on the evening of 24 June, the Duke of Windsor sent another message to Churchill, intimating that he was not being offered the assurances or concessions he wanted, and he prevaricated over returning to the inevitable restrictions he would immediately encounter in Britain:

> Your message and facilities for returning greatly appreciated, but I ask you to consider the following seriously.
>
> My visits to England since the war have proved my presence there is an embarrassment to all concerned, myself included, and I cannot see how any post offered me there, even at this time, can alter this situation.[16]

Yet again Churchill limited his reply to: 'It will be better for Your Royal Highness to come to England as arranged, when everything can be considered.'[17]

The belligerent communications continued over the next twenty-four hours with a further four messages passing between the two men – all closed until 2016.[18]

In an effort to break the impasse, Sam Hoare intervened, sending:

IMMEDIATE.

> *Following for Prime Minister:*
> Impossible to persuade Duke to leave Madrid before Sunday
> and Lisbon before Wednesday. He insists there is no need for
> such haste unless there is some job for him in England or the
> Empire. I could not have put more strongly case for immediate
> departure but with no result.[19]

The Duke of Windsor supplemented Hoare's view by sending
to Churchill the following day: 'Regret that in view of your reply
to my last message I cannot agree to returning until everything
has been considered and I know the result.'[20]

Edward's 'negotiations' with his own government were, of
course, a device to avoid a return to Britain and the immediate
restrictions that would be placed upon his activities. It must also
be said that the Duke's past activity had taken him over the brink
of what was deemed acceptable, and it is not improbable to
speculate that he was by now too afraid to return to Britain under
the current circumstances. Eventually Sam Hoare, who became
extremely nervous as reports began to appear in the European
press declaring he and the Duke had been meeting with German
officials to arrange a negotiated peace, cabled Churchill:

> The Duke has been to see me again and has raised further
> questions about his status and financial position [Edward was
> still grousing over his lack of income from the civil list, despite
> the fact he was a millionaire and cash-strapped Britain now
> needed every penny to fight a war she couldn't afford] . . .
> I informed him that I would quote these views to you as he
> gave them to me but that I would not have anything to do with
> his personal finance. This must be settled when he is in
> England. As a result he agreed to drop the financial question. I
> have again told him that . . . he ought not to stop here; that his
> place is in England particularly as he is official[ly a] General,

and that when the world is crashing this is no time for bargaining.

Can you help me with a friendly message that will get him back to England? Could Monckton also help?[21]

However, nobody's patience is endless, particularly Winston Churchill's when trying to defend Britain against imminent invasion and defeat, and he finally threatened the Duke in guarded language, sending:

SECRET & PERSONAL

Your Royal Highness has taken active military rank and refusal to obey direct orders of competent military authority would create a serious situation. I hope it will not be necessary for such orders to be set. I most strongly urge immediate compliance with wishes of the government.[22]

It must have been a chastening experience for the Duke, for no one had ever dared give him a direct order before, let alone threaten him if he did not obey. What his actual reaction was on reading Churchill's message can only be guessed, but he must have realized full well that he was now playing a desperate endgame that could result in the ultimate of repercussions. The response to Churchill's cyphered cable is yet another of those held under the seventy-five year rule – withheld until 2016. However, whatever Churchill's cable said, it either frightened the Duke, or made him more determined, for Hoare followed up the message with a further emphatic: 'I do not believe that they will return to England without further assurances.'[23]

From the known facts about the Duke's actions throughout the winter of 1939 and spring of 1940 it would not be unreasonable to assume that the 'assurances' were some form of immunity – some wiping clean of the slate. In anyone else's cases there could have been little easing of the rules, little turning of a blind eye, but royalty still had an overawing effect in those dark days of 1940, and even if in the Duke of Windsor's case that reverence had begun to pale, who during Britain's most dangerous of times could face charging their former king with treason?

Despite the clear chronology of events that is documented in the messages that were flying through the ether between Madrid and London, there were other less seemly events taking place behind the scenes. The first was that during their week in Madrid, the Windsors ignored the protocol of being at war, and engaged the services of the Italian Chargé d'Affaires, Count Zuppo, to safeguard their beloved Riviera home La Croë. Count Zuppo was asked to contact the Windsors' old friend Count Ciano, Mussolini's Foreign Minister, and request that La Croë be placed under the protection of the Italian Government. La Croë would remain safe until the Windsors' return in 1945. In Paris, the Windsors' bank accounts in the Banque de France were scrupulously protected and not once looted by Carl Schaefer, the German Alien Property Custodian, whose job was to confiscate the assets of foreign nationals that had been left in France, despite ample opportunity during four years of occupation. Every other foreigner with accounts at the Banque de France lost their money – but not the Duke and Duchess of Windsor.

Incredibly and ludicrously, even Winston Churchill would become sucked into the Duke's schemes to protect his lifestyle and assets, now abandoned in occupied France, and he acted in breach of his own wartime Trading with the Enemy Laws. In the spring of 1941, at a time when every Briton was being told to tighten their belts, living under the austerity of tight rationing, and Britain was counting every penny, Churchill arranged to pay the Duke's rent for his Boulevard Suchet home out of government funds, as the following document makes clear:

> Mr Winston Churchill presents his compliments to His Excellency the United States Ambassador and, with reference to Mr Achilles letter of 1st March to Sir George Warner of the Foreign Office concerning the property in Paris of His Royal Highness the Duke of Windsor, has the honour to request that the United States Embassy in Paris may be asked to be so good as to make the following payments on behalf of the Duke of Windsor, from British funds at their disposal, the payments to be shown as separate items in their account with the Foreign Office:
>
> 1. Rent of 55,000 Francs for the current year, but not to continue the purchase option.
>   Renew the insurance, costing 10,000 Francs.
>   Pay back wages to Ferdinand Lolorrain at the rate of 2000 Francs monthly.
> 2. The Duke of Windsor would also be grateful if the United States Embassy could enquire the situation regarding his possessions in the Banque de France and pay 15,000 Francs for the current year's rent of his strong room there, which expired last November.[24]

The last major event that took place behind the scenes in Madrid that last week of June of 1940 was that Sam Hoare organized a grand reception for his former king. Whilst Britons were being told to be prepared to make the ultimate sacrifice, and misery abounded across a Europe where people were dying by the thousand, Sam Hoare began laying in the preparations of a super party – a grand reception staged at the British Embassy on Friday, 28 June. However, in Madrid poverty and starvation lurked just beneath the surface and food was scarce. Undaunted, the embassy hired a lorry to bring in bountiful produce and delicacies from neighbouring Portugal. On that Friday night, 28

June 1940, whilst France lived up to the reality that the Germans had taken the last French outpost on the Atlantic coast, that Hitler now ruled from Norway to the Spanish frontier, and Britain was beginning to come under nightly air raid, the Duke and Duchess of Windsor, bedecked in all their finery, were chauffeur driven from the Ritz in their Buick limousine to attend a grand reception for over 300 guests at the British Embassy, complete with hired caterers and musicians in the delightfully warm Spanish summer evening.

If ever the phrase 'to fiddle while Rome burned' applied, it was to this night.

A.W. Weddall, the American Ambassador to Spain, engaged the Duke in discussion during the reception. What the Duke told him he reported back to the State Department in Washington in a secret memorandum that said:

> In conversation last night, the Duke of Windsor declared that the most important thing now was to end the war before thousands more were killed or maimed to save the faces of a few politicians.
>
> With regard to the defeat of France ... the Duke stated that stories that the French troops would not fight were not true. They had fought magnificently, but the organization behind them was totally inadequate. In the past ten years Germany has totally reorganized the order of its society in preparation for this war. Countries which were unwilling to accept such a reorganization of society and concomitant sacrifices should direct their policies accordingly and thereby avoid dangerous adventures. He stated this applied not merely to Europe, but to the United States also.
>
> The Duchess put the same thing more directly by declaring that France had lost because it was internally diseased and that a country which was not in a condition to fight a war should never have declared war.[25]

It was a speech that could have been mouthed by Charles Bedaux at his most obdurate, and all it did was to substantiate the claim circulating in certain corners that the Duke and Duchess of Windsor were a hard-nosed pair, for whom only the wonders of a totalitarian state held any attraction – so long, of course, as they were at the top of the heap.

However, the Duchess did have one other thing on her mind, one she tackled Weddall about, and which became notoriously known as 'The Cleopatra Whim'. She asked Weddall to contact the American Consul in Nice, and request that he go to La Croë to recover her green swimsuit which she had forgotten to pack, and which she felt she would soon need. History does not record what the overworked US Consul in Nice made of the request.

Meanwhile, the ever efficient ant-heap that was Nazi Germany had been far from complacent or inactive during the Windsors' sojourn in Madrid, and neither had their SD's or Abwehr's actions been impinged upon, as had British activity by Hoare's shutting down of the intelligence operations during the Duke's visit. That the Duke, contrary to what was considered acceptable behaviour in a time of war, was in touch with the German authorities while his fellow countrymen fought to the death is without a doubt, for he had his own private business with which to attend.

The German Foreign Ministry Secretariat teletyped:

With reference to telegram No. 2140 of 29 June from Madrid, on the protection of the [Boulevard Suchet] residence of the Duke of Windsor. The Foreign Ministry requests first that [Otto] Abetz be instructed to undertake unofficial and confidentially an unobtrusive observation of the residence of the Duke. Secondly, Ambassador [to Madrid] von Stohrer is to be instructed to have the Duke informed confidentially through a

Spanish intermediary that the Foreign Ministry is looking out for its protection . . .[26]

This was followed up a few days later by a telegram from Stohrer back to Ribbentrop's Ministry:

Windsor told the [Spanish] Foreign Minister that he would return to England only if his wife were recognized as a member of the royal family and if he were appointed to a military or civilian position of influence. The fulfilment of these conditions was practically out of the question. He intended therefore to return to [Spain] . . . where the Spanish government has offered him the Palace of the Caliph at Ronda as a residence for an indefinite period. Windsor has expressed himself to the Foreign Minister and other acquaintances in strong terms against Churchill and against the war . . .[27]

Back at the British Embassy, Hoare drafted yet another telegram to be cyphered and sent to Churchill, saying:

I did my best in long conversation to persuade [the] Windsors to return immediately, but I found him completely rigid on the following lines. He says if he returns now he will probably not be able to leave England again during the war. This being so, his position must be regularized and he will not return unless it is . . . I hope he will leave for Lisbon on Sunday or Monday, and I have told him that I think it both dangerous and unsuitable for him to prolong his visit here.[28]

On 2 July, under extreme pressure from the British government, the full details of which will probably never be known, the Duke and Duchess of Windsor were at last pried out of their suite at the Madrid Ritz, to hit the road for Lisbon. Persistent negotiation and discussion had established that the safest course of action for the British government would be to banish the recalcitrant Duke to the far side of the Atlantic, and the position of Governor of the Bahamas. That the Windsors did not want to go, considered the Governorship an island imprisonment and quarantine for the duration is without a doubt, and Wallis took to calling the appointment the 'St Helena's of 1940', bringing with it the images of a defeated Napoleon Bonaparte banished to an island prison far from intrigue and any chance of escape. Once again assembled into a small convoy of vehicles, with loyal retainers about them and their lorry load of possessions bringing up the rear, the Duke and Duchess of Windsor travelled westward across the heat-blanched Spanish plains past Talavera, over the Sierra de San Pedro, and down into Portugal.

CHAPTER EIGHT

Negotiation

THIS LAST PHASE of the Duke of Windsor's adventure, his month of controversy in Lisbon, is the period of Edward's wartime activity that has been most widely covered and that which, until now, was the most difficult to understand. A large proportion of the difficulty has been in comprehending the motives behind the Duke of Windsor's behaviour and actions. This is because the Duke's dealings have been repeatedly examined and scrutinized through British eyes, yet if one were to look at what the Duke was doing from the German side of the fence, the events of July 1940 begin to make a great deal more sense. The Duke's demands to Churchill for clarification of his position, and the Windsors' enquiries into such trivial details as would their servants be requiring white uniforms in the Bahamas, were just a smokescreen – a blind for what else was happening – and the only effective result the Windsors' demands served was to delay their departure from Europe; which was exactly what they were intended to do. This then poses the question: why? Why was the Duke not keen to take up an appointment that would see him relaxing in Caribbean luxury and sunshine for the duration of the war? Well, that is quite simple. He viewed his own importance as too great to be wasted on a backwater appointment in the middle of nowhere, and he truly believed it was his right as the former British Head of State to get Britain out of the war, to come to some amicable agreement with Germany, allowing Hitler's armies to race off eastward.

On their arrival in Lisbon – a veritable nest of intrigue and activity by July 1940 – the Windsors were met by the British Ambassador, Sir Walford Selby, an old friend from their visits to Vienna. It was through Selby, Wallis later claimed, that the arrangement had been made for them to move into the large and exquisite but curiously named villa at Cascais, the Boca di Inferno – the Mouth of Hell. This beautiful seaside villa, finished in pink stucco and boasting a large swimming pool, was very private, yet it held one other major attraction to the recalcitrant Duke. It once more enabled Edward to throw himself headlong into the midst of intrigue, the company of the Nazi espionage system, and gave his enemies the opportunity to call him imprudent, fool-hardy, and irresponsible. However, contrary to popular myth, the Duke of Windsor was a far from stupid man, and he knew exactly what he was doing. At a time when Britain was fighting for her very survival, Edward, Duke of Windsor, moved into the home of a Portuguese banker named Dr Ricardo do Espirito Santo y Silva (known to British Intelligence as the 'Holy Ghost'), a man with strong German sympathies and who was a constant source of information and intelligence. One of the German cables from von Stohrer back to Ribbentrop reported, 'I immediately got in touch with our confidant the Duke's host, the banker Ricardo do Espirito Santo y Silva . . .'[1]

At the same time as the Duke and Duchess of Windsor moved into Boca di Inferno, Santo y Silva took on a Japanese butler by the name of Jikuro Suzaki to service the Windsors' needs within his home. However, Jikuro Suzaki was no mere innocent servant, for he had been recruited in the early 1930s by one Herr Kurt

Janke of the SD (a veteran spy who had been active since the First World War), further yet, Suzaki had in the past been employed by the SD to infiltrate the French administrative authorities in Morocco and obtain their secrets. Immediately prior to his appointment at Boca di Inferno and the Windsors' company, Suzaki had been active in Lisbon obtaining the confidential dispatches from the Portuguese envoys in London and Washington, and forwarding them to Berlin via Erich Schroeder, the SS Police attaché at the German Embassy.

The Windsor's move into Boca di Inferno set the tone for their next month in Portugal, yet again placing them within easy access of German communication, and enabling the Duke to engage in his last exercise in 'back-room negotiations' before his Bahamas banishment to an island quarantine for the duration.

Lisbon in the summer of 1940 was a stark contrast to dusty Madrid. Where Madrid was damaged, squalid, heat-blanched, and rife with poverty, Lisbon was vibrant, lush, beautiful, cooled by the Atlantic, and restless with activity. From the moment the German war-machine had started to move the previous September, Europeans of all nationalities had been flooding to the safety of Portugal to take refuge whilst the war lasted. As a result, the Portuguese language was corrupted by a multitude of foreign tongues, English, French, German, Hebrew, Dutch, and Belgian. All these people crammed into Lisbon's hotels, boarding-houses, and private homes, all trying to eke out an existence whilst surviving on their savings, and all clamouring to flee across the Atlantic to America. It was a precarious existence where the pawn shops did a rampant trade, and the value of furs, jewels, and family heirlooms plummeted as the market became saturated, with the price of common goods – meat, vegetables and fruit – spiralling upward. Fortunes were made and lost within the confines of Lisbon's city walls, and dozens committed suicide every week, driven by despair and the prospect of starvation when their money ran out.

Meanwhile, nestled into the luxury of Boca di Inferno fifteen miles to the north of Lisbon, the Duke of Windsor had work to do and a future to plan.

Barely a week after the Windsors' arrival in Lisbon, von Stohrer sent a confidential telegram to his Foreign Ministry reporting that Colonel Juan Beigbeder y Atienza, the Spanish Foreign Minister:

> ... told me today that the Duke of Windsor had asked that a confidential agent be sent to Lisbon to whom he might give a communication for the Foreign Minister [Ribbentrop]. The [Spanish] Foreign Minister will immediately fullfill this request.
>
> The [Spanish] Foreign Minister also told me, as [Ramone Serrano Suner] the Minister of Interior had done a few days ago, that right up until the end of his stay here [in Madrid], Windsor was still holding to the decision reported in my telegram No. 2182 [to consider taking up the offer of the Palace of the Caliph at Ronda], and had reiterated his intention to return to Spain.'[2]

Ramone Serrano Suner, the Spanish Minister of the Interior, was a curious individual described by Hoare as 'deliberately ill-mannered, spitefully feminine, small-minded, fanatical, impetuous, and not yet forty with snow-white hair'. However, Suner had one other special attribute that endeared him to the Duke of Windsor – he was the brother-in-law of Generalissimo Franco, and therefore had direct access and the ear of the dictator of fascist Spain. It was to be a character trait that ran throughout the Duke's life, be it dealing with Britain, Germany, or even Spain: he had been brought up to use what the British establish-

ment commonly termed the 'old-boy network', and it was a habit
he fell into time and time again, especially at this most sensitive
of times when confidentiality and a word in the right ear could
make the difference between failure or success.

Suner assured Stohrer that he would get his brother-in-law
Generalissimo Franco 'in on the plot', and would send an
emissary to the Duke in Lisbon – the Duke's long-time friend
Miguel Primo de Rivera, the district leader of the Falange (Spain's
Fascist Party) in Madrid. The Duke's friendship with Rivera was
close and their association had been refreshed only a few days
earlier when the Falange leader had been one of the 300 guests
invited to the Madrid Embassy reception for the Windsors.
Despite Churchill's failed efforts to have the documents destroyed
at the end of the war, the finer details of Rivera's mission were
set down for posterity by Stohrer when he wrote to Ribbentrop:

> The emissary will request the Duke, with the Duchess, to return
> to Spain for a short time 'before his departure for the Bahamas'
> since ... [Suner] would like to discuss with him certain
> questions regarding Spanish–English relations and to give him
> important information affecting the person of the Duke ...
> [Suner] will inform the Duke of a thoroughly reliable report
> (communicated to me in your telegraphic instructions)
> received by the Spanish Security Service concerning the threat
> to the life of the Duke. [Suner] will then add an invitation to
> the Duke and Duchess to accept Spanish hospitality, and
> financial assistance as well.[3]

This most curious of messages refers to a threat to the Duke
not from the Germans, but from the British, for Ribbentrop had
been concerned to inform Stohrer a few days before that:

> A report had reached us today from a Swiss informant who has
> for many years had close connections with the English Secret

Service to the effect that it is the plan of the English Secret Service, by sending him to the Bahamas, to get him into English power in order to do away with him at the first opportunity.

At any rate, at a suitable occasion in Spain the Duke must be informed that Germany wants peace with the English people, that the Churchill clique stands in the way of it, and that it would be a good thing if the Duke would hold himself in readiness for further developments. Germany is determined to force England to peace by every means of power and upon this happening would be prepared to accommodate any desire expressed by the Duke, especially with a view to the assumption of the English throne by the Duke and Duchess. If the Duke should have other plans [Ribbentrop had continued] and be prepared to cooperate in the establishment of good relations between Germany and England, we would likewise be prepared to assure him and his wife of a subsistence which would permit him, either as a private citizen or in some other position, to lead a life suitable to a king.[4]

Not surprisingly, the report that Ribbentrop was referring to is one of those listed as 'Not Found', and any claims since that time that all this was a dastardly plot by the Germans to discredit the British government and/or Edward, must be tempered by the thought that Germany had no concept in 1940 that they would lose the war five years later, and therefore these documents were *never* intended for publication anyway. Indeed, the entire affair only came to light after the war ended in 1945, when it certainly could not assist the Germans in any way.

Could such a plan to 'do away with' the Duke of Windsor have existed?

Because of his intransigent and outspoken attitudes, encouraging enemy belief that he was a serious alternative to the existing government, he could easily have become a focus for defeatism and collaboration in the mould of Pétain ... Had he been anyone but a key member of the royal family, it is unimaginable that his loose talk and seditious behaviour would have been tolerated.[5]

However, as Britain's former king and elder brother of the reigning monarch, there was very little that could be done whilst he was at liberty on the European continent to restrain or censure his comments without playing into German hands, and freely supplying Germany's propaganda minister, Goebbels, with a vast scoop that would cause considerable harm in Britain, the Dominions, and Churchill's efforts to obtain aid from the United States.

If he would not quickly go to the Bahamas, where he could do comparatively little harm, doing away with him may have indeed been a real and only alternative. He certainly could not be allowed to go on making traitorous remarks, for in the event of invasion his role might have become critical. British files on this aspect are not available; some never will be. Nevertheless, it is worth considering that in 1945, Polish General Sikorsky was shot down over the Mediterranean after leaving Gibraltar in an act which has persistently been attributed to Churchill, and equally persistently denied.[6]

It is also pertinent to note that at this time the Portuguese government ordered their Customs Service to search and disarm any British Secret Service personnel entering their country. The intimations that the Duke could be placed in danger by Britain is understood when it is known that Windsor himself was not beyond making statements that threatened Britain directly. Hoynigen von Huene reported in a 'Strictly Confidential' memo to Ribbentrop that:

The Duke intends to postpone his departure for the Bahama Islands as long as possible, at least until the beginning of

August, in hope of a turn of events favourable to him. He is convinced that if he had remained on the throne war would have been avoided, and he characterizes himself as a firm supporter of a peaceful arrangement with Germany.

Huene concluded his memo with the devastating revalation that the Duke of Windsor 'definitely believes that continued severe bombing would make England ready for peace.'[7]

This last line of Huene's memo cannot be construed in any form other than the Duke of Windsor expressing an opinion, and it is clearly the Duke's view that if Britain would not yet come to terms, another turn of the screw should be applied until his former subjects yielded. The significance of his remark was not lost upon the Germans, particularly Hitler who still desperately wanted his forces disentangled from the West. Hitler's attitude was noted by Count Ciano, who recorded that the German Führer 'is rather inclined to continue the struggle and unleash a storm of wrath and steel upon the British. But the final decision has not been reached, and it is for this reason that he is delaying.'[8]

The German offers being made to Windsor at this time, via the emissary, would have been most tempting to almost anyone – to be credited in history as the person who stopped a devastating European war between Germany and Britain – never mind to someone like the Duke who saw himself as a potential head of the Peace Movement, as well as Britain's rightful Head of State, ousted from his position by manipulation and treachery. To any normal person it would have of course been obvious that the Germans were engaged in the strategy of divide-and-conquer on a grand scale, but it must be remembered that the Duke had a very large ego indeed. He was no commoner; he was one born to be king and he thought on a grand scale, thus his concept of what was acceptable to achieve his end result knew no bounds.

These tentative feelers, put out by Ribbentrop to the Duke via de Rivera undoubtedly touched their mark, for the Duke once again threw himself body and soul into the 'salvation' of Britain – one that would find Britain its rightful place in the new world order, where she would look towards her empire and colonies, and not stand in the way of Germany's position as bastion against the Red menace to the East.

On 16 July, Stohrer sent another telegram to Ribbentrop, informing him that the Duke had sent a message through de Rivera to Beigbeder to say that:

> His designation as Governor of the Bahamas was made known to him in a cool and categorical letter from Churchill with the instruction that he should leave for his post immediately without fail. Churchill threatened him with arraignment before a court martial in case he did not accept the post.

Stohrer went on to inform Ribbentrop that Beigbeder had asked the Spanish Ambassador to Portugal 'to warn the Duke most urgently against taking up the post'.[9]

A week later de Rivera undertook another trip from Madrid to Lisbon and back again, solely to visit the Duke and Duchess. Stohrer was able to report to Ribbentrop that:

> The Duke expressed himself very freely. In Portugal he felt almost like a prisoner. He was surrounded by agents, etc. Politically he was more and more distant from the King and the present English government. The Duke and Duchess have less fear of the King who was quite foolish [reichich toricht], than of the shrewd Queen who was intriguing against the Duke . . .
>
> The Duke was considering making a public statement and thereby disavowing present English policy and breaking with his brother.[10]

It is clear from the cable traffic at this time that a consider-able amount of effort was being ploughed into the Duke by the German and Spanish governments to persuade him to take the *right* decision, i.e. to break with George VI, Churchill, and the British government, withdraw to the luxury of a palace in Spain, and await the time when he would play an important part in European politics in the near future. That he did not, is not only down to the fact that he was still undecided as to the best course of action, that if he *did* throw in his lot with the Germans he would be committed for ever, but also that the Duke of Windsor was now coming under pressure from the British government as well.

Despite the precautions of the Germans and the Duke, it did not escape British attention what was going on in Lisbon, for whilst Churchill probably did not know the full intricate details, he had an advantage that the Germans were unaware of, and that was called Ultra, based at Bletchley Park. Ultra, one of the best kept secrets of the Second World War, was quietly and methodi-cally using the captured German Enigma technology to decode all the German diplomatic signals flowing between Germany, Madrid and Lisbon, and Churchill was undoubtedly kept fully abreast of the Duke's finagling with the Nazis. In 1981 Freddy Winterbotham (who by spring 1940 had been moved to Bletch-ley) was asked if Ultra had been listening and decoding the German signals about the Duke of Windsor. 'He confirmed that they had indeed intercepted the signals, but, he claimed, never knew what was in them because they were immediately seized by MI5, Britain's internal espionage service.'[11]

If MI5 had the signals, then Churchill knew in July 1940 of the Duke's flirtation and dealings with the Nazis, and that reinforces the 'do away with him' idea. It would also explain why after the war British Intelligence launched themselves on a 'search and destroy' mission of German documents – hence all the 'Not

Found' or 'Missing' cables. 'American sources confirm that, in the wake of their armies, hordes of British Intelligence men descended like locusts on all the German records they could find.'[12] A curious postscript to this scenario is that in 1945, despite the desperate need for Britain to continue to lead the world in code-breaking at Bletchley Park, Winston Churchill crippled Britain's ability to break intelligence codes by personally ordering that every last scrap of the whole etablishment be destroyed. For days the wartime staff of Bletchley Park marched back and forth with every last record, intercepted code, ticker-tape, book, reference, machine, and piece of paperwork, and burned the lot to ashes. The world's first computer – capable of decoding a message by multiple thousand computations per minute – was smashed to bits by sledgehammer and buried. It was State-sponsored vandalism on a grand scale that set back Britain's ability to decode Soviet and Eastern Bloc messages for a decade. And all in the name of what? Nobody will ever know, except that it cannot be a coincidence that this was the very time Churchill was moving heaven and earth to have the captured German records on the Duke of Windsor destroyed. It is therefore not too great a leap of the imagination to deduce this wanton act of destruction originated from the same seed – the need to protect and keep for ever secret the wartime activities of the Duke of Windsor.

On 19 July, Hitler made another attempt at peace with Britain, for now his urgency to disengage his forces from the West had become a desperation to take his armies eastward against Russia. He had sworn himself before the German people never to engage Germany in a two-front war again, yet here he was tied to a war he did not want with Britain. Before an assembled gathering at the Reichstag, Hitler delivered a speech, which though sprinkled with a smattering of insults aimed at Churchill, was modest in tone, craftily phrased to placate Europe's neutrals, and designed to instil appeasing thoughts into the British public. The Reichstag erupted into thunderous applause when he finished, and he left confident that he had opened the way to a coming of terms with Britain.

An hour later the BBC broadcast a swiftly compiled response that avowedly declared a clear and resounding 'No' to the Führer's advances. Furious, Hitler decided to use his own means to assure peace, and, calling in Ribbentrop in accord with the SD, he set in motion a scheme to undermine Churchill and the British government, and use the Duke of Windsor once again in an effort to stop this unwanted war with Britain.

On the morning of 20 July, SS-Brigadeführer, General Walter Schellenberg (the man who had dined with Hitler at the Chancellery in November), a high-ranking officer in the SD, was summoned to Ribbentrop's office in the Foreign Ministry. Schellenberg was no back-room bruiser of the sort normally seen within the higher echelons of the SS, but an educated man who was valued within the SD. He was a meteor within the SS, and at thirty years of age with a degree in law and political science, his high rank was a sign of that value. He was therefore educated, intelligent, and Ribbentrop was well aware of Schellenberg's connections in Spain and Portugal through the Auslandsnachrichtendienst (the SS Secret Service Abroad – of which he would become Head in 1941) that made him a natural for the mission ahead. Before going over to the Foreign Ministry to see Ribbentrop, Schellenberg telephoned his Commanding Officer, and Head of the SD, to tell him of the summons.

'I see,' Reinhard Heydrich had replied coldly, 'the gentleman no longer wishes to consult me – old idiot! Well, go over there and give him my best regards.' Aware of Heydrich's pathological jealousy, Schellenberg assured his boss of a full report of the encounter upon his return.

On Schellenberg's arrival at the Foreign Ministry, he and Ribbentrop had exchanged brief cordialities before the Foreign Minister had quickly got to the point:

'You remember the Duke of Windsor, of course?' he asked Schellenberg suddenly. 'Were you introduced to him during his last visit?'

After Schellenberg replied that he had not met the Windsors during their tour of 1937, Ribbentrop had plunged on asking, 'Have you any material on him?'

'I cannot say at the moment,' Schellenberg had replied.

'Well, what do you think of him personally?' Ribbentrop had persisted. 'How do you evaluate him as a political figure, for instance?'

Schellenberg confessed that he was not sufficiently aware of the subject, but commented that he thought the British had handled the abdication situation sensibly.

> My dear Schellenberg [Ribbentrop interjected], you have a completely wrong view of these things – also of the real reason behind the Duke's abdication. The Führer and I already recognized the facts of the situation in 1936. The crux of the matter is that, since his abdication, the Duke has been under strict surveillance by the British Secret Service.[13]

During the course of the next hour, Ribbentrop gave Schellenberg a detailed briefing on the operation he was to conduct in Spain and Portugal, and if one looks closely at what was said, it does not support the British government's insistence that it was all a dastardly kidnap plot. Schellenberg listened intently as Ribbentrop told him:

> We know what his [Edward's] feelings are ... and we know from our reports that he still entertains sympathetic feelings towards Germany, and that given the right circumstances he

wouldn't be averse to escaping from his present environment
... We've had word that he has even spoken about living in
Spain and that if he did go there he's ready to be friends with
Germany ... The Führer thinks this attitude is extremely
important, and that you ... might be the most suitable person
to make some sort of exploratory contact with the Duke – as
representative, of course, of the Head of the German State. The
Führer feels that if the atmosphere seems propitious you might
make the Duke some material offer if he were ready to make
some official gesture dissociating himself from the manoeuvres
of the British royal family. The Führer would, of course, prefer
him to live in Switzerland, though any other neutral country
would do ...

If the British Secret Service should try to frustrate the Duke
in some such arrangement, then the Führer orders that you are
to circumvent the British plans, even at the risk of your life,
and, if need be, by the use of force. Whatever happens, the
Duke of Windsor must be brought safely to *the country of his
choice* ... It will also be your responsibility to make sure at the
same time that the Duke and his wife are not exposed to any
personal danger.[14]

If one looks at Ribbentrop's statement, it is hard to believe
that the Germans intended to kidnap the Duke for their own
devious and Machiavellian purposes. Additionally, if the Duke
had been threatened by the Germans, it would certainly not have
prevented him making a hue and cry to the British government,
the Portuguese government, the British Secret Service, the Portuguese police, and the world's press. But did he? No he did not.
And the documentary evidence supports that fact.

Whatever else the activity in Lisbon in July 1940 was, it was
certainly *not* kidnap. What emerges from Schellenberg's brief is
that, 'Hitler had decided to send in the SD to *aid* the Duke to get
out of Portugal and away from the security of the British to a
country of his choice. The force which Schellenberg was being

told he must be prepared to use is to be directed against anyone trying to stop getting the Windsors out, not against the Windsors.'[15]

At the end of Schellenberg's briefing, Ribbentrop took up the telephone, asked his switchboard to connect him with the Führer, and handed Schellenberg the earpiece to listen into the conversation. When Hitler answered, Ribbentrop reported on his briefing to Schellenberg, who listened as the German Führer interjected, 'Yes – certainly – agreed.' Then Hitler added: 'Schellenberg should particularly bear in mind the importance of the Duchess's attitude and try as hard as possible to get her support. She has great influence over the Duke.'

'Very well, then,' Ribbentrop replied. 'Schellenberg will fly by special plane to Madrid as quickly as possible.'

'Good. He has all the authorization he needs,' the Führer added, before concluding, 'Tell him from me that I am relying on him.'[16]

When the German documents relating to this episode were eventually cleared for publication in 1956, as 'Documents German Foreign Policy, Series D, Volume X', after Britain's repeated blocking tactics used in America until the documents' release could be stalled no longer, the British Foreign Office took the extraordinary step of issuing a statement expressly to denigrate the German documents as a 'tainted source', and to insist that the Duke of Windsor had always been loyal to Britain's cause:

Statement to be made by Her Majesty's Government on Publication of Volume X of the German Documents

Certain papers in Series D, Volume X of the documents of the German Ministry of Foreign Affairs, published under the joint auspices of Her Majesty's Government, the French Government and the Government of the United States of America, show that in the summer of 1940 the Germans were engaged in various schemes to exploit the Duke of Windsor, then temporarily resident in Portugal. The Duke was subjected to heavy pressure from many quarters in Europe, where the Germans hoped that he would exert his influence against the policy of His Majesty's Government. His Royal Highness never wavered in his loyalty to the British cause or in his determination to take up his official post as Governor of the Bahamas on the date agreed. The German records are necessarily a much tainted source. The only firm evidence which they provide is of what the Germans were trying to do in this matter, and of how completely they failed to do it.

What must be thrown into this unwholesome brew is the realization that the vast majority of damaging documents that referred to the Duke of Windsor had already been comprehensively looted from Germany, firstly by Blunt and Morshead in 1945 for George VI, then by agents of British Intelligence, the 'Marburg File' had been destroyed, and yet publication of the remaining scraps of German diplomatic communication was still enough to cause paranoia and concern in Whitehall, Downing Street, and Buckingham Palace. However, minimal as these scraps are they can be supported by a much more comprehensive, and far more illuminating source – Schellenberg's intelligence reports, and they tell an entirely diffent story from what the British establishment would proffer as the 'truth'.

As soon as Schellenberg left Ribbentrop's office, he swiftly went to report on the meeting to Heydrich, at the SS Headquarters office on Prinz Albrecht Strasse.

'Well,' Heydrich had asked, 'and how did you get on with our old idiot gentleman?'

After hearing Schellenberg's report, Heydrich had given his subordinate a brief lecture on the way that Ribbentrop always wanted 'to use our people when he gets an idea like this'. He continued, 'You are really much too valuable to me to waste on this affair. I don't like the whole plan. Still, once the Führer gets hold of such a notion it's very difficult to talk him out of it, and Ribbentrop is the worst possible adviser . . .' A few minutes later the interview finished and Schellenberg left, glad to be out from under Heydrich's 'reptilian gaze', remembering someone had once said of his SS boss that, 'Two people are looking at me simultaneously.' Yet despite his curious and disturbing personality, it must be remembered that Heydrich was a genius in the art of deception, and his fertile mind was far from inactive.

Before the week was out, he would make his presence felt in Portugal.

On Thursday, 25 July, Schellenberg flew to Madrid aboard a Junkers 52 of the Transport Flight, flying firstly to Bourges where it landed at 1.30 p.m. to refuel, before continuing onto Spain and landing at Madrid at 6 p.m. The pilots of the JU52 were all special couriers for the Secret Service and known to Schellenberg, who frequently visited Spain for his job within the SD, and so the whole experience was not new to him. After landing Schellenberg was driven into Madrid, and on to the Germany Embassy for a meeting with the Ambassador, von Stohrer.

Stohrer had been far from idle in the previous few days, and forty-eight hours prior to Schellenberg's arrival had reported that:

The Duke and Duchess were extremely interested in the secret communication which the Minister of the Interior [Suner]

272

promised to make to the Duke ... The Duke and Duchess said they very much desired to return to Spain and expressed thanks for the offer of hospitality. The Duke's fear that in Spain he would be treated as a prisoner was dispelled by the confidential emissary, who in response to an enquiry declared that the Spanish government would certainly agree to permit the Duke and Duchess to take up their residence in southern Spain (which the Duke seemed to prefer), in Granada or Malaga, etc.

The Duke said that some time previously he had surrendered his passports to the English Legation with a request that Spanish and French visas be secured (for a possible personal visit to his Paris residence).

This, of course, despite the fact that Paris and most of France was under German occupation, and that French territory and airfields were being used to launch air-raids upon Britain. Not surprisingly, Stohrer revealed that the Duke's request to journey back to occupied Paris had not been smiled upon by Britain and:

The English Legation was clearly unwilling [to help]. In these circumstances he [the Duke] asked the Spanish Minister of the Interior, who is unusually interested and active in this case ... [to] at once send another confidential emissary to Lisbon in order not to attract [British] attention by again sending the first emissary, who is well known. This new confidential emissary is to persuade the Duke to leave Lisbon as if for a long excursion in an automobile and then to cross the border at a place which has been arranged.[17]

These do not seem to be the actions and statements of a man under threat of forcible removal from his country for an enforced comfortable residency in sunny Spain, indeed, Stohrer supplemented his message a mere twenty-four hours later reporting to Ribbentrop:

273

The new confidential emissary ... will take to the Duke of Windsor a detailed letter from the first confidential emissary. In this letter the first confidential emissary says that he has not yet heard what the important message which [Suner] ... wants to give the Duke, but he has the impression that it has to do with a warning of the great danger which threatens the Duke and Duchess. In the letter the Duke is further urged to go with the Duchess to a well-known resort in the mountains near the Spanish frontier, and from there make excursions which will bring him suddenly to a certain place on the frontier where by accident one of the secretaries of [Suner] ... together with the first emissary will meet him 'by chance', and invite the Duke and Duchess for a short visit at an estate near the frontier on the Spanish side ...[18]

Before the full plot to assist the Duke and Duchess of Windsor to flee across the frontier into Spain is further examined, however, it is important to look at the other side of the coin – at what else was taking place at this time, for the Duke had been far from reticent and unobtrusive in his activities or his opinions. On 20 July, the Windsors had put on a dinner party at Boca di Inferno, to which they invited the American Ambassador to Portugal, Herbert Claiborne Pell, in addition to a member of the British Embassy, David Eccles. Over the course of dinner the Duke and Duchess made no secret of their feelings for Britain, or Churchill's war effort, causing Claiborne Pell to immediately report back to Cordell Hull in Washington that:

The Duke and Duchess of Windsor are indiscreet and outspoken against the British government. Consider their presence in United States might be disturbing and confusing. They say that they intend remaining in the United States whether Churchill likes it or not and desire apparently to make propanganda for peace ...

An account of this unwholesome conversation eventually made its way back to London, and caused much consternation among the men in Whitehall who read it. Clearly, it declared in guarded language the Duke and Duchess of Windsor would make publicity in America for Britain to come to terms and capitulate before Hitler's forces. The prospect of the pair making such statements in a country whose aid was vital if Britain were to survive could not be tolerated, and the very thought of such an eventuality sent shudders through the men in power. Churchill drafted a telegram to be sent to President Roosevelt enumerating his concerns about the Duke, and explained the Bahamas appointment by saying:

> The activities of the Duke of Windsor on the Continent in recent months have been causing H[is] M[ajesty] and myself grave uneasiness as his inclinations are well-known to be pro-Nazi and he may become a centre of intrigue. We regard it as a real danger that he should move freely on the continent ...

Before sending the cable, Churchill experienced a pang of unease at exposing Britain's dirty washing to the Americans, and he scrubbed out the sentence mentioning the Duke's pro-Nazi sympathies, changing it to state that though 'his loyalties are unimpeachable, there is always a backwash of Nazi intrigue which seeks to make trouble about him'.[19] Despite this change, the implications of what Churchill now felt for his former king were no longer hidden in the shadows. Mindful of what the Duke of Windsor had already accomplished in France, Churchill undoubtedly now saw the Duke as a very real complication to his efforts to ensure Britain's survival.

In the meantime, the Duke of Windsor evidently decided to keep his options open despite his fears of British intent towards him, and mindful of the attractive advances being made to him by the Fascist states of Germany and Spain. On 4 July he appeared to relent before Churchill's threats of dire consequences, court martials, or possibly worse (for the majority of Churchill's telegrams are still under censor), and telegraphed Churchill from Lisbon saying:

> I will accept appointment as governor of Bahamas, as I am sure you have done your best for me in a difficult situation. I am sending Major Phillips to England tomorrow, and will appreciate your receiving him personally to explain some details.[20]

However, on 22 July, Ribbentrop received a memorandum from a secret contact in London which clearly stated that the Duke of Windsor had sent a confidential message to his brother, George VI, urging him to sack Churchill and the current coalition Cabinet, and replace it with a new pro-Hitler Cabinet that would be more amenable to end the war. The memo stated that this stance was being supported and urged upon George VI by Lloyd George. This memo by the agent in London was corroborated by a report Ribbentrop received from his ambassador to Ireland, who confided that:

> Such a revised cabinet would be prepared to make immediate peace with Germany. Among those who would be willing to make such a peace were Lord Halifax, Sir John Simon and Sir Samuel Hoare.[21]

In Italy on the same day, the newspaper *Gazetta del Popolo* printed a story claiming that the Duke of Windsor wanted a new Fascist government in Britain, with Lloyd George appointed as prime minister.[22] Quite how these claims came to be made is not at all clear, for too many of the telegrams, memos, and communications are listed as 'Not Found', 'Lost', or still 'Withheld'.

However, there are clues that point to the direction of the Duke's activities.

Espirito Santo, owner of Boca di Inferno, later confided that he had invited the German Ambassador Hoynigen-Huene to meet the Duke. Worse still, in the midst of a war in which Britain was being pummelled to destruction by the German Luftwaffe, Edward, Duke of Windsor, actually returned the courtesy, visiting Huene in his own home, and like Bedaux before him had the misfortune of being spotted when he least expected it.

In 1940 Hoynigen-Huene lived in the Sacramento a Lapa region of Lisbon, and it was here that the Duke was seen by a Briton living nearby, Mrs Judith Symington, who recalled:

> I was driving home one day when I caught sight of a man in the car in front. I thought I recognized him. Isn't that the Duke of Windsor? I asked, nudging my husband. The car stopped some distance from the German residence, and sure enough, it was he who got out. He was wearing a navy suit, and he walked along the street, up the steps and into the house. Obviously he didn't want to be seen. It wasn't the only occasion, either, that I spotted him going to see Hoynigen-Huene.[23]

David Eccles later recalled that the Duke of Windsor 'spent his days intriguing. We wanted to get him out. We knew once we had him on the other side of the Atlantic, we could watch him.'

It is evident then, that if the Duke could be spotted so easily cavorting with Britain's enemy, that the German cyphered messages were being intercepted by Bletchley Park and decyphered by Ultra, then Churchill *must* have known what the Duke was doing, must have realized the very real danger he posed. However, all this activity was not merely about whether the Duke and Duchess would flee to the security of Spain for the duration, possibly to become a puppet manipulated by Hitler's machinations, for a much more sinister chain of events was to take place during that last week of July 1940. A frantic race against the clock had been started by none other than Schellenberg's boss, the arch genius of deception, Reinhard Heydrich. He had arrived in Lisbon by special plane, but his arrival was merely the prelude to the arrival of a much more important person.

Throughout the latter part of July, Schellenberg had been sending special telexes back to Berlin, some of them clearly intended for Hitler himself for they were typed on a machine nicknamed the 'Führer-type', with a specially enlarged typeface that enabled Hitler to read the communications without having to put his glasses on. During this time Schellenberg's messages became most interesting for they repeatedly referred to people under their code names.

Now, to understand these messages and what they mean, it is firstly important to know *who* the code names referred to, particularly two gentlemen known as 'Willi' and 'C'.

'Willi' we have already met, for he is the Duke of Windsor. This can be clearly established not only by the Walbach document of 4 April that declared: 'Z[ech] B[urkesroda] accidentally referred to B[edaux's] source as Willi', but also from the Schellenberg messages that refer to meetings between 'Willi' and Rivera, reference to Wallis as 'Willi's wife', and lastly the message that Willi left on *Excalibur* – the liner used the day the Duke departed Lisbon bound for the Bahamas.

'C', on the other hand, can clearly be established as Heydrich, for within the SD Heydrich was known under that code letter because of his fascination in times past with the British Secret Service – the Head of which is always known as 'C'. Within the SD, everyone knew that 'C' was Heydrich, and there are numerous examples in the SD archives of 'C has ordered' such and such, or 'The decision concerned C personally...' There was even a special rubber stamp made that directed documents to Heydrich which said: 'SUBMIT TO C'.[24]

There are two other major characters mentioned in Schellenberg's memos, a man called 'Winzer', and a mysterious figure code-named 'Viktor'. 'Winzer' was in fact Paul Winzer, the SS Police Attaché to the German Embassy in Madrid, known as a Kriminalkommisar whose job was to oversee embassy security and to keep tabs on the embassy staff and diplomats; a task which unsurprisingly did not endear him to his fellow embassy workers. 'Viktor' on the other hand was an altogether much more important person, and for that reason his identity will take a little explaining, but only after first examining some of Schellenberg's memos.

Armed with the knowledge of whom some of the coded persons were, it is possible to look at the Schellenberg confidential memos back to Berlin in a much more informed light. On Friday, 26 July Schellenberg reported:

> 'C[Heydrich] in complete agreement, declares himself able to guarantee security for Willi. Consultation with von Huene. Heineke and Bocker [two of Schellenberg's men] leave Madrid by car at 15.30 hrs. Badajos by 22.00 hrs. They stay overnight there.[25]

On Saturday the 27th, Schellenberg sent:

> Depart Badajos 08.30 hrs to arrive Lisbon at 15.00 hrs. [Paul] Winzer arrives in Lisbon at 19.00 hrs. Detailed discussion with C[Heydrich] about security, etc, for Willi. Telegram to Madrid with the request to forward it to Berlin . . .[26]

Then, on Sunday the 28th, Schellenberg reported that:

> Viktor is expected. Telegram to Madrid; 11.00 hrs to Berlin. Two possibilities were described and guidance was requested.

Discussion with C[Heydrich] and [Paul] Winzer. Viktor was with Willi. The latter asked for 48 hours time to think it over.[27]

Sunday, 28 July 1940 was to become the climax of the Duke's intrigues with Germany and the Nazis. It was a watershed date, for never again would the Duke be quite so embroiled in behind-the-scenes dealing with Britain's enemy. Not since the Napoleonic Wars had Britain faced a threat of the magnitude that it did that long hot summer of 1940, when Britain's very survival hung precariously in the balance. Yet on that quiet Sunday morning in Lisbon, Edward, Duke of Windsor, engaged in discussions with Britain's most dangerous of enemies – an enemy that could have paved the way to Britain's defeat – for he met with 'Viktor'.

The identity of 'Viktor' needs to be clearly established to assertain the importance of the Duke's discussions, for Schellenberg reported 'Victor was with Willi', and that 'Willi' – the Duke – needed forty-eight hours to think over whatever had been discussed.

A clue to who 'Viktor' was comes from Schellenberg himself, who on the 28th sent another message back to Germany, this time addressed to someone known as 'A.H.', which said:

> Just a note to keep you informed. Our friend Tomo met with C and Willi this morning. Seven point plan was discussed in detail. Meeting again on 29.7 . . .[28]

A.H. was not as one might suppose *Adolf Hitler*, but rather a very close friend of 'Viktor' – a man named *Albrecht Haushoffer*. Albrecht Haushoffer was the son of Professor-General Karl Haushoffer, an expert in Geopolitics based in Munich. After the end of the First World War Professor-General Karl Haushoffer had taught many of the men who would become the bright lights, so to speak, of the new Germany. Amongst these bright lights was a certain Rudolf Hess, who had fought with valour through the First World War, and in the early 1920s had returned to Munich to take up his studies under the esteemed Professor Haushoffer.

Despite the apparent eccentricities of Hess's flight to Britain in 1941, the ruination of his reputation at the Nuremberg Trials, during which he was virtually written-off as deranged, Rudolf Hess was no mental lightweight, no mean political mover, and had been the very man to coin the phrase 'Führer'. Hess had been a brilliant student, and his education under Haushoffer was to earn him considerable respect and influence in foreign policy decisions of the new Reich under Hitler. Haushoffer was to become a great influence in Hess's life, a mentor if you like, and he became firm friends with the old Professor's son, one Albrecht Haushoffer.

By the latter half of the 1930s, Albrecht's close association with Hess (by now Deputy-Führer), in conjunction with his own eminence as an expert on foreign affairs and Geopolitics, resulted in his being sent on various missions to Prague on behalf of the Reich in 1936 and 1937. The two Haushoffers, son and father, corresponded regularly, and by virtue of their high-brow existence and caution when corresponding in Hitler's Germany, they invented a code of their own when referring to men of importance. Basing their code on Japanese, of which the intelligent Albrecht was an expert, their code took the following form: Adolf Hitler, they named 'Master Great Spirit' translated as O'Daijin; with evident humour at Ribbentrop's posturing, they termed him, 'I will not deviate', translated as Fukon; and Hess became 'Friend' known as Tomodaichi – shortened in their correspondance to Tomo.[29]

So where then did the code name 'Viktor' come from?

One of Hess's pleasures in life was to fly himself in his own plane, and Freddy Winterbotham commented that Hess, who he knew well, 'was a good pilot and used to fly his own aeroplane about Germany...' The plane that Hess flew all over Germany was his new 'toy', a Messerschmitt 110 fighter-bomber with the registration number VJ-OQ. And Hess's call sign? Obvious really ... 'V' for 'Viktor'.

We therefore have an equation: 'V' for 'Viktor' is Hess in the air; 'Tomo' is also Hess to the Haushoffers. Schellenberg's memos: 'Viktor is expected' is Hess flying to Lisbon; 'Viktor is with Willi' on the morning of the 28th – communicated to Hitler, followed by 'Tomo met with C and Willi this morning' – communicated to Albrecht Haushoffer.

And where did they meet? Well, probably far from prying eyes at the Sacramento a Lapa home of Hoynigen-Huene, only 'Willi' – the Duke – was seen by Judith Symington, arriving for the meeting dressed in his proverbial best-blue Sunday-suit.

To understand why Rudolf Hess flew all the way to the south-western extremity of Europe to meet the Duke of Windsor on the morning of Sunday, 28 July 1940, it is first necessary to understand Hess's importance in German foreign affairs, for he was not merely the saturnine Deputy-Führer who followed his Führer about and stood with folded arms glaring at Hitler's audiences – the common image of him. Hess was one of Hitler's closest confidants, and beyond the symbolic title of being Deputy-Führer, Rudolf Hess was very important in matters of foreign affairs. Early within the formation of Hitler's new Nazi state, Rudolf Hess had been the man who decided that the SD was to become the Nazi's own counter-intelligence service, a Party organ directly under the wing of the Nazi Party. He was therefore in on the very inception of the SD. In addition it should be remembered that on Hitler taking power in 1933, there had been three services created within the Nazi Party structure to look after the interests of Germans abroad: the Foreign Organization (Auslandsorganisation), the Foreign Political Office (Aussenpolitisches Amt), and the Committee for Germanism Abroad (Veiein für das Deutschtum im Ausland), known as the VDA. However, these three organs, each with a responsibility for German interests abroad, could not help but step on one another's toes, and so the whole set-up was very inefficient. In 1936 Hitler ordered Hess to reorganize the whole structure, which Hess did by bringing all three organizations under the umbrella of one body – the Volkdeutsche Mittelstelle (the Office for Germans by Origin Resident Abroad), commonly known as the VOMI.

During the very earliest years after its creation, the VOMI had been ineffectual under a variety of inefficient chiefs until Hess decided that a stronger personality was needed to instil some discipline and efficiency into the new organization, and he therefore put it under the auspices of Himmler's SS. Not very long after, VOMI became absorbed into the SS, and the SD (a branch of the SS) utilized the VOMI's connections in foreign countries to increase its intelligence network. This was epecially fortuitous for Schellenberg, for he was able to use the VOMI's extensive network in Spain and Portugal, where it was particularly active, to give him a ready-made intelligence system. 'This also consolidated the link with Hess who technically was still the overseer of VOMI, and it can be seen that Portugal brought together all the essential elements of Hess's special "empire" – VOMI, the SD, and Schellenberg's connections.'[30]

The Duke of Windsor had met Hess on his visit to Germany in 1937. At that time the Duke had attended several receptions at which Hess had been present, indeed, the Duke had even been to Rudolf Hess's home where the two men had mysteriously descended into the privacy of Hess's wine cellar for a discreet discussion. Hess was therefore well known to the Duke (Wallis described him as 'charming of manner and good-looking'), and was undoubtedly the highest-ranking Nazi that could, firstly, surreptitiously travel beyond the Reich's borders without attracting too much attention, and secondly, that the Duke could be given access to a man he already knew, a man he knew had Hitler's ear, and a man he knew had the eminence and power to issue orders and take decisions on his own authority.

The last element of Hess's connection to the Duke of Windsor, why Hess was in Portugal at all, was his association with A.H. – Albrecht Haushoffer. On the Nazis coming to power in 1933, Rudolf Hess had put his old friend Haushoffer in touch with Ribbentrop, and Haushoffer duly became an adviser to the Dienstelle Ribbentrop, which was also a Nazi government branch under Hess's office. Haushoffer was extremely pleased with his new job, which he saw as serving a more important and influential role in foreign affairs than if he had joined the Foreign Ministry, and he became increasingly involved in surreptitious foreign relations deals. Hitler encouraged Hess and Ribbentrop to develop these alternative diplomatic manoeuvres and to recruit specialists like Haushoffer, who could determine and advance Nazi Foreign Policy. In 1936 Haushoffer was sent on Hitler's orders to contact the Czechs for secret talks, but he was 'strictly forbidden to have any contact with the German diplomatic mission in Czechoslovakia and with the German Foreign Minister, von Neurath.'[31] By 1936 Hitler had therefore taken to using his own foreign affairs experts to bypass his own Foreign Ministry, just as he would in 1940 Portugal. Therefore, from these two examples we have a good idea of the extent to which Hess was the power behind the façade of VOMI, operating on an independant and surreptitious level for Adolf Hitler.

However, Czechoslovakia and central Europe aside, it was with regard to Britain and British policy that Haushoffer's contributions must be considered as of the utmost importance. Throughout the 1930s, Haushoffer had repeatedly visited Britain and after 1934 he was a constant source of data and reports on

Britain, often being consulted for background material prior to any diplomatic exchanges or visits by eminent politicians. In April 1935, Haushoffer wrote for the *Zeitschrift für Geopolitik* a 'Report from the Atlantic World', in which he had been at pains to stress that Germany should exist in a state of peaceful co-existence with Britain and that, 'The final decision on the fate of Europe – as was the case at the turn of the century – is in the hands of Britain . . .'

Rudolf Hess, then, was no eccentric, nor was he the ineffectual Nazi marionette that has been characterized over the years since the war; he was an important, though discreet, leading Nazi in the mould of his successor Martin Bormann. He was an efficient politician, an organizer, a specialist on foreign policy, who knew all the important secrets of the Reich, and had within his grasp access to key decisions on foreign policy, the SD, and the VOMI. This then was 'Viktor' – the man with whom 'Willi' met that quiet Sunday morning in Lisbon.

A clue to what the two men discussed during their meeting can be found in the words 'Seven Point Plan'. It is unlikely that Germany was merely offering the Duke sanctuary in Franco's Spain. Could the Seven Point Plan have been a peace plan negotiated by the Duke in an effort to present the British government with a fait accompli? There are several indicators that show this could have been what the Duke did. One such indication can be discerned from Hess's personal view of the war situation that was developing in the West. Barely a month before his flight to Portugal, on the morning of 24 June 1940, Hess had visited his doctor, Dr Kersten. During the course of his treatment, Hess and Kersten had discussed the war, and Kersten recorded for posterity in his dairy that Hess told him:

> We'll make a peace with England in the same way as with France. Only a few weeks back the Führer again spoke of the

great value of the British Empire in the world order. Germany and France must stand together with England against the enemy of Bolshevism. That is why the Führer allowed the British army to escape at Dunkirk. The English must see that and seize their chance. I can't imagine that cool, calculating England will run her neck into the Soviet noose instead of saving it by coming to an understanding with us.[32]

Additionally, on that Sunday, 28 July 1940, Schellenberg's report indicates that discussions took place between Hess and the Duke, whilst Heydrich was with Winzer, thus the two chief negotiators were together while the two senior policemen watched over the security arrangements. At the end of the meeting, the Duke asked for forty-eight hours to think over whatever had been proposed to him. Whatever had been suggested to the Duke it was beyond his power to give an immediate decision, but it is known that Germany was anxious for Britain to pull out of the war, so did the proposition to the Duke allude to this? Hess/ 'Viktor' does not appear in the cables again and evidently he left immediately after the meeting with the Duke, leaving Heydrich and Schellenberg to await the answer.

Later the same day as the meeting, Schellenberg reported that the Duke and Duchess had suddenly decided to move out of Santo y Silva's villa, and into the Hotel Avis in the centre of Lisbon. If this snap decision was taken in response to the Duke's meeting with 'Viktor', then it surely indicates that the Duke suddenly began to feel that he was getting in too deep, even for him. There are clearly two stances that can be taken with reference to the Duke's meeting with 'Viktor'; the first is that 'Viktor' offered, or pressured the Duke into fleeing to Spain, and that finally, after many months of finagling with the Nazis, the actual thought that he would have to irrevocably declare his colours for all the world to see was simply a step too far for the

Duke. If he came out into the open for everyone to see, and fled to Fascist Spain, there would be no going back. It had been quite a different matter to use Bedaux, to remain hidden behind the scenes, and hope that the short-sharp-shock on the battlefields of France would force Britain to come to reasonable terms with Germany and cause the downfall of an irresponsible government that had all too readily declared war on Germany, and also cause the dislodgement of his brother who had supported that government. And yet the Duke could now clearly see that Churchill had no intention whatsoever of coming to terms.

On first hearing of the Windsors' decision to move out of Santo y Silva's Cascais home, Schellenberg immediately arranged for a Portuguese contact to warn the Duke that the Hotel Avis was the centre of British Secret Service activity, and of the 'hostile intentions of the Churchill Government'. The warning had the desired effect, the Duke and Duchess's resolve to be suddenly gone from Cascais wilted, and they decided to remain in Santo y Silva's home a few days more. Schellenberg also reported that the Duke told him that he was expecting the 'pre-arranged arrival of a friendly English minister', and it is certainly possible that he was coming to give the Duke advice on what he should do next – not about the Bahamas appointment, for that is not secret enough for the British documents on the matter to still be closed to public scrutiny. It is therefore not impossible that the Duke of Windsor was being advised on something else – perhaps the Seven Point Plan?

Walter Monckton flew out to Lisbon aboard a flying boat from Poole in Dorset, and stayed for a week with the Windsors at Boca di Inferno. That Monckton felt uncomfortable in his surroundings is without a doubt, commenting after the event that he had felt almost guilty at the sense of liberation in carefree neutral Portugal, where the lights blazed all over Lisbon every night, when compared to blacked-out London. The carefree evenings with the Windsors' evening parties felt most unnatural, the men in white dinner jackets and women *en grande tenue* seemed to belong to a bygone era – the pre-war days of the year before, which seemed a distant memory. However, there were other worries for Monckton, and he later recorded:

> I got very worried by an effort made by the Falangists, no doubt under Axis influence. The Marques de Estella, a son of the old Dictator, Primo de Rivera, flew over from Madrid to persuade the Duke not to go to the Bahamas on the grounds that he had information of a plot by the British government to have him killed there . . .[33]

By July of 1940 Walter Monckton had been made Minister for Information, and in such dire times of war, with Germany threatening to cross the English Channel and invade, it is highly unlikely that Monckton would have been sent all the way to Portugal merely to persuade Edward to discard the rumoured threats to his safety and to depart for the Bahamas. Even Frances Donaldson, author of the renowned *Edward VIII*, who is usually generous to the Duke, queries this, writing:

> All the same, one cannot help wondering if it is true that Monckton was ignorant of everything that was going on except the attempt to persuade the Windsors that they were threatened by the British, because, if so, the Duke withheld a good deal of information from him. [She added in a footnote:] Monckton also withheld a good deal. His notes on the abdication and its aftermath purport to be an account kept at the time for the benefit, it seems reasonable to assume, of future historians. But they regularly stop short of the more interesting facts and it is quite impossible to believe that in July 1940 a member of the government was sent to Lisbon either as a courtesy to the Duke of Windsor or with no particular reason beyond a general desire to speed him on his way.[34]

Donaldson was right. Monckton had been sent there on a much more important mission. The indications are that Winston Churchill knew exactly what the Duke had been up to, for as Winterbotham made clear, Ultra's deciphered messages were being taken by MI5. Churchill therefore learned of the 'Seven Point Plan' via Ultra, or it is even possible that the Duke informed him, convinced as he was that he was doing the right thing, and that once presented with a fait accompli there was every likelihood that Churchill would have no choice but to fall into line.

German Intelligence noted Monckton's arrival in Portugal, and Schellenberg immediately reported: 'Today there arrived at the Duke's as announced the English Minister who calls himself Sir Walter Turner Monckton, a lawyer from Kent.' Santo y Silva, the Duke's host, had promptly called Schellenberg to let him know of Monckton's arrival, but insisted the man was a 'confidential agent'. Schellenberg agreed with Santo that '. . . a cover name is involved. It is possible that it concerns a member of the personal police of the reigning King by the name of Camerone'.[35] It was unlike Schellenberg to make a mistake, especially since he had talked with 'C' and 'Willi' that day 'concerning report to Berlin'. He also reported that 'Willi does not want to go [to the Bahamas]'.[36] Since Schellenberg met with 'Willi' that day, and Windsor had helpfully told him that an 'English Minister' was coming, it also does not seem likely that he would have confused the name Monckton with 'Camerone'. This then poses the question whether there was another man with Monckton, someone who may well have been an agent, or perhaps a representative of the security services or the Foreign Office?

Monckton's official assignment was to counter the German and Spanish influence by persuading the Duke that he was in no danger from the British, and that he should now depart for his appointment as Governor of the Bahamas. However, Monckton failed to persuade the Duke he would be safe and quickly recognized that German interest and influence had rather more effect on the Duke than British.

> The Marques de Estella [Primo de Rivera, the Spanish Falange leader] ... flew in from Madrid to persuade the Duke not to go to the Bahamas on the ground that he had information of a plot by the British government to have him killed there.
>   It sounds fantastic [Monckton wrote], but he [de Rivera] managed to impress the Duke and Duchess.[37]

Unfortunately, Monckton was not one to record everything for posterity, and his published reports were only half facts, as was attested to by Frances Donaldson. The strange truth is that this man who sought to weaken Spanish influence over the Duke had at least one lengthy discussion with de Rivera, and it is known that to allay the Duke's fears of an untimely end Monckton had to 'secure by telegram the attendance of a detective from Scotland Yard to accompany them and look after them.'[38]

It is likely he was in the background to other talks as well, for the Duke was still meeting with German representatives. On Monday, 29 July Schellenberg recorded in his log:

> Discussion with C [Heydrich] and Willi concerning reports to Berlin. Willi does not want to go [to Bahamas]. Madrid transmits at midday the report which von Stohrer gave to Berlin.[39]

Then, on Tuesday, 30 July, Schellenberg recorded:

> Winzer travels back to Madrid at 08.00 hrs. At 16.00 hrs telegram to Berlin via Madrid about the two remaining possibilities, since it has been established without doubt that Willi will co-operate ...[40]

However, by then Monckton had managed to ensure the Duke of Windsor's compliance with Churchill's wish for him to sail on the *Excalibur* on Thursday by promising his safety and by providing a second policeman. Nevertheless, both sides seemed satisfied and began to disperse. Winzer, the SS Police Attaché, left for Madrid on Tuesday, and as he had accompanied 'Viktor' to Lisbon, it is reasonable to assume they left together once their task was done. Certainly the intrigue was nearly over.

Undoubtedly, part of Monckton's task had been to convince the Duke that though beaten on French soil Britain might have been, she was far from finished, and that if the Duke entertained ideas of a triumphal return as Britain's saviour, it was not likely to happen without a life and death struggle, for Churchill had no intention of throwing in the towel yet. Too many documents and records are withheld, or just plain lost to be able to gauge fully what was happening, or what indeed Monckton told his former king to dissuade him from openly coming out on the German side.

During his remaining hours in Portugal the Duke pondered his next move. He walked in the garden at Boca di Inferno, chainsmoking, he wandered deep in thought on the beach frontage of the villa. De Rivera called in every day to visit the Duke, obviously attempting to pursuade him to take the right decision. De Rivera called in the day after Monckton arrived and had another lengthy private conversation with the distressed Duke, who told de Rivera that he had not yet made up his mind. However, he had been deeply disturbed by the reports of British intrigue and no longer felt secure, declaring that he could not move a step without surveillance. Nevertheless, de Rivera was pleased to hear that the Duke had not given up the idea of being an intermediary between Hitler and the British government, and he reported that:

The Duke indicate[d] that he has ... given consideration to the possibility that the role of an intermediary might fall to him. He declared the situation in England at the moment is still by no means hopeless, therefore he could not act now by negotiations carried on contrary to the orders of the English government, and let loose against himself the propaganda of his English opponents, which might deprive him of all the prestige at the period when he might possibly take action. He could, if the occasion arose, take action even from the Bahamas.[41]

When this report reached Ribbentrop, the German Foreign Minister quickly sent a long message back to Hoynigen-Heuene in Lisbon, with instructions to contact Santo y Silva immediately and to talk confidentially with the Duke before his departure for the Bahamas. He was to tell him that:

Basically Germany wants peace with the English people. The Churchill clique stands in the way of this peace. Following the rejection of the Führer's last appeal to reason Germany is now determined to force England to make peace by every means of power. It would be a good thing if the Duke were to keep himself prepared to co-operate with them for further developments. In such case Germany would be willing to co-operate most closely with the Duke and to clear the way for any desire expressed by the Duke and Duchess ...[42]

After their meeting, Santo y Silva reported back that:

The message conveyed to the Duke made the deepest impression on him, and he felt appreciative of the considerate way in which his personal interests were being taken into account ... The Duke paid tribute to the Führer's desire for peace, which was in complete agreement with his own point of view. He was firmly convinced that if he had been king it would never have come to war. However, he requested that it be understood that at the present time ... disobedience [to British government instructions] would disclose his intentions prematurely, bring about a scandal, and deprive him of his prestige in England. He was convinced that the present moment was too early for him to come forward, since there was as yet no inclination in England for an approach to Germany. However, as soon as the frame of mind changed, he would be ready to return immediately. To bring this about there were two possibilities. Either England would call upon him, which he considered to be entirely possible, or Germany would express the desire to negotiate with him ... He would remain in continuing communication with his host [Santo y Silva] and had agreed with him upon a code word, upon receiving which he would immediately come back over. He insisted that this would be possible at any time, since he had foreseen all eventualities and had already initiated the necessary arrangements. The statements of the Duke were, as the confidant stressed, supported by firmness of will and the deepest desire, and included an expression of admiration and sympathy for the Führer.[43]

Evidently the Duke clearly expected a swift change in Britain, perhaps as a result of the Seven Point Plan he had negotiated with Hess. During those last days and hours in Lisbon, Santo y Silva kept almost constant company with the Duke, urging him to accede to the Seven Point Plan, persuading him not to leave, but to remain in Portugal or Spain and hold himself ready to swing into action as Britain's saviour who had negotiated peace.

Edward, Duke of Windsor, former British monarch, finally departed from Europe on 1 August 1940, eleven months to the day since Hitler's forces rolled over the Polish frontier and started the Second World War. He left in the certain belief that his departure was only a convenient interlude, for on 15 August, as soon as he arrived in the Bahamas, Hoynigen-Heuene cabled Berlin:

> The confidant [Santo y Silva] has just received a telegram from the Duke of Windsor from Bermuda asking him to send a communication as soon as action is advisable. Should any answer be made?[44]

The entry in Series D Volume X of the Documents on German Foreign Policy merely states: 'No answer to this telegram from Lisbon has been found.'

Walter Monckton had succeeded in persuading the Duke of Windsor to leave for the Bahamas probably only after assuring him that serious consideration would be given to the proposals contained in the Seven Point Plan. The Duke had therefore gone believing that as a result of the negotiations initiated by himself, a peace formula would be agreed, and his standing as leader material would be reinforced. Though he might have lost his throne, in Britain's darkest hour the Duke of Windsor was determined to project his personality, show that it was his *will* that would determine peace and save Britain from disaster. The 'Churchill clique', would have been discredited, together with the monarch who had supported the policy, and Edward's *dignitas* would be raised to such a level that the British people would have demanded the return of 'Edward the Peacemaker'.

The fact that he alone had caused the disaster that was the Battle for France would be conveniently forgotten – kept forever secret, which indeed it has been up to now.

The Windsors' future adventures in the Bahamas aside, and despite the continued concern that the Duke was pro-Nazi (even resulting in J. Edgar Hoover preventing their dry-cleaning being sent to New York, for fear that the ducal couple might hide secret messages in the lining of the Duke's suits), there were yet two more curious episodes to be played out in this royal saga of 1940.

On 13 September, during a day-time air-raid on London, a lone Messerschmitt 110 fighter-bomber broke formation and dived on Trafalgar Square, passing low over Admiralty Arch. To the amazement of those watching, it thundered along the Mall at nearly 250 miles per hour almost brushing the tree tops, the turbulence from its passing causing leaves to cascade in its wake. At the other end of the Mall, King George VI and Queen Elizabeth stood in one of the sitting rooms at Buckingham Palace together with Sir Alexander Hardinge, watching the raid from a window. They apparently saw the Messerschmitt as it rushed toward them, together with a fleeting recall of seeing objects drop from it as it roared overhead. The objects – bombs – dropped all around them; two exploded in the Quadrangle, thirty yards from where they stood, a third detonated in the chapel killing a workman, and two others landed harmlessly in the grounds. The last, number six, struck the Palace but with the fortunes of war that often go hand in hand with such well-planned attacks, it failed to explode – probably saving the lives of the royal couple.

Whilst George VI was badly shaken by the attack, history records that Queen Elizabeth is said to have commented: 'I'm glad we've been bombed. It makes me feel I can look the East End in the face.' Whether Elizabeth spontaneously said this, or whether it was attributed to her in a public relations exercise will probably never be known, what is known however, is that George VI was convinced that the attack against Buckingham Palace was directed against him personally. His opinions were further reinforced by the suspicion that the pilot 'had local knowledge', and that the attacker was a relation. This belief was reinforced by the knowledge that British Intelligence informed him that his brother, the Duke of Windsor, had been engaged in lengthy and detailed private discussions when he was in Spain during June –

talking to his cousin the Infante Alfonso, a General in the Spanish Air Force.[45] It was rumoured that the attack was part of the Nazis' continuing plans to assist the Duke of Windsor back into power, perhaps, if all else failed, as Regent. After the war it turned out that the navigator of the Messerschmidt 110 was Prince Christopher of Hesse, well acquainted with both Buckingham Palace *and* the Duke of Windsor, and by a strange coincidence, brother to Prince Phillip of Hesse, to whose home George VI sent Anthony Blunt to recover with urgency any royal correspondance that could cause a royal loss of face.

The final incident to be played out in this royal drama occured a little over a month later, at the Château de Candé. On returning from the Spanish frontier after a meeting with Generalissimo Franco, Adolf Hitler, accompanied by Hermann Göring and Joachim von Ribbentrop, interrupted his journey home to stop at a small French town called Montoire. Here, on the afternoon of 24 October 1940, Hitler met an old acquaintance of Bedaux's – Marshal Pétain, now French Head of State and ruler of Vichy France (who, incidentally, Bedaux had been to see the previous week, when he had travelled to Vichy for a confidential meeting with the French leader).[44] After the brief meeting, Hitler, Göring, and Ribbentrop journeyed the thirty-three miles to Bedaux's Château de Candé, where they were to be entertained to dinner. A previously undisclosed OSS document reveals that on arriving, the prestigious guests went into the Candé library, where:

> One of the first things they did was to stand before the portraits of the Duke and Duchess of Windsor and salute them in Nazi fashion.[46]

Silent homage to the man who gave them France.

Epilogue

AFTER THE DUKE of Windsor's banishment to the far side of the Atlantic, his partner in perfidy, Charles Bedaux, was appointed as an economic adviser and production expert within the Greater Reich, as well as being given a staff of one hundred German clerks, a set of offices on the Champs-Elysées, and charged with the responsibility of liquidating Jewish businesses in France. He was thus extremely busy in newly occupied France for the next two years. However, Bedaux's luck only lasted until the autumn of 1942, when he found himself trapped on the wrong side of the Allied lines in North Africa after the successful execution of Operation Torch. On the night of 7 November 1942, Charles Bedaux went to bed in his hotel in Algiers as an expert organizing a joint Germany-Vichy project to build a pipeline across the Sahara Desert from Ougadouga to Algeria, and on the morning of 8 November found himself in newly liberated French North Africa, under Allied occupation. Instantly, and like a snake shedding its skin in the harsh light of dawn, Charles Bedaux became the Allies most obdurate supporter, and he was seen in bars all over Algiers buying rounds for all the gallant Allied soldiers who had 'liberated' him from two and a half years of hell under Nazi rule. Such was Bedaux's eminence, and his name had not been forgotten, that he was even invited to dine with the supreme Allied commander of Torch, Lieutenant-General Dwight D. Eisenhower.

To everyone's acute embarrassment, particularly Eisenhower's, the French arrested Bedaux soon after his dinner with the American General, charging him with collaboration and a whole range of other crimes including outright treason. The next twelve months became the most difficult in Bedaux's chequered career, for having been able to do exactly what he wanted for well over thirty years, he now discovered there was a price to pay and found himself being asked the most difficult and awkward of questions – like why had he supported the Nazis. Of course he had no answer, not one that he could give anyway, and he squirmed left and right, prevaricated, avoided giving direct answers, changed the subject as often as possible, feigned medical conditions, and probably deep down knew he was done for. In December of 1943, after a year of being held by the French, his custody was taken over by the FBI and he was shipped back to Miami for further investigation, where he allegedly committed suicide two months later.

'Dead Men Don't Blab', blared the headlines of the American magazine *The National* on 11 March 1944, which went on to report that:

> It will be too bad if the late Charles E. Bedaux is allowed to sink into limbo without causing more than a one-day ripple in the headlines. For the history of the industrial efficiency expert, who died on 18 February when he was due to face a grand-jury investigation into his relations with the Nazis, is an instructive one . . .

After a very brief résumé of Bedaux's career during the war years from 1940 to 1942, enumerating 'his friendship with Abetz, Wiedemann, and Schacht and his visit to the home of Ribbentrop in August, 1939', *The National* described his appointment as an expert in Economic Projects for the Reich, and how, in 1941, Bedaux travelled to Athens where 'he negotiated the sell-out of two Greek generals' to the Germans. The article went on to detail how after Operation Torch took place in November 1942, Bedaux got himself captured by the Allies, at which time he was arrested 'not by order of General Eisenhower as some reports have stated, but by the Military Security section of the French Deuxième Bureau' (the Intelligence Department). Detailed in the report was the involvement of the FBI, who apparently interfered with the Deuxième Bureau's investigation, and 'attempted to get them to withdraw the charges against Bedaux'. And asked, 'Why, when he was in detention, was he permitted an opportunity to accumulate sufficient luminal to enable him to choose his own time of exit?'

The article concluded with the statement that:

> Charles Bedaux not only had many influential friends but also a vast host of enemies – all the democrats of the world. It is, however, his enemies who should mourn his death for if he had lived until he had told all, they might have learned much to their advantage. Many of his friends, on the other hand, probably heard the news cheerfully. If they sighed at all, it was a sigh of relief.

At the time of Bedaux's death, one of his greatest friends, the Duke of Windsor, was enduring a far more peaceful existence in the Bahamas, quarantined in a gilded cage with golden sands, and protected by a Company of Cameron Highlanders who amused themselves by constantly rehearsing what they would do in the event of an enemy attempt to 'kidnap' the Duke. All in all, it was a very exasperating existence for the Duke and Duchess, and during the closing weeks of the Second World War, on

16 March 1945, the Duke resigned his post as Governor. Within short order the Windsors removed themselves from the Bahamas, travelling to the United States where they remained until sailing back across the Atlantic. They arrived at their Boulevard Suchet home in September, which had remained absolutely untouched despite the ravages of six years of war, and four years of German occupation of Paris. To the Windsors it must have seemed that at last they could return to their pre-war existence of semi-regal opulence, the embarrassment of the Duke's flirtation with Nazism kept secret by the few in the know. The French government, blissfully unaware of what their honoured resident had done, even granted the Duke a tax-free status that was to last for the rest of his life. However, there was one minor fly in the ointment that returned to disturb the Duke. In 1946, Joachim von Ribbentrop requested that the Duke of Windsor appear as a witness on his behalf at the Nuremberg Trials, emphatic that the Duke had evidence to give that was important to his defence. The Duke of Windsor declined to appear.

Throughout the Second World War, the Duke of Windsor had always kept with him a locked metal dispatch case, within which he placed his most private papers. On his return to Paris in the autumn of 1945, these papers were at long last taken from the case and securely locked away in the Duke's private safe, where they remained for the next forty years, beyond his death in 1972 when they passed into Wallis' care. Amongst these papers were two dossiers, one headed 'German Documents', and the other containing 'Correspondence of Sir Samuel Hoare'. When Wallis died in 1986 she left these two dossiers, together with her other private papers and possessions, to be put into the custody of her lawyer, Madame Blum. At this time the British royal family made a concerted effort to take possession of a great many of the items that Wallis left, undoubtedly including the Duke's private papers. It is to Madame Blum's credit that she prevented this happening, and the Windsors' private papers remained untouched and unseen even after her own death; thus her loyalty to the Duchess was absolute.

In an effort to fully unravel all the facts behind the events of 1939 and 1940, I eventually managed to track down where Madame Blum had lodged the remnants of the Duke and Duchess of Windsor's private papers and possessions. When the Duchess of Windsor died she left a very large sum of money to the Institut Pasteur, which they astutely used to pay for the construction of a very fine building at the Hôpital St Jacques, to which the Institut is attached. It was to the Institut Pasteur I now discovered that Madame Blum had passed the care of the Duke and Duchess of Windsor's private papers.

In the early spring of 1999 I contacted the Head of the Legacy Department at the Institut, requesting access to the Windsors' papers. Initially my request for access was turned down, and I was informed that no one had ever been given access to the Windsor papers since their arrival at the Institut some ten years before. However, with perseverance, a great many phone calls over several weeks, and my assurances that I was a bona fide author conducting research for a book, the Institut relented and announced they would give me access to the papers. Within an hour of receiving this news by telephone, I received a nine-page fax detailing their holding, and was staggered at the quantity of material they held: one hundred and sixty-nine items – albums, documents, files, books, dossiers, tins of photographs and boxes of papers, all contained in thirty-two cartons. As I read through the listing I was thrilled to read on page three, itemized as contained within 'Carton No. 2':

Un dossier 'German Documents'
Correspondence de Sir Samuel Hoare concernant
The Duke of Windsor's visit to Madrid

On 5 March 1999, in a Paris wet and humid with pouring rain, I arrived at the Institut Pasteur for my appointment. I passed through the Institut's security and was taken to the second-floor office of the Chef du Bureau de Legacies, where I received a friendly welcome and was presented with a complimentary copy of *A King's Story*, an autobiography written by the Duke in the early 1950s. This was a recent reprint I had not seen before, as the original had long been out of print, and I felt a sense of foreboding for I remembered that the manuscript had been listed as also contained within 'Carton No. 2'. After this breaking of the ice, the initial friendly conversation that enquired about my journey, the Directeur suddenly became serious and informed me that a terrible mistake had occurred; not all the papers on the listing I had been sent were available, specifically those I had requested from 'Carton No. 2'. The papers had been removed from the listing held by the Institut Pasteur. Slowly the story came out, revealing that after Madame Blum's death, representatives of the British royal family had contacted her executors and vetted the papers Madame Blum had protected, removing them back to the Royal Archive in Britain. I realized this was probably going to be another example of documents concerning the Duke of Windsor becoming 'Lost', 'Not Available', or 'Closed' until some distant date.

Eventually, I was shown up a great many flights of stairs to the warren of attic rooms that served as the Institut's archive. Here I was led into a side-room, and, on a table in the middle of the room, permitted to examine two dilapidated cardboard boxes that looked forgotten and abandoned. Within these boxes I found the last remaining personal items of the Windsors left at the

Institut: photographs of an ill-at-ease Duke posing whilst playing golf; pictures of a seated Edward and Wallis laughing while a ball bounced for their dog; a touching photograph of the Duchess, a subtle study in light and shadow; snapshots taken by the Duchess of her pot-plants during the last years of her life. There were other items, too; the letters of condolence to the Duchess on the Duke's death, Buckingham Palace headed notepaper listing the floral tributes at the Duke's funeral, the royal family's names ticked in blue, everyone else ticked in red; the cards from the flowers. Lastly, a battered collection of papers entitled 'EP Ranch' and 'Etoshwa' – the paperwork and accounts of the Duke's Canadian ranch, and his unsuccessful efforts to find oil on this land in the late 1940s and early '50s.

All the papers and photographs were very interesting, but they were not what I had travelled all the way to Paris to see. Where were the contents of 'Carton No. 2'? I asked. For that matter, where were the other thirty-one cartons? The Directeur gave me an embarrassed smile and admitted that this was all they had, just two boxes of bits and pieces out of an original listing of one hundred and sixty-nine items – the royal retainers had taken the lot.

How long ago did this happen? I persisted. After all, the fax to me was a mere three weeks old, and when my assistant had telephoned the Directeur in person, he had given no intimation that there were any items missing at all.

Another smile of embarrassment, a Gallic shrug.

Slowly I realized that the Directeur had not known the items were not there. The listing at the Institut had not been updated, and all that remained were tantalizing clues to documents that were now securely locked away somewhere under royal control.

'You can always ask Windsor Castle for access,' he offered helpfully.

It was still pouring with rain as I walked away from the Institut, down Rue du Dr Roux and left into Boulevard Pasteur to take me back towards the city centre. It was two hours later, and I had examined all the papers and possessions that were left of the Duke and Duchess of Windsor's lives together; placed into the safekeeping of Madame Blum by Wallis, and in turn passed on by her for posterity to the Institut Pasteur. But, I had discovered, the royal family play the long game; all they had done was to await Madame Blum's death, and then requested *her* executors to hand over the Windsors' papers and possessions. These were items that had never belonged to the royal family, and yet still they hoarded – grabbing a document here, a letter there – like jackdaws frightened to let go in case the truth might spill from the royal nest. What I had seen at the Institut was no archive, no legacy, merely two battered cardboard boxes that were considered so insignificant that no one could be bothered to take them away – they had simply been . . . forgotten.

It stopped raining by the time I reached the Eiffel Tower, and I stood below it staring up at the Jules Verne restaurant on the first level, watching as great water droplets plummeted earthward from the vast structure, just as Bedrich Benes had sixty years before. 'Did he slip or was he pushed?' I found myself wondering. A sudden laugh from a group of Japanese tourists brought me back to the present, and I looked about me at the sightseers, the elderly Frenchman walking his dog, the numerous children who stared enraptured at the vast structure. Undoubtedly, the Parisians who had watched as the conquering Germans stared with the same look of wonder on their faces as the children who surrounded me, never realized that the man who had caused the downfall of their Third Republic had actually been born only around the corner, within sight of this very tower.

Time to be gone, I determined. Time to go home and try one last time to track down the Duke of Windsor's private dossiers, which I had now learnt had been removed back to Britain by royal retainers.

I duly wrote to the Keeper of the Royal Archives at Windsor Castle, mentioning that I was an author who had been to the Institut Pasteur to study the Duke of Windsor's papers, and that I would like to read for myself the contents of 'Carton No. 2'; namely the dossiers headed 'German Documents' and 'Correspondence of Sir Samuel Hoare'. It took some time for a reply to my request to make its way back to me, and when I opened the letter richly embossed with the royal coat of arms I realized that the mystery surrounding the Duke of Windsor was not to be solved, for I was informed not only that, 'I am afraid that neither of the two files you describe is here,' but also that, 'No papers have been transferred to the Royal Archives by the Institut Pasteur.'

Where are the Duke of Windsor's wartime dossiers headed 'German Documents' and 'Correspondence with Sir Samuel Hoare concerning the Duke of Windsor's visit to Madrid'? These papers exist, somewhere. They are clearly listed as being within the private papers of the Duke of Windsor, left to the Duchess and then the care of Madame Blum, and they have ultimately ended up back under royal control. The cover-up that began in the Second World War has continued to the present day, and shows every sign of continuing into the future.

Appendix

The 'EP' Letter

THE 'EP' LETTER was given to Peter Allen by Albert Speer in July 1980. At the time Speer refused to elucidate the prominence or importance of the letter, and so, without accurate indentification of 'EP' or access to the various documents that have been released in the last twenty years (such as the one detailing the sighting of Bedaux at the Reich Chancellery on 9 November 1939), the letter's importance was missed and it remained unstudied and filed away.

In early 1999, during the research for *Hidden Agenda*, the 'EP' letter's importance resurfaced again when 'Mr B' was identified, and the letter was properly and professionally translated for the very first time. Although the text of the letter would appear intentionally innocuous, perhaps hiding a series of cryptic messages, the discovery that the writer had not used the initials to his name 'EP', but was indicating *Edward* and his title, *Prince*, meant that the very letter itself became important, for it shows that Windsor was *not* being used by Bedaux, but was inexorably tied to the flow of information to the Germans. The letter reveals that Windsor was not unwittingly being pumped for information by Bedaux, but that he was telling Bedaux the Allies secrets *knowing* that the Germans would in due course receive the intelligence; thus he intentionally betrayed the Allies' defences to Germany.

306

Because of the devastating conclusion that this evidence suggests, it became crucial that the letter was examined by experts who could properly identify and authenticate its authorship. The letter was therefore put under the detailed scrutiny of a forensic handwriting expert, trained in the field of forensic document and handwriting examination. That it originated from the correct period was confirmed, as study of the material of the letter revealed that it had been written on pre-war unbleached paper with an ink of indeterminate, but not modern origin (there were innumerable brands of ink available in Europe in the 1930s, and it is therefore impossible to identify any one manufacturer). That tied the letter down to the period, but what of the writing? Had someone for nefarious purposes attempted to 'frame' the Duke?

This suggestion does not make sense, for one would have thought that if such a plan had existed to incriminate the Duke, surely the letter would at the very least have declared something that proved the Duke had not been entirely loyal to the Allied cause? As it is, the letter is so innocuous that its true meaning is impossible to discern *unless* the other documents are taken into account – and no one in 1939 knew that Bedaux would come under the surveillance of the Dutch GSIII, British Intelligence, or the Field Security Police, let alone that in the distant future those confidential and secret papers, including those of the German Auswärtiges Amt, would become available for public scrutiny.

To fully authenticate the authorship of the letter the expert examined the handwriting, paying particular attention to the characteristics of the writing, design of the individual letter formations, their relative size, proximity to one another and the spacing, as well as the writing's fluency, legibility, pressure, slant, rhythm and speed. This was then compared with other known samples of the Duke of Windsor's handwriting, such as the letters he wrote to Wallis Simpson between 1931 and 1937, as well as a detailed examination of a chain of correspondence written by the

Duke to Winston Churchill in the late 1930s. Examining the letter under these criteria, the expert concluded absolutely and unequivocally that the handwriting was indeed that of the Duke of Windsor, and therefore authenticated the letter.

However, one has to remain objective about this letter, and it is a fact that the one feature common to all experts is that they inevitably disagree with another's findings. The use of experts breeds disagreement, for by the very nature of their business they are perpetually engaged in dispute and argument. If involved in a legalistic matter, be it for civil dispute, a criminal matter, or even a contention over insurance, the one certainty common to all is that one side will always produce an expert to dispute the other side's expert. As time proceeds there will undoubtedly be other professional opinions about this letter's origin, and dispute over one person's findings over another. That is the nature of expert examination. For many the discovery that the Duke of Windsor had his own hidden agenda in 1939 and 1940 will be an unpalatable truth, and this will almost certainly instigate doubt over the 'EP' letter, and possibly repeated examination of the letter until the desired expert opinion is forthcoming. Yet, this must be tempered with the realization that this letter does not stand alone as the only accusing finger, and if it did not exist the remaining documentary evidence from archives in Europe and America would still reveal exactly the same chain of events that culminated in the fall of France.

References

Prologue

1 Sarah Bradford, *King George VI* (Weidenfeld & Nicolson, 1989)
2 Chapman Pincher, *Their Trade is Treachery* (Sidgwick & Jackson, 1983)
3 Bradford, op. cit.
4 Nigel Hamilton, *Monty the Field Marshal*, Vol. III (London, 1983)
5 The Cadogan Papers, Churchill Archives Centre, Churchill Centre, Cambridge
6 Bradford, op. cit.
7 Ibid.
8 Ibid.
9 Doc. no. 841.001/3–1547, Diplomatic Branch, National Archive, Washington, DC
10 Peter Wright, *Spycatcher* (Heinemann Australia, 1987)
11 P. Brendon & P. Whitehead, *The Windsors* (Hodder & Stoughton, 1986)

1: Born to be King

1 Quote from Margot Asquith
2 Sarah Bradford, *King George VI* (Weidenfeld & Nicolson, 1989)

3 J. Bryan and J. Murphy, *The Windsor Story* (Granada, 1979)

4 Ibid.

5 Edward, Duke of Windsor, *A King's Story* (London, 1951)

6 Bradford, op. cit.

7 *The Traitor King* (TV programme), Hart Ryan Productions 1996

8 Mr Kenneth de Courcy, Interview, 1996

9 Bradford, op. cit.

10 Sir Robert Hamilton Bruce Lockhart, *The Bruce Lockhart Diaries*, (Macmillan, 1973)

11 Charles Higham, *Wallis* (Sidgwick & Jackson, 1988)

12 J. and S. Poole, *Who Financed Hitler?* (London, 1979)

13 Charles Higham, *Trading with the Enemy* (Robert Hale, 1983)

14 Poole, op. cit.

15 Ibid.

16 F.W. Winterbotham, *The Nazi Connection* (London, 1978)

17 Ibid.

18 Ladislas Farrago, *The Game of Foxes* (London, 1972)

19 Doc. no. 5482/E382057–78. Auswärtiges Amts Archive, Bonn

20 Ibid., and D.G.F.P., Series C, Vol. IV, Coburg dispatches for Hitler's attention.

21 Albert Speer, *Inside the Third Reich* (Weidenfeld & Nicolson, 1970)

22 Fritz Hesse, *Hitler and the English* (London, 1954)

23 André Francois-Poncet, *The Fateful Years* (London, 1949)

24 Paul Schmidt, *Hitler's Interpreter* (London, 1951)

25 Peter Allen, *The Crown and the Swastika* (Robert Hale, 1983)

26 Robert Rhodes James (ed.), *Chips, The Diaries of Sir Henry Channon* (Weidenfeld & Nicolson, 1967)

27 Doc. no. 8015/E576522–4, Auswärtiges Amts Archive, Bonn

28 Ralph G. Martin, *The Woman He Loved* (London, 1974)

29 *The Traitor King*, op. cit.

30 Ibid.

31 Frances Donaldson, *Edward VIII* (Weidenfeld & Nicolson, 1974)

32 Allen, op. cit.

33 Higham, op. cit.

34 Ibid.

35 Rhodes James, op. cit.

36 Allen, op. cit.

37 Donaldson, op. cit.

38 Ibid.

39 Ibid.

40 Higham, op. cit.

41 Lord Beaverbrook, *The Abdication of King Edward VIII* (London, 1958)

42 Martin, op. cit.

43 Higham, op. cit.

44 James Lees-Milne, *Harold Nicolson* (Chatto & Windus, 1981)

45 Donaldson, op. cit

46 Ibid.

47 The Monckton Papers, Bodleian Library, Oxford

48 Higham, op. cit.

49 Donaldson, op. cit.

50 Ibid.

2: The Efficiency Engineer

1 File no.#10505–27, Military Intelligence Division, National Archive, Washington DC

2 Register of Births, Charenton-le-Pont, Paris

3 Sworn statement by Mr C.E. Bedaux, 23.03.43, Dossier no. 100–49901, FBI Archive, Washington DC

4 Testimony by Mr C. E. Bedaux, 23.03.43, Doc. Ref. 1003/2682, FBI Archive, Washington DC

5 File no.#10505–27, Military Intelligence Division, National Archive, Washington DC

6 Ibid.

7 Ibid.

8 Ibid.

9 Ibid.

10 Ibid.

11 Ibid.

12 Ibid.

13 Ibid.

14 *Grand Rapids Herald*, 22 February 1917, Michigan, USA

15 Kent County Wedding Certificate, State of Michigan, drawn from Ledger 18, p. 242

16 File no.#10505–27, Military Intelligence Division, National Archive, Washington DC

17 Intelligence file no. RG-319 IRR, National Archive, Washington DC

18 Bundesarchiv Militararchiv Correspondence, Ref. MA6/1–6992, 12.03.98

19 Dossier no.100–49901, FBI Archive, Washington DC

20 Mayor's Office, Tourainne, France and FBI interrogation dossier 1003/2682, 28.12.43

21 Bedaulim Ltd, Company Return for 1935, Companies House, Cardiff

22 Doc. no. 9–2498, Department of Justice Archive, The Hague, Holland

23 Charles Higham, *Trading with the Enemy* (Robert Hale, 1983)

24 Intelligence file no. RG-319 IRR, National Archive, Washington DC

25 Higham, op. cit.

26 Intelligence file no. RG-319 IRR, National Archive, Washington DC

27 Ibid.

28 Higham, op. cit.

29 Higham, op. cit.

30 Intelligence file no. RG-319 IRR, National Archive, Washington DC

31 Doc. ref. 1003/2682, 23.12.43, FBI Archive, Washington DC

32 Sworn statement by C.E. Bedaux, 17 July 1943, Doc. no. 100–49901, FBI Archive, Washington DC

33 Intelligence file no. RG-319 IRR, National Archive, Washington DC

34 Dossier no. 100–49901, FBI Archive, Washington DC

3: Marriage and Exile

1 Charles Higham, *Wallis* (Sidgwick & Jackson, 1988)

2 Ibid.

3 J. Bryan & J. Murphy, *The Windsor Story* (Granada, 1979)

4 Interrogation Report, 28.12.43, Dossier no. 1003/2682, p. 32, FBI Archive, Washington DC

5 Higham, op. cit.

6 Frances Donaldson, *Edward VIII* (Weidenfeld & Nicolson, 1974)

7 Ibid.

8 The Duchess of Windsor, *The Heart has its Reasons* (London, 1956)

9 The Messersmith Papers, University of Delaware, USA

10 Ibid., and Higham, op. cit.

11 Barbara Hutton, *The Barbara Hutton Diaries, 1935–1940* as quoted in Higham, op. cit.

12 Doc. no. RG 319–IRR, National Archive, Washington DC

13 Doc. no. FO 826/562057, Public Records Office, Kew

14 Doc. no. FO 328/7655/10, Public Records Office, Kew

15 Doc. no. FO 376/20287/41, Public Records Office, Kew

16 Doc. no. RG 319–IRR, National Archive, Washington DC

17 'The Errol Flynn File', FBI Archive, Washington DC

18 Gwynne Thomas, *King Pawn or Black Knight* (Mainstream Publishers, 1995), and Charles Higham, *Errol Flynn, The Untold Story* (London, 1980)

19 'The Errol Flynn File', FBI Archive, Washington DC, and Ibid.

20 D.G.F.P., Series D, Vol. X

21 *The Times*, 3 October 1937

22 The Sir Robert Lindsay Letters as quoted in Higham, op. cit.

23 J. Bryan & J. Murphy, op. cit.

24 Emmy Göring, *My Life with Göring* (London, 1972)

25 Sir Dudley Forwood, Duke of Windsor's Aide, as quoted in *The Traitor King* (TV programme), Hart Ryan Productions, 1996

26 Ralph G. Martin, *The Woman He Loved* (London, 1974)

27 Doc. no. FO 328/7655/76, Public Records Office, Kew

28 Higham, *Wallis* (Sidgwick & Jackson, 1988)

29 J. Bryan & J. Murphy, op. cit.

30 Sir Dudley Forwood, Duke of Windsor's Aide.

31 *The Daily News*, 12 December 1966

32 *The New York Times*, 23 October 1937

33 *The New York Times*, 27 October 1937

34 *The Baltimore News*, 2 November 1937

35 *The Times*, 10 November 1937
36 Testimony by Mr C.E. Bedaux, 29.12.43, Doc. no. 1003/2682, FBI Archive, Washington DC
37 Report no. 521 by Henri Sibour, Doc. no. RG 226, National Archive, Washington DC
38 Statement to Leonard Greenburg, Doc. no. 100/2682, FBI Archive, Washington DC
39 Doc. no. RG 319–IRR, Security Intelligence, National Archive, Washington DC

4: War

1 Diplomatic doc. no. 242, French Yellow Book, 1938–1939
2 B.H. Liddell Hart, *The Other Side of the Hill* (Cassell, 1948)
3 Ibid.
4 André Brissaud, *Histoire du Service Secret Nazi* (Plon, Paris, 1972)
5 *Volkischer Beobachter*, 1.09.39
6 Liddell Hart, op. cit.
7 Doc. no. 106, Documents on German–Polish Relations, HMSO
8 Frances Donaldson, *Edward VIII* (Weidenfeld & Nicolson, 1974)
9 Ibid.
10 Ibid.
11 Ibid.
12 The Duchess of Windsor, *The Heart has its Reasons* (London, 1956)
13 Doc. no. WO 106/1655/23, Public Records Office, Kew
14 Brigadier Davy's notes, Doc. no. WO 106/1782, Public Records Office, Kew
15 J. Bryan and J. Murphy, *The Windsor Story* (Granada, 1979)
16 Doc. no. 7N2817, Service de 3 Armées, Vincenness
17 Doc. no. WO 106/1653/19, Public Records Office, Kew
18 Sarah Bradford, *George VI* (Weidenfeld & Nicolson, 1989)
19 Ibid.
20 Donaldson, op. cit.
21 Ibid.

22 Bedaux interrogation, 29.12.43, Doc. no. 1003/2682, FBI Archive, Washington DC
23 Ibid.
24 D.G.F.P., Doc. no. 134, Series D, Vol. IIIV
25 D.G.F.P., Doc. no. 203, Series D, Vol. IIIV
26 D.G.F.P., Doc. no. 235, Series D, Vol. IIIV
27 D.G.F.P., Doc. no. 318, Series D, Vol. IIIV
28 F.W. Winterbotham, *The Nazi Connection* (London, 1978)
29 F.W. Winterbotham Interview, conducted by Peter Allen, 5.01.81
30 Doc. no. WO 106/1655/21, Public Records Office, Kew
31 Donaldson, op. cit.
32 Ibid.
33 Doc. no. W.O. 106/1678/1A, Public Records Office, Kew
34 Doc. no. W.O. 106/1678/2A, Public Records Office, Kew

5: Betrayal

1 B.H. Liddell Hart, *History of the Second World War* (Cassell, 1970)
2 B.H. Liddell Hart, *The Other Side of the Hill* (Cassell, 1948)
3 RG-319 IRR OSS, US National Archive, Washington DC
4 Ibid.
5 Memorandum by L.L. Laughlin, 22.3.44, Doc. no. 100–49901, FBI Archive, Washington DC
6 Doc. no. 100–49901, FBI Archive, Washington DC
7 Report by J. Wenger-Valentine, 26.2.43, Doc. no. 100–49901, FBI Archive, Washington DC
8 André Brissaud, *Histoire du Service Secret Nazi* (Plon, Paris, 1972)
9 Ibid.
10 Ibid.
11 Ibid.
12 Ibid.
13 Ibid.
14 Ibid.
15 Ibid.
16 Albert Speer Interview, 27.07.80.

17 Brissaud, op. cit.

18 Doc. no. WO 160/1678/2B, Public Records Office, Kew

19 Brissaud, op. cit.

20 Doc. no. FO 371/28741, Public Records Office, Kew

21 Doc. no. FO 2880/7/49, Public Records Office, Kew

22 Brissaud, op. cit.

23 Frances Donaldson, *Edward VIII* (Weidenfeld & Nicolson, 1974)

24 Gwynne Thomas, *King Pawn or Black Knight* (Mainstream Publishers, 1995)

25 Donaldson, op. cit.

26 Ibid.

27 Doc. no. 1003/2682, FBI Archive, Washington DC

28 Michael Bloch, *The Duke of Windsor's War* (Weidenfeld & Nicolson, 1982)

29 Donaldson, op. cit.

30 Liddell Hart, *The Other Side of the Hill*, op. cit.

31 Ibid.

32 Ibid.

33 Ibid.

34 Ibid.

35 Donaldson, op. cit.

36 Doc. no. WO 208/609, Public Records Office, Kew

37 Donaldson, op. cit.

38 Doc. no. WO 208/2036A, Public Records Office, Kew

39 M. Anton Muret Interview, 17.04.98

40 D.G.F.P., Doc. no. 528, Series D, Vol. III

41 Liddell Hart, op. cit.

42 Ibid.

43 Report ref. no. R/990228, Institut Royal Météorologique de Belgique

44 D.G.F.P., Doc. no. 528 Enclosure, Series D, Vol. III

45 Ibid.

46 Liddell Hart, op. cit.

47 *General Ironside's Diaries 1937–1940* (Constable, 1962)

48 Ibid.

49 Donaldson, op. cit.

50 Ibid.

51 Chisolm and Davie, *Beaverbook: A Life* (Hutchinson, 1992)
52 D.G.F.P., Doc. no. 580, Ref. 122667, Series D, Vol. III
53 D.G.F.P., Doc. no. 582, Ref. 122669, Series D, Vol. III
54 Wilhelm Heottle, *Die Gehiem Front* (Germany, 1953)
55 Doc. no. FO 371/28741, Public Records Office, Kew
56 D.G.F.P., Doc. no. 584, ref. 122671, Series D, Vol. III
57 Doc. no. WO 106/1678, Public Records Office, Kew
58 Doc. no. FO 371/28741, Public Records Office, Kew
59 *Ciano's Diary 1939–1943*, 10.05.40 (Heinemann, 1947)
60 D.G.F.P., Doc. no. 212, Ref. E694560, Series D, Vol IX

6: Disaster

1 D.G.D.P., Doc. no 214, Ref. 215794, Series D, Vol. X
2 *General Ironside's Diaries 1937–1940* (Constable, 1962), Entry date, 10.06.40
3 Ibid., Entry date, 11.06.40
4 Doc. no. WO 106/1655, Appx 2 iii, Public Records Office, Kew
5 Doc. no. WO 106/1655 08.03.40., Public Records Office, Kew
6 J. Bryan & J. Murphy, *The Windsor Story*, (Granada, 1979)
7 Philip Ziegler, *Diana Cooper* (London, 1981)
8 D.G.F.P., Doc. no. 152, Ref. B002549, Series D, Vol. X
9 Philip Warner, *The Battle of France* (London, 1988)
10 Bedaux interrogation, 12.29.43, Doc. ref. 1033–2682, FBI Archive, Washington DC
11 J. E. Hoover letter, 6.02.43, Doc. no. 100–49901, FBI Archive, Washington DC
12 *General Ironside's Diaries*, op. cit., Entry date, 15.06.40
13 Liddell Hart, *The Other Side of the Hill* (Cassell, 1948)
14 Ibid.
15 Ibid.
16 Interview, Brigadier M.R. Lonsdale, DSO, OBE, 12.03.80
17 Liddell Hart, op. cit.
18 *General Ironside's Diaries*, op. cit., Entry date, 21.06.40
19 Warner, op. cit.

20 Liddell Hart, op. cit.
21 Ibid.
22 *General Ironside's Diaries*, op. cit., Entry date, 23.06.40
23 Doc. no. WO 160/1678, Public Records Office, Kew
24 Liddell Hart, op. cit.
25 Liddell Hart, *History of the Second World War* (Cassell, 1970)
26 *General Ironside's Diaries*, op. cit., Entry date, 26.06.40
27 Warner, op. cit.
28 J. Bryan & J. Murphy, op. cit.
29 Charles Higham, *Wallis* (Sidgwick & Jackson, 1988)
30 Ian Ousby, *Occupied* (John Murray, 1992)

7: Flight

 1 Doc. no. FO H/XLI/11, Public Records Office, Kew
 2 Churchill quotation from BBC broadcast, 04.06.40
 3 D.G.F.P., Doc. nos. 378, 456, Series D, Vol. IX
 4 Noel Barber, *The Week France Fell* (London, 1976)
 5 Letter by J.E. Hoover, 02.02.43, RG 319 IRR, National Archive, Washington DC
 6 RG 226, OSS Report 15.01.43, National Archive, Washington DC
 7 Doc. no. FO H/XLI/5, Public Records Office, Kew
 8 Doc. no. FO PA/XLI/13, Public Records Office, Kew
 9 RG 319 IRR, Central Files Report, National Archive, Washington DC
10 The Templewood Papers, Cambridge University Library, Cambridge
11 Ibid.
12 Doc. no. 100–49901, FBI Archive, Washington DC
13 Doc. no. FO H/XLI/6, Public Records Office, Kew
14 Doc. no. FO H/XLI/10, Public Records Office, Kew
15 Doc. no. FO PD/XLI/15, Public Records Office, Kew
16 Doc. no. FO PD/XLI/17, Public Records Office, Kew
17 Ibid.
18 Doc. nos. FO H/XLI/18, 19, 20, & 21, Public Records Office, Kew

19 Doc. no. FO PD/XLI/18, Public Records Office, Kew
20 Doc. no. FO PD/XLI/19, Public Records Office, Kew
21 Doc. no. FO PD/XLI/21, Public Records Office, Kew
22 Doc. no. FO PD/XLI/23, Public Records Office, Kew
23 Doc. no. FO H/XLI/25, Public Records Office, Kew
24 US State Department, Doc. no. NND 70032L, National Archive, Washington DC
25 Charles Higham, *Wallis* (Sidgwick & Jackson, 1988)
26 D.G.F.P., Doc. no. 66, Series D, Vol. X
27 D.G.F.P., Doc. no. 86, Series D, Vol. X
28 Doc. no. FO PD/XLI/20, Public Records Office, Kew

8: Negotiation

1 D.G.F.P., Doc. no. 276, Series D, Vol. X
2 D.G.F.P., Telegram no. 2298, Ref. B15/002545, Series D, Vol. X
3 D.G.F.P., Doc. no. 159, Series D, Vol. X
4 D.G.F.P., Doc. no. 152, Series D, Vol. X
5 Peter Allen, *The Crown and the Swastika* (Robert Hale, 1983)
6 Ibid.
7 D.G.F.P., Doc. no. 152, Series D, Vol. X
8 *Ciano's Diary 1939–1943* (Heinemann, 1947)
9 D.G.F.P., Doc. no. 175, Series D, Vol. X
10 D.G.F.P., Doc. no. 211, Series D, Vol. X
11 F.W. Winterbotham Interview, conducted by P. Allen, 5.01.81
12 Allen, op. cit.
13 Walter Schellenberg, *Memoirs* (London, 1956)
14 Ibid.
15 Allen, op. cit.
16 Schellenberg, op. cit.
17 D.G.F.P., Doc. no. 211, Series D, Vol. X
18 D.G.F.P., Doc. no. 216, Series D, Vol. X
19 Charles Higham, *Wallis* (Sidgwick & Jackson, 1988)
20 Doc. no. FO PD/XLI/24, Public Records Office, Kew
21 *Gazetta del Popolo*, Turin, 22 July 1940

22 N. Shakespeare, *The Men Who Would Be King* (Sidgwick & Jackson, 1984)

23 Josef Wulf, *Die SS* (Bonn, 1969)

24 Document no. R SS/1236, 26.7.40, Bundesarchiv, Koblenz

25 Ibid.

26 Ibid.

27 Document no. E 147120, Bundesarchiv, Koblenz

28 James Douglas-Hamilton, *Motive for a Mission* (London, 1971)

29 Allen, op. cit.

30 Douglas-Hamilton, op. cit.

31 Felix Kersten, *The Kersten Memoirs* (London, 1956)

32 The Monckton Papers, Bodleian Library, Oxford

33 Frances Donaldson, *Edward VIII* (Weidenfeld & Nicolson, 1974)

34 D.G.F.P., Doc. no. 254, Series D, Vol. X

35 Doc. no. R SS/1236, 29.07.40, Bundesarchive, Koblenz

36 Donaldson, op.cit.

37 The Monckton Papers, op. cit.

38 Doc. no. R SS/1236, 29.07.40, Bundesarchive, Koblenz

39 Doc. no. R SS/1236, 30.07.40, Bundesarchive, Koblenz

40 D.G.F.P., Doc. no. 264, Series D, Vol. X

41 D.G.F.P., Doc. no. 265, Series D, Vol. X

42 D.G.F.P., Doc. no. 276, Series D, Vol. X

43 D.G.F.P., Telegram no. 884 (B15/B002655), Series D, Vol. X

44 Gwynne Thomas, *King Pawn or Black Knight* (Mainstream Publishers, 1995)

45 RG 226, Report no. 521, OSS Files, National Archive, Washington DC

46 RG 226 OSS E92, Box 214 Folder 43, National Archive, Washington DC

Bibliography and Sources

Algemeem Rijksarchief, The Hague, Holland

Allen, Peter, *The Crown and the Swastika: Hitler, Hess and the Duke of Windsor* (Robert Hale, 1983)

Archive of Auswärtiges Amt, Bonn, Germany

Archives Diplomatique, Paris, France

Archives Generales du Royaume, Bruxelles, Belgium

Archivex SSRO, Prague, Czech Republic

Barber, Noel, *The Week France Fell* (London, 1976)

Bezy, Jean, *Le S.R. Air* (Editions France-Empire, 1979)

Bloch, Michael, *The Duke of Windsor's War* (Weidenfeld & Nicolson, 1982)

Bloch, Michael, *Wallis & Edward Letters 1931–37* (Weidenfeld & Nicolson, 1986)

Bradford, Sarah, *George VI* (Weidenfeld and Nicolson, 1989)

Brendon, P. & Whitehead, P., *The Windsors* (Hodder and Stoughton, 1986)

Brissaud, André, *Histoire du Service Secret Nazi* (Plon, Paris 1972)

Bryan, J. and Murphy, J., *The Windsor Story* (Granada, 1979)

Bundesarchiv, Berlin, Germany

Bundesarchiv, Bonn, Germany

Bundesarchiv, Koblenz, Germany

Bundesarchiv Militararchive, Freiburg, Germany

Butcher, Harry C., *My Three Years with Eisenhower* (Simon & Schuster, 1946)

Chisolm, A. and Davie, M., *Beaverbrook: A Life* (Hutchinson, 1992)

Colvin, Ian, *Chief of Intelligence* (Victor Gollancz, 1951)

Costello, James, *Ten Days that Saved the West* (Bantam, 1991)

Companies House, Cardiff, United Kingdom

D'Archives de Paris, Paris, France

Documents on German Foreign Policy (London HMSO)

Donaldson, Frances, *Edward VIII* (Weidenfeld & Nicolson, 1974)

Douglas-Hamilton, James, *Motive for a Mission* (London, 1971)

Downes, Donald, *The Scarlet Thread* (London, 1954)

Edward, Duke of Windsor, *A King's Story* (London, 1951)

Farrago, Ladislas, *The Game of Foxes* (London, 1972)

Federal Bureau of Investigation, Washington DC, USA

Francois-Poncet, André, *The Fateful Years* (London, 1949)

French Yellow Book, Diplomatic Documents 1938–39 (Hutchinson, 1947)

Garret, Richard, *Mrs Simpson* (Arthur Baker Ltd, 1979)

Gazetta del Popolo, Turin, Italy

Geheimes Staatesarchiv Preussischer Kulturbesitz, Berlin, Germany

Göring, Emmy, *My Life with Göring* (London, 1972)

Hamilton, Nigel, *Monty the Field Marshal* (London, 1983)

Hart Ryan Productions, *The Traitor King* (Hart Ryan Productions, 1996)

Heottl, Wilhelm, *Die Geheim Front* (Germany, 1953)

Hesse, Fritz, *Hitler and the English* (London, 1954)

Hibbert, Christopher, *Edward the Uncrowned King* (Macdonald & Co, 1972)

Higham, Charles, *Trading with the Enemy* (Robert Hale, 1983)

Higham, Charles, *Wallis* (Sidgwick & Jackson, 1988)

Hoch, Anton, *Das Attent auf Hitler im Munchen Bergerbraukeller 1939* (Vierteljahrshefte fur Zeutgeschichte, 1969)

Hoover Institution, Stanford, USA

Imperial War Museum, London, United Kingdom

Institut Pasteur, Paris, France

Institut Royal Météorologique de Belgique, Bruxelles, Belgium

Jacobsen, Hans Adolf, *Falle Gelb* (Weisbaden, 1957)

Kent County Clerks Office, Grand Rapids, USA

Kersten, Felix, *The Kersten Memoirs* (London, 1956)

Lees-Milne, James, *Harold Nicolson* (Chatto & Windus, 1981)

Liddell Hart, B. H., *The Other Side of the Hill* (Cassell, 1948)

Liddell Hart, B. H., *History of the Second World War* (Cassell, 1970)

Martin, Ralph G., *The Woman He Loved* (London, 1974)

Marwick, A. and Simpson, W., *Documents 2:1925–1959* (Open University Press, 1990)

Ministerstvo Vnut SR, Bratislava, Slovak Republic

National Archives, Washington DC, USA

National Security Agency, Maryland, USA

N.S.D.A.P. (files of the Central Archive), Berlin, Germany

Ousby, Ian, *Occupied* (John Murray, 1992)

Pincher, Chapman, *Their Trade is Treachery* (Sidgwick & Jackson, 1983)

Public Records Office, London, United Kingdom

J. and S. Poole, *Who Financed Hitler?* (London, 1979)

Rhodes James, R., *Chips, The Diary of Sir Henry Channon* (London, 1967)

Rijksarchief, Den Haag

Schellenberg, Walter, *Memoirs* (London, 1956)

Schmidt, Paul, *Hitler's Interpreter* (London, 1951)

Service Historique de 3 Armées, Paris, France

Shakespeare, N., *The Men Who Would Be King* (Sidgwick & Jackson, 1984)

Smith, R. Harris, *OSS* (California Press, 1972)

Speer, Albert, *Inside the Third Reich* (London, 1970)

Thomas, Gwynne, *King Pawn or Black Night* (Mainstream Publishing, 1995)

Vansittart, Lord, *Lessons of my Life* (Hutchinson, 1946)

Vintras, Roland, *The Portuguese Connection* (Bachman & Turner, 1974)

Volkischer Beobachter, Berlin

Wallis, Duchess of Windsor, *The Heart has its Reasons* (London, 1956)

Warner, Philip, *The Battle for France* (London, 1988)

Westphal, General Siegfried, *The German Army in the West* (Cassell, 1951)

Winterbotham, F. W., *The Ultra Secret* (Weidenfeld & Nicolson, 1974)

Winterbotham, F. W., *The Nazi Connection* (London, 1978)
Wright, Peter, *Spycatcher* (Heinemann Australia, 1987)
Wulf, Josef, *Die SS* (Bonn, 1956)
Ziegler, Philip, *Diana Cooper* (London, 1981)

Index